The Revolution Within

Why do some individuals participate in risky anti-regime resistance whereas others abstain? *The Revolution Within* answers this question through an in-depth study of unarmed resistance against Israeli rule in the Palestinian Territories over more than a decade. Despite having strong anti-regime sentiment, Palestinians initially lacked the internal organizational strength often seen as necessary for protest. This book provides a foundation for understanding participation and mobilization under these difficult conditions. It argues that, under such conditions, integration into state institutions – schools, prisons, and courts – paradoxically makes individuals more likely to resist the state. Diverse evidence drawn from field research – including the first large-scale survey of participants and nonparticipants in Palestinian resistance, as well as Arabic-language interviews and archival sources – supports the argument. The book's findings explain how anti-regime resistance can occur even without the strong civil society organizations often regarded as necessary for protest and, thus, suggest new avenues for supporting civil resistance movements.

Yael Zeira is Croft Assistant Professor of Political Science and International Studies at the University of Mississippi. Her research examines the causes and consequences of public opinion and political behavior in authoritarian and conflict settings, with a regional focus on the Middle East. Her other research on this topic has been published in leading academic journals, including *Comparative Political Studies* and the *Journal of Conflict Resolution*.

T0349299

The Revolution Within

State Institutions and Unarmed Resistance in Palestine

YAEL ZEIRA

University of Mississippi

CAMBRIDGE
UNIVERSITY PRESS

University Printing House, Cambridge CB2 8BS, United Kingdom

One Liberty Plaza, 20th Floor, New York, NY 10006, USA

477 Williamstown Road, Port Melbourne, VIC 3207, Australia

314–321, 3rd Floor, Plot 3, Splendor Forum, Jasola District Centre,
New Delhi – 110025, India

79 Anson Road, #06–04/06, Singapore 079906

Cambridge University Press is part of the University of Cambridge.

It furthers the University's mission by disseminating knowledge in the pursuit of
education, learning, and research at the highest international levels of excellence.

www.cambridge.org
Information on this title: www.cambridge.org/9781108472197
DOI: 10.1017/9781108559492

© Yael Zeira 2019

First published 2019

Printed in the United Kingdom by TJ International Ltd. Padstow Cornwall

A catalogue record for this publication is available from the British Library.

ISBN 978-1-108-47219-7 Hardback
ISBN 978-1-108-45912-9 Paperback

Contents

Figures

Tables

Acknowledgments

A great many people contributed to the writing of this book in ways I can only begin to acknowledge here. First and foremost, this book could not have been written without the extraordinary trust and generosity extended to me by many Palestinians and also Israelis during the course of my field research. Ziad Abu Zayyad, Hillel Schenker, Gershon Baskin, Munther Dajani, Ghassan al-Khatib, Fadwa al-Labadi, Maya Rosenfeld, and Hanna Siniora all opened doors for me on my first trip to East Jerusalem and the West Bank (and in many cases thereafter) and made my subsequent research possible. Although he always brushed off my many American "thank yous," particular thanks are owed to Ziad Abu Zayyad, who has always been ready to help me in any way he can and treated me like family. I am also grateful to Adnan Milhelm at al-Najah University, Aissa Abu Zahera of Al-Quds University and the Abu Jihad Museum of the Prisoners' Movement, and the al-Masri family of Nablus for their support. Finally, the survey that this book draws upon would not have been possible without the dedicated leadership and staff at Al-Maqdese Center for Society and Development and particularly my tireless project manager, Anas Abdeen. Anas helped me train and manage a talented and hardworking group of survey interviewers, including Ruʾa Abbas, Rami Abu Ahram, Samer Ahwedat, Tahani Balableh, Mutasem Fanasha, Laila Hammad, Tareq Kahala, Malek Kawameh, Dima Masri, Nadi Othman, Dana Tabari, Athar Zaghal, and Suha Zidan. In addition to this team, I also benefited from the advice of two experienced survey practitioners in the West Bank, Manal Warrad and Olfat Hammad, who generously shared their expertise with me.

In Palestine and Israel, I am also indebted to the capable help of four research assistants, Raja᾽ Abdel Aziz, Manar Al Kawasmi, Mahmoud Ramahi, and Inbar Noy. Beyond research assistance, Raja᾽ Abdel Aziz also offered patient Arabic language practice, good hummus, and incomparable friendship. In addition, I was also fortunate to meet Ahmad Abu Galia and Daniel Weishut during my first research trip to Jerusalem and to count them among my dear friends ever since. The Albright Institute also provided me with a home away from home during my many trips to the area, owing in large part to the warm hearts and capable hands of Hisham Jibrin, Nadia Bandak, and the Albright staff and community of scholars. In addition to the Albright, I am also grateful to Nahed Abu Asbeh for opening her home to me and for her friendship, as well as to the staff and scholars at the Kenyon Institute. Finally, to all of my anonymous interviewees, others who I cannot name here, or those whose names I never learned in the first place but who shared their stories and hospitality with me – thank you.

This book grew out of a dissertation written in the Department of Politics at New York University. I owe a huge debt of gratitude to the members of my dissertation committee, who each shaped the writing of this book in important ways: Kanchan Chandra, Bruce Bueno de Mesquita, Michael Gilligan, Alexandra Scacco, and, from outside NYU, Macartan Humphreys and Amaney Jamal. I would like to extend particular thanks and recognition to my dissertation chair, Kanchan Chandra, whose intellectual integrity and commitment to combining rigorous theory with deep area knowledge have shaped and inspired my own. Without Kanchan's advice to overcome my theoretical stumbling blocks by returning to a case I know well (even though that case was Palestine and not India), this book would not have been written, and I would not today be a Middle Easternist. Particular thanks are also owed to Alexandra Scacco, who generously gave of her time as an assistant professor to mentor me through the ins and outs of doing sensitive survey research. I cannot thank her enough. In addition to my advisers, I also benefited from the knowledge, mentorship, and support of other NYU faculty, including Bernd Beber, Neal Beck, Cyrus Samii, Eric Dickson, Sandy Gordon, Sally Merry, Becky Morton, Jonathan Nagler, Alastair Smith, David Stasavage, and Joshua Tucker. I would like to particularly acknowledge Neal Beck, who patiently answered my methodological questions in his own incomparable way and has always been a friend to me. Finally, both this book and I would have been poorer without the contributions and friendship of an exceptional group of NYU colleagues, particularly Daniel Berger, Anjali Thomas Bohlken, Ana Bracic, Julie Browne, Simon Chauchard, Anna Getmansky, Robin Harding, Kristin Michelitch, Tolga Sinmazdemir, and Manuela Travaglianti. From NYU, I am especially grateful to Anjali Thomas Bohlken and Simon Chauchard for providing feedback at multiple stages of this project and for their enduring friendship.

After leaving NYU, the University of Mississippi and Stanford University have both provided an excellent home for the continued evolution of this research. It is difficult to imagine a more supportive or collegial group of colleagues than I have found at the University of Mississippi. Special thanks are owed to the stalwart chair of the department of political science, John Bruce, who has always found a way to say "yes," as well as to the former director of the Croft Institute for International Studies, Kees Gispen, for his support. My students at Mississippi have also contributed to the writing of this book, including an outstanding group of undergraduate and graduate RAs: Nichole Gligor, Lauren Newman, Kate Noonan, and Connor Somgynari.

As a postdoctoral fellow at Stanford University, I was fortunate to have Jeremy Weinstein as my mentor, as well as to take part in conversations and discussions around this project with Byron Bland, Lisa Blaydes, Lina Khatib, Lee Ross, Michael Tomz, and Allen Weiner. Jeremy Weinstein also organized a workshop of extraordinary junior comparative scholars who helped shape the contents of this book including Grant Gordon, Jessica Gottlieb, Eric Kramon, Avital Livny, Amanda Robinson, Anoop Sarbahi, Bilal Siddiqi, and Manuela Travaglianti. In addition, Adi Greif, Aila Matanock, and Brenna Powell also provided valuable feedback and warm friendship during my time at Stanford. Finally, my year at Stanford was also greatly enriched by my affiliations with the Center for Democracy, Development and the Rule of Law (CDDRL), the Center for International Security and Cooperation (CISAC), and the Stanford Center on International Conflict and Negotiation (SCICN).

A large community of scholars beyond these institutions has also shaped this book in important ways. Wendy Pearlman, Jake Shapiro, and Mark Tessler, as well as my Mississippi colleagues Susan Allen, Vivian Ibrahim, and Greg Love, all provided invaluable feedback on an early version of this manuscript during a book conference held at Mississippi in Spring 2016. Without their insightful comments and warm encouragement, the final product may never have seen the light of day. I was also fortunate to be selected to participate in the 2016 POMEPS Junior Scholars Book Development Workshop held at Princeton University. Special thanks are owed to my discussants, Mark Beissinger and Kathleen Cunningham, who pushed me to situate the book more deeply in comparative perspective, as well as to Marc Lynch and all the conference participants. As I presented parts of this project over the years, I also received valuable feedback from many other individuals. With apologies to those I am surely forgetting, I would like to acknowledge Nathan Brown, Dan Corstange, Cassy Dorff, Amaney Jamal, Stathis Kalyvas, Peter Krause, Timur Kuran, Quinn Meacham, Jeremy Pressman, Jim Ron, Nadav Shelef, and Libby Wood, as well as my colleagues in the IR/CP workshop at Mississippi, including Susan Allen, Jeff Carter, Matt DiGiuseppe, Ben Jones, and Greg Love. Consuelo Amat, Dina Bishara, Rana Khoury, and especially Devorah Manekin also provided helpful feedback on various pieces of the manuscript. During the process of preparing for my initial field research for this project, I also benefited enormously from conversations with other scholars of Palestine, including Wendy Pearlman, Avram Bornstein, Rochelle Davis, Randa Farah, and Frances Hasso. Finally, during the course of my field research, I was also lucky to be able to share ideas and friendship with a terrific group of colleagues and friends, including Sarah Bush, Angel Foster, Elias Gabriel, Eleanor Gao, Sean Kirkland, Peter Krause, Lisa Mahoney, Devorah Manekin, Stefanie Nanes, Julie Peteet, Michael Robbins, Yorke Rowan, Alex Winder, and many others whom I do not have room to name or am regretfully forgetting. Sarah Bush, especially, continued to offer her sage advice on the project as it developed from dissertation to book, as well as her steady friendship and support. Finally, although my research in Jordan never made it into this book, its contents were nonetheless touched by my time there, and I owe additional thanks to Mohammad Azraq, Katie Touchton-Leonard and Hisham Kassim, Hala Salem and the leadership of the al-Quds Center for Political Studies, and Barbara Porter and the scholars and staff at ACOR.

Various institutions also contributed funding to support this project. At New York University, I was fortunate to receive a Torch Fellowship for Dissertation Field Research from the NYU Graduate School of Arts and Sciences. Without this generous fellowship, I would not have been able to spend nearly a year in the field and to conduct the survey on which this book draws extensively. A subsequent postdoctoral fellowship with the Empirical Studies of Conflict Program at Stanford University provided me with the financial and intellectual support I needed to begin transforming my dissertation project into a book. Finally, the Department of Political Science and the Croft Institute for International Studies at the

University of Mississippi contributed funding for an additional wave of field research conducted in 2014, as well as for a book conference that was invaluable to me in transforming a rough manuscript into a polished book.

Finally, I could not have written this book without the encouragement and support of my friends and family outside the academy. I am so very lucky to have all of you in my life. In particular, I am grateful to Louise Story-McKee for her helpful editorial advice on the dissertation, as well as her steadfast friendship through the years. Words are also not enough to express my thanks to my family and particularly to my parents, Ariela and Eldad Zeira. No matter what, they have always been 100 percent behind me. Likewise, my extended family in Israel gave me a loving home away from home and a welcome respite from the pressures of conducting field research abroad. Lastly, I want to express my deep appreciation to my husband, Tom, who helped me realize my passion for the Middle East and endured my many absences, deadlines, and doubts with his characteristic patience, good humor, and love. Our son, Oscar, was born during the final revisions to this book, and I am profoundly grateful to him as well.

I

Introduction

I.I INTRODUCTION

To the world, the first Palestinian intifadah is a young man, arm bent back to throw a stone, his face masked in a black-and-white checkered kaffiyeh. He is one of the "children of the stones" described in a popular poem.[1] His image has been writ large into a generation rising in rebellion, a universal spirit carrying an entire people into a movement of protest. As Joost Hiltermann wrote of the first intifadah, "it was remarkable that the entire population could be mobilized simultaneously" (Hiltermann, 1993, 173). Yet most Palestinians did not, in fact, pick up stones or don the kaffiyeh. Most did not directly participate at all. Indeed, while participation was high relative to other uprisings, nonparticipation was still far more common: at the peak of the revolt, only 35 percent of Palestinians are estimated to have taken part.[2]

Who is the young man behind the kaffiyeh, and why does he, rather than his neighbor, take to the streets? Why do some individuals choose to participate in anti-regime resistance whereas other similar individuals do not? The answers to these questions bear on fundamental puzzles about collective action. Participants in the first Palestinian intifadah took part in demonstrations, sit-ins, and strikes at great personal risk, facing near-certain arrest or violence. Yet, the potential benefits of participation – an end to Israel's military occupation of the Palestinian Territories and the establishment of an independent Palestinian state – were far from certain.

[1] Nizar Qabbani, reprinted in Lockman and Beinin (1989).
[2] This participation rate was calculated using the Nonviolent and Violent Outcomes (NAVCO) 1.1 dataset (Chenoweth, 2011).

I

Moreover, those benefits would be shared by all Palestinians, regardless of whether or not they bore the risk.

This book draws on an in-depth study of unarmed protest against the Israeli occupation of the Palestinian Territories to explain why individuals resist repressive regimes. Unarmed resistance against repressive regimes differs fundamentally from other kinds of contentious collective action. In contrast to social movement activism in liberal regimes, it takes place in a context of repression, media censorship, and lack of information. Information about anti-regime movements, protests, and the number of participants is not reported in the mass media or other sources, and even obtaining such information can be a dangerous act. Yet, unlike armed resistance that takes place within a similar environment, unarmed resistance requires mass participation to succeed. Tens of thousands of individuals must expect others to participate and choose to participate themselves. Prospective participants must obtain information about the occurrence, size, and strength of protests in the face of repression, censorship, and surveillance.

This book advances and tests a new theory that explains how and why some individuals are able to overcome these challenges. The book's main argument focuses on the facilitating role of *state-controlled mass institutions*: large heterogeneous organizations run or controlled by the state such as schools, prisons, and courts.[3] It argues that, when groups have strong anti-regime sentiment but lack the internal organizational strength often seen as necessary for protest, integration into state institutions paradoxically makes individuals more likely to resist the state. Integration into these institutions joins individuals in wider and more information-rich social networks, facilitates communication and coordination, and reduces the risks of participation in protest. Thus, all else equal, individuals who are integrated into these institutions have greater access to information about resistance and are better able to participate in protest than individuals who are not. As a result, the probability that they will begin to participate in protest is higher than that of similar individuals outside this institutional context, and this tendency to protest persists over time.

While integration into state institutions makes individuals more likely to participate in anti-regime resistance in lasting ways, there are also important limits on its impact. This book further argues that, while state institutions facilitate mass protests among organizationally weak

---

[3] See Section 1.4 for a formal definition.

groups without strong civil society organizations, such organizations are needed in order to *subsequently* link disparate protests into a nationwide campaign. As mentioned previously, individuals inside state institutions possess greater access to scarce political information about protest. However, without strong civil society organizations and networks, existing institutional and geographic divisions are still likely to circumscribe the content and flow of this information. News about anti-regime activities may not enter state institutional networks to begin with, and information that does enter may not travel far beyond neighboring and proximate institutions. Thus, in the absence of strong civic organizations and networks to connect them, state institutions may still give rise to mass protests, but these protests will tend to remain relatively localized and uncoordinated.

These arguments are based on diverse evidence collected over twelve months of field research in the Palestinian Territories. The centerpiece of this field research is an original, large-scale survey of former participants and nonparticipants in unarmed resistance to Israeli rule in the West Bank. The survey is the first large-scale poll of participants and nonparticipants in Palestinian resistance, as well as one of only a few systematic surveys of anti-regime resistance conducted worldwide. As such, it offers rare, fine-grained data on participation in resistance that are usually not available to scholars. In this book, I complement these survey data with insights drawn from over forty in-depth interviews with Palestinian political leaders and activists, teachers and students, former prisoners, and civil society members.

The book's findings explain how organizationally weak groups typically thought to lack the capacity for protest are able to mobilize against powerful regimes. According to canonical social movement theories, social movements emerge among groups with internal organizational strength: strong autonomous institutions, organizations, and networks of a group's own, which provide its members with the capacity for protest (McAdam, 2010; Tilly et al. 1975; Oberschall, 1973). For example, in the paradigmatic case of the American civil rights movement that helped shape this perspective, scholars trace the movement's emergence to the growing strength of the Southern black church and other "indigenous" institutions (McAdam, 2010; Morris, 1984). Similarly, as Zhao has noted, scholars also often invoke the rise of civil society to explain the Eastern European revolutions of 1989 (Di Palma, 1991; Ost, 1991), as well as the Chinese prodemocracy movement of the same year (Zhao, 1998, 1494). Yet, in contrast to these prominent cases, civil society organizations are often weak in the authoritarian environments in which anti-regime protest tends to take place. Increasingly, they are banned or harshly repressed and, therefore, have only limited size and influence. This book shows that, under these difficult conditions, integration into state institutions under the ruling regime's control paradoxically facilitates anti-regime resistance. Thus, while they do play a coordinating role, independent institutions and organizations of a group's own may not be as important for explaining the emergence of mass protest as many scholars have traditionally thought. In advancing our understanding of mass mobilization and participation among organizationally weak groups, the book also illuminates the sources of anti-regime protest in cases that are not fully explained by existing theories, including Palestine, South Africa, and Egypt.

1.2 CASE SELECTION

The Israeli–Palestinian conflict is one of the most intractable ongoing global conflicts.[4] Before his death, Nelson Mandela called a just solution to the conflict "the most important issue of our time" (quoted in Pilger 2007, 74.) Similarly, at the height of the Arab Spring protests, Jordan's King Abdullah declared, "[N]o matter what's happening in the Middle East – the Arab Spring… the economic challenges, high rates of unemployment – the emotional, critical issue is always the Israeli–Palestinian one."[5]

While the Israeli–Palestinian conflict did not originate with Israel's military occupation of the Palestinian Territories, the over fifty-year-old Israeli occupation underlies the modern dispute between Israel and the Palestinians. In 1967, during its second war with its Arab neighbors, Israel conquered the West Bank and the Gaza Strip and placed them under military rule. Claiming the eastern half of Jerusalem as part of Israel's undivided capital, it also annexed East Jerusalem and placed it under Israeli civil law. Since then, Israel has continued to exert effective control over these territories, even as it has ceded some sovereignty to the Palestinian Authority in the West Bank and withdrawn Israeli forces

---

4 The UCDP/PRIO Armed Conflict Dataset lists an active civil conflict between Israel and Palestinian actors for nearly every year from 1949 to 2014.

5 King Abdullah II. 2011, September 22. "King Abdullah: Jordan Needs 'Stable Middle Class' [Interview by D. Greene and S. Inskeep, Transcript]." NPR.org. www.npr.org/2011/09/22/140670554/king-abdullah-jordan-needs-stable-middle-class (accessed March 26, 2017).

and settlers from the Gaza Strip. Meanwhile, the mainstream Palestinian national movement – originally formed to "liberate" all of historic Palestine from Israeli sovereignty – has embraced ending the Israeli occupation of the Palestinian Territories and establishing an independent Palestinian state in its place as its primary goal.

Broad-based participation is critical to the success or failure of anti-regime movements such as the Palestinian national movement. Recent research suggests that such movements are more successful in ending military occupations and other forms of non-democratic rule when they use unarmed resistance rather than armed violence. Unarmed resistance is also associated with more desirable post-campaign outcomes, including, importantly, a lower risk of conflict recurrence (see e.g. Chenoweth and Stephan, 2011). In order for unarmed campaigns to succeed, however, they must attract wide participation (Chenoweth and Stephan, 2011; Pearlman, 2011). Identifying the conditions that support Palestinian participation in unarmed resistance can thus help to illuminate not only the trajectory of the ongoing Palestinian campaign against Israeli occupation but also the prospects for more comprehensive conflict resolution.

This book examines the determinants of participation in unarmed resistance against the Israeli occupation of the Palestinian Territories during more than a decade leading up to and culminating in the first Palestinian intifadah (1978–89). In addition to its geopolitical significance, the Palestinian case offers several advantages for studying the drivers of participation in unarmed resistance. As shown in Figure 1.1, Palestinians had ample opportunities to participate in unarmed resistance during the period from 1978 to 1989. Throughout this period, organized demonstrations, strikes, and other unarmed protests occurred with regular and increasing frequency throughout the Occupied Territories. By studying a case in which there were wide opportunities for participation over a sustained period of time, this book identifies why, given similar opportunities, some individuals participate whereas otherwise similar individuals do not. More generally, by focusing on a single case, this study is better able to hold constant country-level, contextual factors that may affect participation in resistance, such as colonial legacies. As a result, it can better isolate the individual-level characteristics and attributes that distinguish participants in resistance from nonparticipants and, therefore, explain their participation.

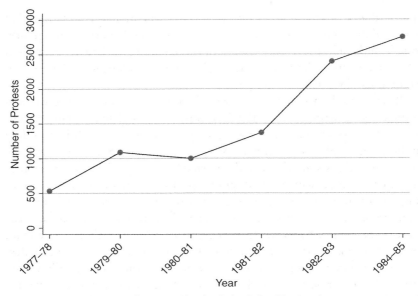

FIGURE 1.1 Unarmed protests in the Palestinian Territories, 1977–1985
Source: Israel Government Yearbooks, in Frisch 1996, 8.

In addition to these empirical advantages, a case study of the Palestinian Territories also offers advantages when it comes to theory-building. As Section 1.3 will describe, leading explanations for participation in political conflict and violence do not fully explain variation in participation in resistance among ordinary Palestinians. While nationalist grievances were strong in the Palestinian case, such grievances were pervasive while participation in resistance was relatively rare. Thus, while nationalist sentiment was an important contributing factor in the Palestinian case, it cannot explain why, given near-universal Palestinian support for the PLO-led nationalist movement, only a minority of Palestinians participated in resistance.[6] Similarly, the material incentives provided to motivate participation in many armed campaigns were also, generally, not offered to Palestinian participants in unarmed resistance. Finally, while civil society associations did help to coordinate participation in resistance, these

---

[6] The Palestinian Liberation Organization (PLO) is an umbrella organization consisting of the main Palestinian nationalist factions, which claims to be "the sole and legitimate representative of the Palestinian people." For a comprehensive history of the Palestinian national movement and the PLO, see Sayigh (1997), Brand (1991).

associations were still in their infancy as protest began to escalate in the late 1970s and generally too weak to support mass participation. Thus, existing theories of participation in political conflict do not fully account for participation in the Palestinian case. As such, a study of the Palestinian case offers a theoretical opportunity to identify new, causal variables that may better explain protest participation in this and other similar cases (see e.g. Seawright and Gerring, 2008).

Some readers may be wary of extrapolating from the Palestinian case to explain other cases of anti-regime resistance in this manner. Given the long duration of the Israeli–Palestinian conflict, the wide media coverage of its developments, and the high degree of international involvement throughout its many stages, it is reasonable to wonder whether the Palestinian case is an "outlier." Yet, while the larger context surrounding the Israeli–Palestinian conflict is indeed unusual, many of the dynamics underlying the political behavior of conflict actors are not. The basic problems that Palestinians had to overcome in order to participate in protest – repression, media censorship, and lack of information – are common to many autocratic regimes. And, while some nondemocratic regimes allow relatively greater space for civil society to develop, the weak, independent institutions and organizations present at the onset of Palestinian mobilization are hardly unique in nondemocratic societies. As such, this book joins the growing number of volumes focused on Palestine that seek to generalize from the Palestinian case and situate it in wider comparative perspective (see e.g. Ron 2003; Jamal 2007; Pearlman 2011; Krause 2017; Manekin, in press). Toward this goal, the book's conclusion discusses the relevance of its arguments for understanding participation in anti-apartheid protests in South Africa and labor strikes in prerevolutionary Egypt.

1.3 EXISTING EXPLANATIONS FOR PARTICIPATION IN UNARMED RESISTANCE

There is growing interest among political scientists in understanding why nonviolent resistance occurs and succeeds (see e.g. Pearlman, 2011; Chenoweth and Stephan, 2011; Nepstad, 2011; Cunningham, 2013). One pivotal condition for success is wide participation. Wide participation allows anti-regime movements to remain resilient in the face of repression, impose greater pressure on repressive regimes, and ultimately extract more meaningful concessions. In contrast, without broad-based participation, anti-regime movements often fail to achieve their goals and may not survive as political movements (Chenoweth and Stephan, 2011).

Who participates in unarmed resistance against repressive regimes, and why? Under which conditions are anti-regime movements most likely to achieve broad participation? The voluminous interdisciplinary literature on political conflict and violence offers a number of compelling answers to these questions. These explanations can be grouped together into three broad schools of thought: grievances, selective incentives, and social structures.

1.3.1 Grievances

Classical explanations for participation in political conflict highlight the role of shared grievances among participants. In cases of anti-occupation, anti-colonial, or nationalist resistance, group grievances rooted in a shared ethnic identity offer perhaps the most common explanation for why individuals resist. A long and illustrious research tradition links ethnic grievances stemming from ethnic discrimination, dominance, and exclusion to group-based mobilization (see e.g. Horowitz, 1985; Gellner and Breuilly, 2008; Gurr, 1970; Petersen, 2002). More recently, Adria Lawrence has persuasively argued that, in French colonies, nationalist movements emerged in response to the political exclusion of colonial subjects (Lawrence, 2013). Similarly, Cederman, Weidmann, and Gleditsch find that "horizontal inequalities" between ethnic groups – that is, "inequalities in economic, social or political dimensions or cultural status between culturally defined groups" (Stewart, 2008) – are associated with a higher probability of ethnonationalist conflict across a large sample of countries (Cederman, Weidmann, and Gleditsch, 2011, 480). While Cederman et al.'s analysis is restricted to civil war, its logic, which argues that inequalities between ethnic groups fuel resentment that promotes conflict, also applies to participation in unarmed resistance. Consistent with this logic, conventional accounts of the sources of the first Palestinian intifadah also often depict the uprising as an outpouring of simmering nationalist resentments and tensions.[7]

Economic grievances may also motivate participants in unarmed resistance, even in nationalist conflicts such as the Israeli–Palestinian conflict. As several scholars have shown, there is often a disjuncture between

---

[7] See e.g. Alimi (2007) for a critique of this perspective.

macro-level grievances and micro-level motivations for participation in conflict (Kalyvas, 2006; Beissinger, 2013; Mueller, 2013). For example, Lisa Mueller finds that participants in Niger's recent prodemocracy movement were driven less by democratic fervor than by more mundane economic demands (2013). Economic dissatisfaction can also intensify political grievances, decreasing support for the ruling regime and increasing the popularity of opposition candidates who are more likely to organize protests (Brancati, 2016). Thus, while the Israeli–Palestinian conflict is fundamentally a conflict between two national groups, it is also possible that participants in the first Palestinian intifadah were driven as much by economic considerations as by national ones. In line with classical theories of revolution, participants could have been motivated by poverty, inequality, landlessness, or other objective economic conditions (Paige, 1978; Scott, 1976; Wickham-Crowley, 1992). Or, they may have been moved to protest by a more subjective sense of economic deprivation, stemming from the gap between individual expectations and economic realities (Gurr, 1970).[8] In keeping with both these perspectives, Israeli authorities have tended to see economic factors as the key to ensuring Palestinian quiescence (Hiltermann, 1993, 18; Khawaja, 1995).

Economic factors appear to have played a relatively minimal role in the Palestinian case, however. While Israeli economic policies in the Palestinian Territories undermined the development of an independent Palestinian national economy, they also initially sought to promote individual prosperity as a means toward social stability (Roy, 1995; Gordon, 2008). Toward this goal, during the first decade of occupation (1967–76), Israeli authorities introduced a number of economic development programs intended to increase Palestinians' economic productivity. Israeli officials established vocational training programs and New Deal–style relief programs, offered low interest-rate loans, and introduced programs to improve agricultural productivity. More importantly, as part of its wider policy of maintaining open borders with the Palestinian Territories (and, therefore, also erasing these borders), Israel permitted Palestinians in the Occupied Territories to work in Israel, where they could earn significantly higher wages. As a result, between 1968 and 1980 the Palestinian economy expanded rapidly, substantially raising standards of

---

[8] More recently, influential work by Elisabeth Wood (2003) and Wendy Pearlman (2011) has also stressed the importance of subjective, psychological, and emotional factors arising from broader political, economic, or social conditions.

living for many Palestinian households (Gordon, 2008, 62–67).[9] Growth did eventually stall out in the early 1980s, causing economic distress and, according to some analysts, leading to the outbreak of the first intifadah in 1987 (Schiff and Yaari, 1991, 87–95). Yet, while hard economic times may have helped cause the intifadah, the Palestinian economy was strong as resistance to Israeli rule first intensified in the late 1970s. Thus, while economic grievances may also drive ethno-national protest, there was not an objective economic basis for such grievances until after protest was well underway.

Nationalist grievances, in contrast, were much more important. Consistent with grievance theories, public opinion surveys show rising levels of nationalism and support for the PLO in the Palestinian Territories as early as 1973. For example, a survey conducted by Israel's *Ma'ariv* newspaper in the wake of the 1973 War found what it called an "extensive and alarming" shift in public support for the PLO and its goal of establishing an independent national Palestinian state (Gordon, 2008, 102). Three years later, in 1976, pro-PLO candidates swept to victory in local municipal elections held in the West Bank. By the early 1980s, polls showed nearly universal support for a Palestinian state under the leadership of the PLO. For example, in a 1982 *Time* magazine poll, 98 percent of Palestinians surveyed favored a Palestinian state, and 86 percent believed that state should be governed by the PLO (Tessler, 1994, 567).

Public opinion surveys, local elections, and other barometers of public opinion thus showed strong support for the PLO-led nationalist movement preceding the rise in unarmed resistance in the late 1970s. Without this strong nationalist sentiment, many Palestinians would surely have been unwilling to incur the high risks and costs of participating in resistance against Israeli rule. Yet, as in other uprisings, this high level of support did not translate into universal participation. Despite wide participation in the first intifadah as compared to other uprisings, the majority of Palestinians did *not* participate in protest even at the revolt's height.[10] Thus, while national grievances may well be a necessary condition for participation, they are not, in and of themselves, sufficient to

---

[9] Between 1968 and 1972, the gross national product (GNP) of the Palestinian Territories increased annually by a whopping 18 percent; between 1973 and 1980, economic growth continued at a slower but still impressive annual rate of over 7 percent (Gordon, 2008, 66).

[10] As mentioned earlier, 35 percent of Palestinians are estimated to have participated in protests at the peak of the first intifadah. Participation rate calculated using the NAVCO 1.1 dataset (Chenoweth, 2011).

explain individual variation in participation in the Palestinian case. Building on grievance theories, this book develops an explanation of why, given such pervasive grievances among members of a group, some group members participate while others abstain.

1.3.2 Selective Incentives

Selective incentives offer a second, possible explanation for participation in anti-regime resistance. In *The Logic of Collective Action*, Mancur Olson famously argued that, because successful collective action yields benefits for participants and nonparticipants alike, rational individuals will be tempted to "free-ride" off others' participation (i.e. "the free-rider problem"). To motivate rational individuals to act in the collective interest, groups must thus offer "selective incentives" – private material goods available only to those participating (Olson, 1965, 51). Applying Olson's framework to the study of revolution, Samuel Popkin argued that armed groups overcome the free-rider problem by offering individuals selective incentives contingent on their participation (Popkin, 1979). More recently, Mark Lichbach has documented the use of such incentives across many forms of contentious politics, including unorganized protests, workers' movements, strikes, and riots (Lichbach, 1998*a*, 217–26).

At the same time, as Mark Beissinger has pointed out, selective incentives may be more likely to operate in some contexts than others. In particular, mass movements are likely to face greater challenges deploying selective incentives than revolutionary vanguard parties, armed militias, or conventional armies. Unlike these latter movements, mass movements typically cannot monitor participation, differentiate between participants and nonparticipants, or provide powerful selective incentives (Beissinger, 2013). As such, selective incentives may be less important motivations for participation in unarmed resistance than armed resistance.

Consistent with this perspective, selective incentives do not appear to have been an important motive for participation in unarmed protest in the Palestinian Territories. Such incentives were not wholly unavailable. Scholarships to attend university abroad, provided to the PLO by various Arab states and the Soviet Union, were allocated firstly to PLO members and their families. PLO members also received salaries and other fringe benefits, and families of killed or imprisoned PLO members received financial assistance (Sayigh, 1997, 458; Jamal, 2005, 70.) While before

1982 the greater part of PLO resources flowed into Lebanon (Frisch, 2012), PLO members in the Occupied Territories were also sometimes rewarded with such benefits. Yet, these benefits were rarely extended to ordinary participants in unarmed resistance, who were generally not formally affiliated with PLO factions. Nor is there any evidence that these participants systematically engaged in looting or other forms of self-enrichment. Thus, to the extent they matter at all, material incentives seem to provide a better explanation for participation in the PLO's formal political and military structures than in mass protest against Israeli rule.

1.3.3 Social Structures

A third set of explanations highlights the role of a community's social structures in shaping participation among its members. Political process theory, arguably the dominant paradigm on social movement mobilization to date, posits that strong independent institutions and organizations provide communities with the valuable resources – leaders, financial resources, communication networks, and, most importantly, members – required for social movements to emerge (see e.g. Oberschall, 1973; Tilly et al., 1975; McAdam, 2010). For example, in the paradigmatic case of the American civil rights movement, the expansion of African American churches, universities, and other autonomous black institutions during the first half of the twentieth century is thought to have afforded the incipient movement with the critical resources it needed to embark in protest (Morris, 1984; McAdam, 2010). Absent such internal organizational strength, some scholars argue, communities will lack the capacity for collective action even in the face of favorable political opportunities for protest. Subsequent revisions to social movement theory have taken a more dynamic and contingent approach, showing how, in the absence of strong preexisting organizations, such institutions can be appropriated or even created (McAdam, Tarrow, and Tilly, 2003). Yet, to a significant degree, internal organizational strength is still seen by many social movement scholars as a prerequisite for protest (see e.g. Tilly and Tarrow, 2007; Nepstad, 2011, 6).[11]

While social movement theories are primarily concerned with explaining why social movements emerge rather than why individuals participate

---

[11] See also Diani and McAdam's review of this literature (2003).

in them, they have important implications for understanding individual participation decisions. In particular, these theories suggest that members of preexisting community institutions and organizations should be more likely to participate in social movement activism than nonmembers. Through their integration into preexisting community institutions and organizations, organization members are more readily available for recruitment into a movement. That is, they are more likely to have been in contact with the movement and its activists – arguably, the most important predictor of recruitment and participation (McAdam, 2010, 44). They can be recruited to the movement en masse using "bloc recruitment" rather than through the slow task of recruiting "isolated and solitary individuals" (Oberschall, 1973, 125). And, due to their existing relationships with organization leaders already active in the movement, they will also tend to be more willing to participate in its activities (McAdam, 2010, 132–33).

Similarly, many social scientists have emphasized the importance of civil society organizations in driving participation in high-risk activism more generally. Membership in civil society associations is often argued to increase the prospects of participation in risky collective action, including both nonviolent protest (Tilly, Tilly, and Tilly, 1975; McAdam, 1986; McAdam and Paulsen, 1993) and violent conflict (Petersen, 2001; Laitin, 1995; Scacco, n.d.). Membership in civil society associations can serve as a source of social pressure – or, conversely, social rewards – to participate in high-risk collective action, rendering civil society members more willing to accept the risks of participation (McAdam, 1986; Petersen, 2001; Scacco, n.d.). Civil society associations can also play a key role in coordinating protest and contacting and organizing prospective protestors, making them more likely to participate (Beissinger, 2011; Beissinger, Jamal, and Mazur, 2015; Mueller, 2013). While scholars may disagree about the specific mechanisms by which civil society associations promote participation, almost all systematic survey research on this topic has found a strong empirical relationship between membership in civil society associations and participation in high-risk collective action (McAdam, 1986; Beissinger, 2011, 2013; Mueller, 2013; Scacco, n.d.).

Membership in civil society associations can also give rise to the strong face-to-face ties that may, more generally, shape the decision to participation in high-risk collective action (McAdam, 1986; Opp and Gern, 1993; Petersen, 2001; Laitin, 1995). Like formal membership in civil society associations, strong ties between individuals can provide social rewards for participation as well as social sanctions for abstention (McAdam, 1986; Opp and Gern, 1993). And, strong ties within groups can build the collective identity and group solidarity that enables group members to join together in collective endeavors (Goldstone, 1994). Consistent with this perspective, empirical studies have found evidence of the importance of strong ties for both unarmed protest (McAdam, 1986; Opp and Gern, 1993) and armed resistance (Petersen, 2001; Laitin, 1995).

In contrast, other scholars have suggested that weak ties, or a combination of strong and weak ties, may be more important in pulling individuals to participate in revolutionary protest (Goldstone, 1994; Beissinger, 2013). Drawing on influential social network theories that argue that larger, more diverse networks are also richer in information (Granovetter, 1973), these scholars contend that weak ties between individuals or groups are important for spreading information and coordinating action during revolutionary processes. In accordance with this argument, Beissinger (2013) finds that internet usage had a larger impact on participation in Ukraine's Orange Revolution than membership in a civil society association, which he interprets as evidence of "the strength of weak ties" (Granovetter, 1973).

In line with the previously discussed social structure theories, scholars of Palestinian politics have also emphasized the importance of Palestinian civil society for the evolution of the first intifadah. For example, in his study of the Palestinian labor and women's movements, Joost Hiltermann argues that the years of institution-building that preceded the first intifadah produced an "institutional infrastructure of resistance" that helped sustain the uprising (Hiltermann, 1993, 13–14). As the uprising began, Hiltermann shows, local trade union branches, women's associations, and other civil society institutions transformed into new "popular committees" that worked to support the uprising (Hiltermann, 1993). In line with this argument, Khawaja (1995) finds that Palestinian West Bank communities that were home to more civil society associations and had greater organizational strength were more likely to participate in local collective action against the Israeli occupation.

Yet, contrary to most social structure theories, the civil society associations and high levels of community organization that ultimately helped propel participation in the first intifadah were still weak as resistance to Israeli rule began to intensify in the late 1970s. Frozen after decades of war, authoritarian rule, and military occupation, Palestinian civil society began to thaw earlier in the decade due to the organizing efforts of pro-PLO nationalist activists. Yet, in the late 1970s, few civic organizations "of any size or influence" existed in the Palestinian Territories (Hiltermann, 1993, 14). Trade unions were small in size and confined to the main Palestinian cities (Hiltermann, 1993, 64). Although the vast majority of West Bank Palestinians lived in rural villages, rural areas had few associations of any kind until well into the 1980s (Al-Sha'bani and Khadr, 1982). Thus, when unarmed resistance to Israeli rule began to escalate in 1978, Palestinian civil society was still too weak to promote participation on a mass level. While those in civic associations and networks were indeed more likely to protest (as predicted by social structure theories), involvement in these nascent structures does not well explain participation among the majority of Palestinians, who were not involved in and were oftentimes completely unaware of them.

Many scholars and observers of Middle East politics have pointed to the role of mosques as mobilizing institutions in revolutions and uprisings around the region (see e.g. Kurzman, 1994; Wiktorowicz, 2004). Mosques were generally more widely present in the Palestinian Territories than other kinds of civic institutions. In the Gaza Strip in particular, the number of mosques doubled between 1967 and 1987 in tandem with the growth of the Islamic movement (Mishal and Sela, 2006, 21). Beginning in the mid-1970s, this increase in mosque construction was also accompanied by the development of new mosque-based social service institutions in Gaza, such as kindergartens and nursery schools (Abu-Amr, 1994, 14–16). Islamist attempts at institutional penetration came later in the West Bank; however, some Islamist institutions were also formed there around this time (Mishal and Sela, 2006, 25).

Yet, unlike the black churches at the core of the American civil rights movement, Palestinian mosques and their institutions were not widely used for mobilization until the first intifadah. Before the uprising began in 1987, Palestinian Islamists and nationalists were involved in a contentious, and sometimes violent, ideological and political struggle. Palestinian Islamists vehemently opposed the PLO and its goal of establishing an independent national (and secular) Palestinian state (Sahliyeh, 1988, 143, 151–58). Rather than use the mosques to mobilize Palestinians to support the nationalist cause, PLO supporters charged, Islamist activists used them to "spread hatred and divide Palestinians" (Sahliyeh, 1988, 156). By the mid-1980s, violent clashes between supporters of the two groups had become routine (Mishal and Sela, 2006, 23–25).

Thus, similarly to Iranian mosques during the early phases of the Iranian Revolution, Palestinian mosques may be considered to have been a "latent resource" as resistance to Israeli rule began to intensify (Kurzman, 1994). Between 1978 and 1987, mosques were occasionally used to protest specific Israeli settler attacks on Muslim religious sites (Sahliyeh, 1988, 147). Yet, only when Islamists joined forces with nationalists in the first intifadah did they provide a basis for more widespread mobilization.

In sum, as unarmed resistance to Israeli rule first intensified in the late 1970s, Palestinians lacked the internal organizational strength that is often thought to be necessary for protest. While beginning to expand, Palestinian civil society was still nascent, largely restricted to urban areas, and lacking in wide influence as more Palestinians began participating in resistance. The mosque network was relatively more developed, but it too was much stronger in the Gaza Strip than in the West Bank and was dominated by Islamist supporters opposed to the PLO and the PLO-led protest movement. Thus, in order to explain how and why some Palestinians participated in unarmed resistance to Israeli rule, we first need to explain how people resist in the absence of strong supportive organizations and networks.

This book builds on prior social structure theories to explain mobilization and participation in anti-regime resistance among organizationally weak groups. Drawing on well-established social movement and network theories, it argues that, in the absence of strong independent institutions and organizations, state institutions can facilitate anti-regime protest. Consistent with theories that point to the utility of weak ties for protest, integration into these institutions joins previously unconnected individuals in larger, more diverse, and information-rich social networks. Similarly, in line with resource mobilization and political process theories, these institutions, despite their state control, provide resources that facilitate communication and coordination under repression. In contrast, as this book will go on to show, integration into state institutions does not uniformly give rise to the strong anti-regime grievances that are also necessary for protest. Instead, like other previously studied "mobilizing structures" (McCarthy, 1996), integration into these institutions makes regime opponents better able to act on their existing grievances, thereby making it more likely that they will participate in protest. After defining what I mean by state institutions more precisely, the next section further develops this argument.

1.4 DEFINITIONS

1.4.1 State-Controlled Mass Institutions

This book focuses on the role of state-controlled mass institutions in shaping participation in anti-regime resistance. Institutions are "systems of established and prevalent social rules that structure social interactions" (Hodgson, 1988, 2).[12] They include organizations, formal rules such as laws, and informal rules such as social norms and conventions. Some examples of institutions are language, money, law, systems of weights and measures, table manners, and firms and other organizations (Hodgson, 1988, 2).

Organizations belong to a subset of institutions defined by three additional features.[13] According to Geoffrey Hodgson, organizations are "special institutions" that develop criteria to establish their boundaries and distinguish members from nonmembers, involve principles of sovereignty concerning who is in charge, and possess chains of command delineating responsibility within the organization. They include political parties, firms, trade unions, schools, and universities (Hodgson, 1988; North, 1994).

Organizations may be either controlled by, or independent of, the state. Examples of state-controlled organizations include schools, prisons, and courts, although these organizations may also be independent (e.g. private schools, private prisons, etc.). Some examples of independent organizations are religious institutions such as churches or mosques, firms or factories, trade unions, or other civil society organizations. However, in totalitarian regimes, many authoritarian societies, and even some democratic systems, such organizations may also be controlled by the state. Thus, whether or not a given organization is state-controlled depends on its context.

Drawing on these distinctions, I thus define a state-controlled mass institution as a large, heterogeneous organization that is run or controlled by the state or government. Any single organization such as a particular school is thus a state-controlled mass institution if it has three qualities: (1) it is public; (2) it is large in size; (3) it has a heterogeneous membership, constituency, or population that draws from multiple

---

[12] See also Knight (1992, 2).
[13] See Hodgson (1988) for an exchange between Hodgson and Douglass North affirming the consistency of organizations with North's definition of institutions.

segments of society (i.e. it is mass-based). A system of organizations such as "schools," "the school system," or "the educational system" can be said to be a mass institution to the extent that the organizations that make up the system are generally mass institutions (e.g. if a majority of schools are mass institutions).

This book focuses on two types of state-controlled mass institutions: educational institutions and disciplinary institutions. During the period of study, most Palestinian students attended state-controlled educational institutions under Israeli administration. With access to education beyond the primary level limited in rural areas (as it is in many developing countries), most intermediate and higher-level schools were based in cities and large towns. Consequently, these schools drew a heterogeneous population of urban students and rural students from outlying villages. Moreover, due to little state investment in education, Palestinian schools were generally quite large and overcrowded (Rosenfeld, 2004, 116; Graham-Brown, 1984, 65). Thus, like schools in many other developing countries, Palestinian schools can be considered to be state-controlled mass institutions.

Similarly, in the Palestinian case, prisons, courts, and other disciplinary institutions may also be considered state-controlled mass institutions. As incarceration widened as a means of control over the Palestinian Territories, these institutions came to resemble a diverse cross section of Palestinian society (Rosenfeld, 2004). Within their walls, prisoners and detainees from cities, villages, and refugee camps throughout the Palestinian Territories mixed with one another, bridging existing ethnic, social, and geographic divides. These social interactions were not only limited to prisoners, however. As a result of their relationships with prisoners, family members and friends of detainees were also, indirectly, integrated into prisons and courts and, in turn, came into contact with one another. Chapter 4 of this book focuses on these wider interactions between previously politically uninvolved family members and friends of prisoners and shows that they resulted in greater participation in protest.

At the same time, there are also important differences between educational and disciplinary institutions. In particular, we may be more likely to see mobilization in schools than in prisons or courts for a number of reasons. First, whereas students are integrated directly into schools, prisoners' families and friends are only indirectly incorporated into disciplinary institutions. Second, school students are also younger and more "biographically available" for protest than prisoners' families (see e.g. McAdam, 1986). Finally, students may also be less constrained from participating in anti-regime resistance than prisoners' families and friends in other ways. For example, the imprisonment of a family member or friend could constrain individuals from participating in resistance for fear of further retaliation against their loved one. Thus, disciplinary institutions such as prisons and courts may represent a relatively "hard case" in which to test the impact of integration into state institutions on participation in protest. To the extent we see mobilization around these institutions as well as around schools, we can thus be more confident of a common institutional and informational explanation for participation in resistance in both cases.

1.4.2 Anti-regime Resistance

This book argues, when groups have high anti-regime sentiment and low organizational strength, that integration into state institutions makes individuals better able, and thus more likely, to participate in anti-regime resistance. I conceptualize anti-regime resistance as risky unarmed collective action targeted against repressive regimes, such as demonstrations, marches, strikes, and sit-ins. Anti-regime resistance is similar to but broader than the concepts of "nonviolent resistance" and "civil resistance" used in much of the literature. Like nonviolent resistance, anti-regime resistance includes acts of unarmed nonviolence, such as demonstrations and marches, sit-ins, and strikes and boycotts (Sharp, 1973).[14] However, anti-regime resistance can also include acts of what some have called "unarmed violence" that use physical force but no weapons, such as the stone-throwing clashes that were an important tactic in the first Palestinian intifadah (Pressman, 2017). Like many forms of unarmed nonviolence, clashes involving stone-throwing are an instance of "crowd collective action" and also involve high risks of participation. Consequently, the logic of participation in such events should be similar to the logic of participation in unarmed nonviolence. As such, this study takes participation in unarmed resistance against repressive regimes – encompassing both unarmed nonviolence and unarmed violence – as its dependent variable.

This definition of anti-regime resistance includes rebellion against both domestic regimes and foreign powers (i.e. occupying regimes). Whether domestic or foreign, unarmed resistance against repressive regimes involves high risks of participation: it is "intense and extreme"

---

[14] See also Pearlman (2011, 3).

and often provokes state violence (Chenoweth and Stephan, 2011, 13). Both domestic and foreign regimes also often seek to limit the flow of information available to citizens and shape the informational environment in similar ways. While this book is based on a detailed study of participation in anti-occupation resistance, its conclusions should therefore apply to anti-regime resistance in general.[15]

1.5 THE ARGUMENT

Having defined state-controlled mass institutions and anti-regime resistance, I now develop a theory that explains how such institutions promote resistance. This theory is expected to apply when groups have high anti-regime sentiment but lack the internal organizational strength often thought to be necessary for protest. Under these conditions, it holds, integration into state institutions will make individuals more likely to participate in anti-regime resistance by lowering informational and organizational barriers to collective action. Integration into these institutions joins individuals in new, more information-rich social networks that persist over time, facilitates communication and coordination, and reduces the risks of protest. As a result, integration into state institutions makes individuals more likely to begin participating in anti-regime resistance even without the benefit of strong civil society organizations, and these initial patterns of participation tend to endure. Yet, while integration into state institutions facilitates participation in mass protests among organizationally weak groups, state institutions alone cannot well support a more comprehensive national uprising. For such an uprising to evolve, groups must therefore develop independent organizations that can subsequently link disparate protests into a coordinated nationwide campaign.

Unarmed resistance against repressive regimes requires mass participation to succeed (Chenoweth and Stephan, 2011; Pearlman, 2011). Yet, anti-regime movements, including anti-occupation movements such as the Palestinian national movement, face challenges in mobilizing participants that social movements in democracies do not. Unlike social movements in democracies, anti-regime movements cannot publicize their activities to prospective participants. Repression and media censorship limit the availability of information. For example, describing the

---

[15] For other studies that generalize from anti-occupation resistance to resistance against other regimes, see Petersen (2001), Laitin (1995), and Darden (2013).

Soviet occupation of Lithuania, Roger Petersen writes that "the biggest problem became the total lack of information. Previously, news traveled through national organizations or papers or radios. Soon after their arrival, the new Soviet regime banned the Young Farmers and Sauliai groups (and all other organizations) and controlled all newspapers and radios" (Petersen, 2001, 115). Likewise, nearly fifty years later, Palestinians confronted a similar information problem. With "almost nothing" about the swelling intifada protests published in the mass media, Palestinian journalist Daoud Kuttab observed that "the Palestinian press was the last place anyone would turn to in order to find out what was happening" (1998).

As these examples suggest, prospective participants in anti-regime resistance face formidable informational and organizational barriers to collective action. These barriers can be thought of as comprising two interrelated informational problems. First, individuals lack basic information about when, where, and how to participate in resistance (i.e. "information on tactics").[16] Under repressive regimes, information about protests is not widely available in the mass media or other sources, leaving most individuals uninformed about where, when, and how they will take place – if they will take place at all. For example, Petersen notes that few citizens heard the appeal issued by the Lithuanian Activist Front to "take independent initiative" to "create the links of a secret activist chain" (Petersen, 2001, 101). With the national leadership banned, organizations removed, and newspapers and radio stations "muzzled," Lithuanians were forced to rely on the "clues emanating from their local environment" (Petersen, 2001, 101). More recently, during the Arab Spring protests in Morocco, Adria Lawrence reports that few rural residents were aware of the ongoing demonstrations – despite the fact that these demonstrations lasted for several months and spread to over one hundred Moroccan towns (Lawrence, 2017, 5).

Second, given information about an impending demonstration or protest, individuals may lack information about the number of other likely participants (i.e. "information on numbers"). Expectations about the number of participants in protest activity are paramount to participation decisions. As the number of participants grows, protestors enjoy

---

[16] This formulation borrows from Little's term "coordination on tactics" (Little, 2016). Because anti-regime resistance in the Palestinian Territories was often organized as opposed to spontaneous, I prefer the term "information on tactics" to (spontaneous) "coordination on tactics."

greater "safety in numbers" and their individual risks of participation fall (Kuran, 1989, 1991). Expectations of large crowds – being "one of many" – can also overcome the "barrier of fear" that may thwart participation in resistance (Pearlman, 2013). And, expectations of crowds should also increase the perceived efficacy of resistance, making individuals more likely to participate (McAdam, 2010; Tucker, 2007). Yet, forming reliable expectations about the number of protestors is difficult under repressive regimes. Prospective dissidents may be uninformed about the nature of the regime (Lohmann, 1994), the preferences of their fellow citizens (Kuran, 1989, 1991), or whether their compatriots will act on these preferences despite the risks.

This book argues that integration into state institutions makes individuals more likely to participate in anti-regime resistance by improving information about both tactics and numbers, thereby lowering informational and organizational barriers to collective action. Integration into state institutions can overcome these barriers through at least three interrelated pathways, which are summarized in Figure 1.2. First, integration into such institutions can provide individuals with novel information about protest from outside their immediate social networks. Second, it can facilitate communication and coordination among large numbers of people and allow information to spread more quickly. Finally, in a context where assembly is otherwise restricted, integration into state institutions can reduce uncertainty about the size and strength of protests and lower the risks of protest participation.

The first way in which integration into state institutions facilitates participation is by joining individuals in new, more diverse and information-rich social networks. According to influential network theories, new information and opportunities must come from "weak ties" from outside an individual's immediate social networks. As a result, broader and more heterogeneous social networks tend to provide more novel information than more narrow and homogenous networks (Granovetter, 1973; Burt, 2009). This book argues that integration into state institutions connects individuals in such wider and more diverse social networks. As public institutions, state institutions tend to have a large, heterogeneous membership that draws from multiple segments of society. For example, in developing countries with limited access to education, public schools typically gather together urban and rural youth from a variety of geographic and social backgrounds. Similarly, in the course of prison visits and court sessions, prisons and courts also bring family members and friends of accused prisoners together and foster unexpected connections

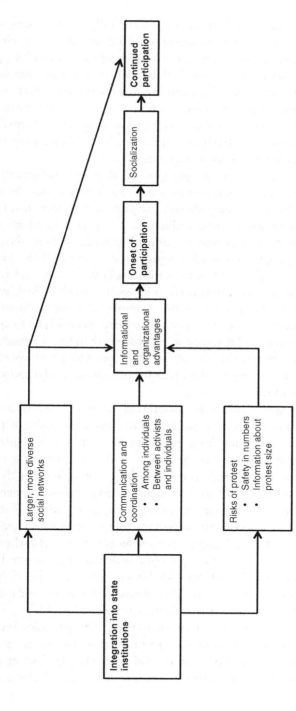

FIGURE 1.2 How integration into state institutions leads to participation in anti-regime resistance

between them. Finally, if initially organizationally weak groups subsequently develop independent organizations and networks of their own, integration into state institutions may also bring individuals into politicized civic networks that are particularly rich in political information. Consequently, individuals inside state institutions are more likely to hear about anti-regime protests and the size and strength of the crowds gathered than individuals outside these institutions. Thus, all else equal, they are better able and more likely to participate in resistance than similar individuals outside this institutional context.

In addition to connecting people in more diverse networks that are richer in information, integration into state institutions also allows this information to be more easily shared. Integration into state institutions facilitates communication and coordination. In societies in which assembly is restricted, these institutions gather hundreds or even thousands of like-minded people in a single geographical location. This "ecological concentration" allows for information to flow quickly and reduces organizational and transaction costs (Lichbach, 1998*b*). Thus, when a "trigger event" sparks protests – for example, a shooting by security forces – individuals inside state institutions are more likely to quickly hear about this event and the impending protests than those outside these institutions. As a result, the probability that they will participate in the demonstrations is also higher than that for otherwise similar individuals outside these institutions.

Finally, integration into state institutions also reduces uncertainty about the size and strength of protests and lowers the risks of protest participation. By gathering large numbers of people in a single location, these institutions provide the people within them with a relative degree of "safety in numbers." As one in a large crowd, individuals inside these institutions face lower risks of identification and punishment and, in turn, of political participation (Gurr, 1970, 265). State institutions are likely to play a particularly important role in cases where assembly is otherwise restricted and groups cannot legally gather elsewhere. For example, were it not for the unique concentration of large numbers of students in Beijing's university district, Zhao argues that the 1989 Chinese prodemocracy movement would not have been nearly as capable of confronting China's powerful state apparatus (Zhao, 1998).

Similarly, integration into state institutions also provides individuals with "information on numbers" in mass demonstrations, reducing uncertainty about the size of protests and lowering the risks of participation. Suzanne Lohman argues that individuals take "informational cues" about opposition to repressive regimes from changes in the size of a protest movement over time (Lohmann, 1994). Yet, under repressive regimes, such changes may not be easily observable. For example, information about the size of protests may not be reported in the media due to censorship. And, direct personal observation may be risky: in many contexts, even being in the vicinity of a demonstration is grounds for arrest and abuse (see e.g. Opp and Gern, 1993, 676). Within this low-information environment, integration into state institutions offers an informational advantage. Inside these institutions, large numbers of prospective protestors can legally gather, observe how many others are gathered, and assess their risks of participation before facing the state's coercive apparatus. For example, even in prisons, prisoners' family members and friends can often congregate together on the prison grounds and, thereby, take the measure of their group. In contrast, outside state institutions, obtaining reliable "information on numbers" often involves greater risks.

As a result of these informational and organizational advantages, individuals who are incorporated into state institutions are better able to participate in anti-regime resistance than similar individuals outside these institutions. This, in turn, increases the likelihood that they will begin participating in resistance. Building on this general argument, the next section traces how these organizational and informational benefits operate more specifically within two key types of state institutions: educational institutions and disciplinary institutions.

1.5.1 Educational Institutions

Educational institutions offer a classic example of how state institutions provide informational and organizational advantages that foster collective dissent. In repressive societies that place limits on assembly, schools offer substantial advantages for information-sharing. As Lipset has written, school and university campuses offer "an ideal place in which to find large numbers of people in a common situation" (1971). "Like a vast factory, a large campus brings together great numbers of people in similar life situations, in close proximity to each other ... *It is relatively easy to reach students; leaflets handed out at the campus gate will usually do the job. These facilitate quick communication*, foster solidarity and help arouse melodramatic action" (Lipset, 1964, 35; my emphasis). As Lipset's observation suggests, information spreads quickly across students, and there are lower organizational and transaction costs of collective action (Lichbach, 1998*b*). As a result, students are more likely to know about impending protests and participate in them than nonstudent youth.

The concentration of large numbers of youth in schools also provides young dissidents with a degree of "safety in numbers" and reduces the risks of protest. As one of many, students face lower risks of identification and punishment than nonstudent youth. The school environment also provides students with valuable "information on numbers" that is not generally available to nonstudents. Because students may legally gather in schools, they can assemble, take measure of their strength, and assess the risks of protest before facing the state's coercive apparatus. In contrast, in repressive societies that limit assembly, obtaining reliable "information on numbers" outside schools is far more risky. For this reason, organized protests often begin from schools and universities, which allow for a "critical mass" of protestors to form before marching out into the street (see e.g. Zhao, 1998).

In addition to these advantages, schools also join youth in wider and more information-rich social networks, which give them access to scarce information about protest. In developing countries where access to education is limited, intermediate and higher-level schools are typically located in urban centers and draw students from both the city and the surrounding villages. As a result, they bring together students from a variety of different geographic and social backgrounds. Indeed, for youth in Palestine and elsewhere, schools often serve as the "primary source of social interaction beyond the family" (FACTS Information Committee, 1990*b*, 337).[17] In contrast, without this forum for social interaction, youth outside schools tend to have smaller, more homogeneous social networks and less access to political information than youth inside schools. As a result, they are worse able and less likely to participate in protest than their student peers.

In sum, integration into educational institutions provides youth with the "information on tactics" and "information on numbers" that are necessary for unarmed protest and lowers their informational and organizational barriers to participation. As a result, students are better able

---

[17] The FACTS Information Committee describes itself as belonging to "a network of popular information committees that arose as a result of the popular organization movement during the intifada or Palestinian uprising" (FACTS Information Committee, 1990*c*, 1). This description indicates that the committee sees itself as part of the Palestinian national movement in the Occupied Territories and that it is likely associated with a Palestinian political faction or group of factions.

to participate in unarmed protest than their nonstudent peers. Consequently, the probability that they will begin participating in protest is also higher than that of otherwise similar youth outside schools. This impact of integration into educational institutions, however, is not uniform but varies across different levels of schooling.

Intermediate Schooling and Protest

Building on this book's more general theory, this book further argues that the impact of integration into educational institutions on anti-regime resistance varies with different levels of schooling. Specifically, as Chapter 3 will show, individuals who were integrated into intermediate schools should be significantly more likely to participate in protest than their peers with less schooling. However, due to the persistence of participation, additional schooling over and above this intermediate level should not further raise their prospects of participation. As a result, the relationship between integration into educational institutions and participation in protest is expected to take on a curvilinear shape, with the probability of participation rising with intermediate schooling and subsequently diminishing.

Different levels of schooling vary in their impact because, in part, primary schoolchildren are generally too young to participate in protest.[18] Regardless of whether or not they are integrated into schools, their probability of participation is low. As children enter adolescence, however, those who pursue additional intermediate levels of schooling are integrated into an institutional environment that facilitates mass mobilization. As previously discussed, they face lower informational and organizational barriers to collective action. Thus, all else equal, they are better able to participate in anti-regime resistance than youth who do not further continue their schooling and are not exposed to this institutional environment. As a result, the probability that they will begin participating in resistance is also higher than that of otherwise similar youth with less schooling.

As I will argue later, these initial forays into protest tend to forge persistent patterns of political participation. Because the social networks formed within intermediate schools remain in place even after individuals

---

[18] In addition, primary schools tend to be local institutions, which engender more narrow social networks than higher-level schools. Thus, while integration into these schools could promote participation in protest by lowering informational and organizational barriers to collective action in other ways, it does not provide students with novel information from outside their community to the same degree.

leave these institutions, and because participation itself may be habit-forming in various ways, youth who begin participating in protest in intermediate schools are likely to continue doing so afterward. Consequently, while they should be more likely to protest than youth with less schooling, their propensity for protest should be similar to that of more educated youth. This produces a curvilinear relationship, with the probability of participation rising at intermediate schooling and subsequently flattening out.

Schools are not the only state institutions to foster persistent habits of political participation, however. Under repressive regimes with high incarceration rates, integration into prisons, courts, and other disciplinary institutions also facilitates collective action and makes some individuals better able to engage in political activism. At the same time, integration into these institutions can also subject these individuals to greater control by the state, potentially deterring them from resisting. In the next section, I explain why, paradoxically, integration into these institutions tends to promote rather than stifle protest.

1.5.2 Disciplinary Institutions

A large body of literature argues that mass imprisonment, like other forms of state repression, may provoke resistance rather than pacify it. When states imprison large numbers of their own citizens, these works suggest, they transform "latent grievances into active antagonisms" (Thoms and Ron, 2007). Dissidents become unwilling to tolerate the status quo, and opposition groups no longer see any other outlets for positive change (White, 1989; Goodwin, 2001). As a result, these scholars argue, they are also more likely to turn to violence. This perspective is also shared by world leaders, including former UN Secretary General Kofi Annan, who cautioned that the rising use of mass imprisonment constitutes "a root cause of conflict."[19]

Imprisonment also figures largely in the academic and popular literature on Palestinian resistance. Among both scholars and the wider Palestinian public – including, first and foremost, prisoners themselves – prisons are widely seen as "universities" (see e.g. Peteet 1994, 39; Collins 2004, 127–30). Through political education and socialization in prison,

[19] Annan, Kofi, 2006, Progress Report on the Prevention of Armed Conflict, https://reliefweb.int/sites/reliefweb.int/files/resources/EAF731628872FF08852571D3006D2418-UNGA-conflictprev-July2006.pdf (accessed March 26, 2019).

prisoners are argued to develop their ideological understandings and increase their commitment to political activism. As one member of the Palestinian branch of the Jordanian Communist Party (JCP) who was imprisoned for his activism stated, "Prison was like a university with many courses. This made me more committed to the JCP" (Interview 13, PPP, Ramallah, October 22, 2009).[20] Such processes of political and ideological transformation may also extend beyond the prisoner to the broader family unit. For example, in *Confronting the Occupation*, the Israeli sociologist Maya Rosenfeld traces how the imprisonment of male relatives sparked the politicization of Palestinian women in the West Bank's Dheisheh refugee camp and, consequently, their initiation into organized political activity (2004).

Consistent with these perspectives, I argue that the imprisonment of a family member or friend makes previously politically inactive individuals more likely to begin participating in anti-regime resistance. However, whereas existing accounts largely focus on the ways that imprisonment strengthens and deepens activists' grievances, I highlight the informational and organizational consequences of a policy of mass imprisonment on a wider group. My argument begins with the premise that imprisonment is a collective experience that affects not only the individual but also the entire family: when a loved one is imprisoned, his relatives and friends visit him in jail, attend court sessions, and are generally integrated into the state's disciplinary institutions. As Rosenfeld (2004) shows in her ethnography, this process also connects prisoners' loved ones in new interfamilial networks of prisoners' families, which cut across existing, more parochial lines of interaction and affiliation.

Building on this observation, I argue that – similarly to educational institutions – integration into disciplinary institutions makes prisoners' relatives and friends more likely to protest by lowering informational and organizational barriers to collective action. Because integration into these institutions gives rise to new interfamilial networks that transcend existing social boundaries, prisoners' relatives and friends have access to political information that is not widely available through other sources. Similarly, because prisoners' relatives and friends interact with

[20] For similar sentiments, see Interview 24, PPP, Ramallah, October 15, 2009; Interview 17, Fatah, Tulkarm, October 29, 2009; Interview 16, Fatah, Ramallah, November 3, 2009; Interview 25, Fatah, al-Ram, November 5, 2009. For interviews by other researchers, see e.g. Collins (2004, 127–30). The PPP (Palestinian People's Party) is the successor to the JCP. All anonymous interviews were assigned a random number for identification.

one another within the close confines of these institutions – for example, waiting for hours on end together to see their loved ones – they can more easily communicate and coordinate with one another than members of other groups generally can. Finally, as imprisonment becomes more widespread and larger numbers of people are affected, prisoners' relatives and friends may also benefit from a degree of "safety in numbers" and face less uncertainty about the risks of protest. As a result of these advantages, prisoners' family members and friends have greater access to information about protest and are better able to participate than individuals outside disciplinary institutions. As a result, the probability that they will begin to protest is higher than that of similar individuals outside this institutional context.

To conclude, like integration into educational institutions, incorporation into disciplinary institutions makes individuals more likely to begin participating in anti-regime resistance. When an individual is imprisoned, his relatives and friends become more likely to participate in protests than they had been before his arrest. Moreover, as the next section further argues, this newfound political activism may not end with a prisoner's release.

1.5.3   The Persistence of Participation

This book contends that individuals who begin participating in anti-regime protest while in state institutions are likely to continue doing so even after exiting these institutions. Research shows that many forms of political participation are highly persistent (see e.g. McAdam, 1986; Davenport and Trivedi, 2013; Niemi and Hepburn, 1995; Alwin and Krosnick, 1991; Sears and Funk, 1999; Gerber, Green, and Shachar, 2003). Participation in protest is also likely to persist for at least three reasons. First, as previously discussed, integration into state institutions links individuals in new, more diverse social networks that are richer in information. When individuals exit these institutions – for example, when students complete their schooling – these networks and relationships remain. Second, the experience of participating in protest may also incorporate individuals into politicized opposition networks, as well as increase their antagonism to the regime. As Doug McAdam has argued, new participants in political activism are likely to meet dissidents they did not know previously, listen to persuasive speeches, discuss and exchange views with other participants, and "try on" activist identities. As a result of these socializing experiences, new participants in political activism become "better integrated into the movement and more ideologically and personally disposed towards participation" (McAdam, 1986, 69). More recently, Davenport and Trivedi (2013) have found that the experience of participating in nonviolent resistance makes participants more aware of discrimination and injustice around them. This perspective suggests that, as participants in protest come to see more prejudice and inequity around them, they may in turn feel compelled to continue participating.

Third, participation in risky collective action can also generate strong emotions that motivate individuals to keep participating even as they face higher costs and risks. For example, in her influential study of popular support for insurgency in El Salvador, Elisabeth Wood found that the rural *campesinos* who actively supported the country's insurgents did so out of what she terms "pleasure in agency" – the pride and pleasure of successfully asserting one's interests and identities. As Wood writes, "Through rebelling, insurgent campesinos asserted, and thereby constituted in their own eyes, their dignity in the face of repression, condescension, and indifference" (Wood, 2003, 18–19). Because pride, dignity, and pleasure are achieved through the act of rebellion, this perspective implies that participation begets more participation. More recently, Wendy Pearlman has argued that emotions lead individuals to prioritize moral values over safety and security, emboldening them to participate in anti-regime protests (Pearlman, 2013). As participation itself generates powerful emotions, this perspective also suggests that, having begun to participate, protestors are likely to continue their participation.

Finally, research suggests that patterns of participation in protest forged during an individual's school years should be especially likely to endure. Research on political socialization identifies adolescence as the key period when political attitudes and behavior form (Sapiro, 2004; Niemi and Hepburn, 1995). According to the "impressionable years" hypothesis, the socializing experiences that people have when they are young powerfully influence their future political orientations. Once this early period of socialization is over, their basic attitudes, values, and worldviews become "sticky" and are unlikely to change. In line with this perspective, in a set of widely cited articles, Jon Krosnick and Duane Alwin find strong support for the impressionable years hypothesis compared with other models of attitudinal formation and change (Krosnick and Alwin, 1989; Alwin and Krosnick, 1991).[21] Since integration into schools socializes youth to protest during their impressionable

---

[21] See e.g. Sears and Funk (1999) and Gerber, Green, and Shachar (2003) for other influential studies showing that political attitudes and behavior persist across the life cycle.

years, it is thus especially likely to forge long-term habits of political participation.

In sum, patterns of political participation that arise in state institutions are likely to persist even after individuals exit these institutions. In addition, patterns of participation formed in state schools – and, therefore, during the "impressionable years" of adolescence – should be especially likely to endure. While state institutions may have a lasting impact, however, there are also important limits on their effects.

1.5.4   Civil Society and the Nationwide Diffusion of Protest

State institutions facilitate mass protests against repressive regimes, but they cannot, on their own, sustain a nationwide uprising. To connect disparate protests into a national protest movement, a strong network of civil society organizations is also needed. As argued earlier, integration into state institutions provides individuals with important informational and organizational advantages that make them more likely to participate in protest. However, without strong civil society networks, the content and flow of political information will still be constrained by existing institutional and geographic divisions (McAdam, 2003). Even though individuals in state institutions have wider networks and can more quickly and easily share information with one another, news about anti-regime activities may not always enter these networks to begin with. And, while whatever information does enter institutional communication channels will spread quickly to neighboring and proximate institutions, it may not travel much further. Thus, in the absence of strong civic organizations and networks to connect them, state institutions may still give rise to mass protests, but these protests are likely to remain relatively localized and uncoordinated.

Social movements scholars have long noted the importance of communications networks for social movements to spread and cohere (Freeman, 2015; McAdam, 2010).[22] According to these scholars, communications networks connect geographically and institutionally distinct groups, transcending existing societal cleavages and boundaries (McAdam, 2003). As Jo Freeman put it, without a communications network, protest may "not become generalized: it remains a local irritant or dissolves completely" (Freeman, 2015, 14). Communications networks are likely to be particularly important for anti-regime movements,

---

[22] See also McAdam (2003).

which must organize under conditions of repression and media censorship. Under these difficult conditions, anti-regime movements are unable to reach prospective participants through the mass media or other widely available sources. In this limited information environment, civic networks should play a particularly important role as conduits of information.

Under repressive regimes, civil society organizations can serve as the backbone for a broader communications network linking political activists, state institutions, and local communities. While these organizations may be at least outwardly apolitical (permitting them to survive under repression), they can nonetheless play an important communicative and connective role. By working through permitted or tolerated civic organizations, activists can forge "vertical ties" to state institutions and local communities and, in turn, better communicate with and coordinate prospective protestors.[23] Civic organizations can also serve as a bridge between different state institutions and give rise to new "horizontal ties" between them. Through these horizontal ties, information about protest can spread not only between proximate institutions but also to more distant ones.

The case of the Shabiba movement, a youth movement affiliated with the Palestinian Fatah party, illustrates this connective function of civic organizations. Through the movement's open structures, political activists affiliated with Fatah – then an illegal, underground party within the Occupied Territories – forged new connections to school students and prisoners' families that they subsequently used to spread information about protest (Interview 11, Fatah/Shabiba activist, Anabta, March 17, 2014). Shabiba's organizational framework also allowed students from different schools to form new relationships with one another, thereby connecting their schools and communities. Thus, with the expansion of the Shabiba movement, state institutions were incorporated into a broader communications network linking political activists, students, the prisoners' movement, and local communities into a national protest movement.

The case of Shabiba suggests that individuals within civic networks should be more likely to participate in anti-regime resistance than those outside these networks. Like students and prisoners' families, these more socially connected individuals possess important informational and

---

[23] See Staniland (2014) for a similar argument about how political activists can use preexisting vertical ties to mobilize support during civil wars.

organizational advantages that make them better able to participate in high-risk protest. In addition, at the meso- or movement level, the growth of civil society organizations should also be associated with rising coordination among dissidents and the geographic diffusion of protest. While this book's individual-level survey data is better suited to testing the first proposition than the second, Chapter 5 also presents suggestive qualitative evidence in support of the latter claim.

1.6 SCOPE CONDITIONS

This book's arguments should apply when groups have widespread anti-regime sentiment and low internal organizational strength. This book argues that, under these conditions, integration into state institutions makes individuals better able, and thus more likely, to protest. Despite their control by the state, integration into these institutions provides individuals with novel information about numbers and tactics that is needed for protest and, thereby, lowers informational and organizational barriers to collective action. Thus, in the absence of independent institutions and organizations that can play such a role, state institutions are, paradoxically, expected to become key nodes of anti-regime mobilization and resistance.

In contrast, state institutions are expected to play a less important role among organizationally strong groups, which have strong autonomous institutions and organizations of their own. State institutions and independent organizations can both provide individuals with informational and organizational advantages for participating in high-risk collective action. However, even under state repression, independent institutions are typically freer from regime control and penetration and may be more easily appropriated by anti-regime actors than state institutions. Thus, where independent institutions have more room to exist, state institutions should be relatively less likely to become a basis for participation and mobilization.

Finally, the theory is also less likely to apply to cases in which anti-regime sentiment is not pervasive. In such cases, integration into state institutions should still provide individuals with informational and organizational benefits that make them better able to engage in high-risk protest. Without a strong motivation to protest, however, it seems unlikely that individuals would choose to take advantages of these benefits and participate in the face of high risks and costs. For example, while integration into state schools may provide youth with "safety in numbers" and reduce uncertainty about the risks of protest, it does not eliminate these risks altogether. Thus, integration into state institutions is unlikely to produce protest in the absence of strong anti-regime sentiment. Indeed, in the Palestinian case, schools did not become important sites of rebellion until after the resurgence of nationalist sentiment in the mid-1970s.

This combination of pervasive anti-regime sentiment and organizational weakness can be found in several important cases in addition to the Palestinian case, including South Africa and Egypt. In South Africa, by the 1970s, black South Africans shared a common antipathy to the ruling apartheid regime irrespective of their social status or background (Marx, 1992, 47–55; Hirschmann, 1990, 8). Yet, battered by increasing government repression throughout the previous decade, black political organizations, trade unions, and other civic groups had withered (Hirson, 1979). Against this backdrop, in the Soweto Uprising of 1976, black public school students initiated the largest demonstration against South Africa's apartheid regime in over fifteen years and helped ignite a national uprising (Glaser, 1998, 15). Similarly, in Egypt in the 2000s, state workers and employees were responsible for the largest protests against the Mubarak regime and its policies that decade, and they also participated at high rates in the Egyptian revolution of 2011 (Beinin and Duboc, 2013; Beinin, 2015; Beissinger, Jamal, and Mazur, 2015). While the Egyptian regime was relatively more tolerant toward civil society than the South African apartheid government, civil society organizations did not organize or initiate these protests, and participants were not drawn from their ranks. Rather, as in the Palestinian and South African cases, protest originated from inside state institutions. This book's conclusion discusses each of these cases in more detail, situating the book's theoretical argument in more comparative perspective.

1.7 STUDY DESIGN

Although this book's theory is presented deductively, it was not developed in a purely deductive manner. Rather, it was developed and tested using what scholars have variously described as an integrative or complementary mixed-method design, in which findings from the initial phases of research inform subsequent phases of data collection and analysis in a more inductive and iterative fashion (see e.g. Seawright, 2016; Small, 2011). Integrative mixed-method designs draw on different forms of data and/or modes of analysis with distinct complementarities in order to arrive at more sound causal conclusions. While these data may be collected and analyzed either concurrently or sequentially (see e.g. Small, 2011), they are usually processed sequentially and, more importantly, iteratively. That is, the findings of one component shape research decisions in the next component in an "indefinite cycle of discovery and refinement" (Seawright, 2016, 10). Such designs are thus also a form of "inductive iteration," involving disciplined, analytic departures from the deductive ideal (Yom, 2015). As several scholars have recently argued, such iteration is how most political scientists actually conduct their research in practice and is at the heart of most field research in the discipline (Kapiszewski, MacLean, and Read, 2015; Yom, 2015). Yet, perhaps because it is often conflated with other, less principled research practices, it is rarely explicitly acknowledged or discussed. Following these and other scholars' calls for greater transparency about the role that induction and iteration play in the production of knowledge, I describe their contribution to this book's conclusions here.

The analysis conducted for this book combines quantitative analysis of original survey data with in-depth analysis of a variety of primary qualitative data and sources, including original interviews, newspaper reports, and other materials. In Fall of 2011, after an initial round of exploratory interviews, I conducted an original, large-scale survey in order to examine the determinants of participation in the Palestinian nationalist movement against Israeli occupation. Drawing on the previous literature, which asserts an important role for formal education in shaping political participation of various stripes, I was particularly interested in the role that education may play in shaping individual participation designs. This analysis revealed that, while education did indeed appear to influence participation decisions, it did so in an unexpected way. In particular, whereas prior research suggested that participants in resistance should be either highly educated and aggrieved or poorly educated and marginalized, the survey's results suggested they were neither. Instead, it demonstrated a more complex, curvilinear relationship between education and participation in resistance, with the probability of participation rising at average, intermediate levels of education and flattening with additional, higher levels of education. As seen in Chapter 3, a variety of robustness checks confirmed this initial result.

Determined to understand the survey's findings and the social reality underlying them, I returned to the field in early 2014 for a second round of interviews. In this round, I sought to interview ordinary participants

and nonparticipants in resistance from diverse educational and socioeconomic backgrounds, teachers, and other relevant actors. I also sought
to interview activists and participants in the Shabiba movement, the
largest student and youth movement in the Palestinian Territories during the time period of interest. Drawing on the literature on nationalism,
my initial hypotheses centered on the role of education in strengthening and deepening Palestinian national identity and grievances, which
may motivate participation in resistance to Israeli rule. Knowing that the
Israeli authorities strictly controlled the educational curriculum during
the period of interest, however, I sought to uncover the presence of a
"hidden curriculum," in which teachers imparted nationalist ideas and
messages to their students informally and/or indirectly (see e.g. Gordon,
2008; Peteet, 2005).[24]

Contrary to my expectations, however, both teachers and students
consistently denied the presence of a hidden curriculum – a denial made
more plausible by the fact that acknowledging such a curriculum was
no longer risky and may even have been socially desirable. Similarly,
other key explanations derived from the existing literature emphasizing the nationalist or political content of education also did not seem
to bear out. In contrast to explanations emphasizing political knowledge
and interest, nearly all of my interviewees – from the most educated to
the least – professed and displayed an avid interest in politics (a fact
which will hardly be surprising to other scholars of the Palestinian case).
Similarly, as additional survey analysis later confirmed, most interviewees harbored strong, subjective economic grievances against Israelis
regardless of their level of education or the extent of their political participation. Thus, at odds with relative deprivation theory, education also
did not seem to give rise to the higher expectations and more intense feelings of deprivation vis-à-vis out-group members that may sometimes fuel
protest.

In contrast to these explanations focusing on the content of education, the interviews pointed to its structure and the ways in which
schools provide students with informational and organizational advantages for collective action. These advantages, however, are not unique

---

[24] The term "hidden curriculum" derives from literature in the academic field of education,
such as Philip Jackson's *Life in Classrooms* (1990), where it was reportedly first used.
Whereas the term often has a negative connotation in this literature (e.g. as in a hidden
curriculum that perpetuates inequities between students), such a negative connotation is
not my intention here.

properties of schools. Rather, they should be present in any institution that repeatedly brings a large, heterogeneous group of people face-to-face with one another in a context where assembly is otherwise restricted. Drawing on these insights as well as prior research on the Palestinian case, I theorized that other state institutions should impact participation in resistance in similar ways as schools and sought to test this hypothesis and the causal mechanisms underlying it. In particular, given the central role that prisons and courts (unfortunately) play in Palestinian society, I wanted to examine whether integration into these institutions also affected participation in resistance in similar ways.

With these new hypotheses in mind, I turned again to analyzing the survey data. In this latter stage of analysis, I tested the relationship between integration into disciplinary institutions and participation in anti-regime resistance. I also inferred multiple, new, observable implications of the causal mechanisms underlying my argument (see e.g. King, Keohane, and Verba, 1994) and tested whether or not they were at work in the case of both types of institutions. These additional tests supported my theoretical explanation – derived through both deductive theorizing and inductive field research – that integration into state institutions made individuals better able and, thus, more likely to participate in unarmed protest. Additional qualitative research, including analysis of newspaper reports, community diaries, and other primary sources, also increased my confidence in this conclusion. By combining different data sources and analytic techniques in this way, and moving critically and deliberately between them in an iterative fashion, I was thus able to form a much more comprehensive picture of the causes of protest participation than would have been possible using a deductive approach alone. In the next section, I provide a brief overview of these data sources and how they were collected.[25]

1.7.1 Field Research and Methods

This book's analyses are based on extensive field research in the Palestinian Territories. Between 2008 and 2014, I made five research trips to the West Bank and East Jerusalem, spending a total of about one year in the region. By making many successive trips over a period of years, I was able to build long-term, trusting relationships with local actors and stakeholders. These relationships, in turn, were pivotal in gaining me the

---

[25] For additional details about the survey, see Chapter 3 and the methodological appendix.

access I needed to carry out sensitive research on individual participation in political conflict.

The centerpiece of my field research is an original, large-scale survey of former participants and nonparticipants in anti-regime resistance in the West Bank that I conducted in 2011. The survey is the first representative, individual-level study of participants and nonparticipants in Palestinian resistance, as well as one of only a few systematic surveys of anti-regime resistance conducted worldwide. Due to the difficulties of gathering appropriate survey data, few systematic studies of participation in anti-regime resistance have been conducted to date.[26] A large number of studies have investigated attitudinal support for resistance, both violent and nonviolent, in Palestine and the broader Muslim world (Shamir and Shikaki, 2002; Nachtwey and Tessler, 2002; Tessler and Robbins, 2007; Telhami, 2010; Jaeger et al., 2012; Blair et al., 2013; Longo, Canetti, and Hite-Rubin, 2014; Hoffman and Nugent, 2017; Shelef and Zeira, n.d.). However, because participation in resistance imposes costs and risks that support does not, the factors that drive attitudinal support for resistance likely differ from those that drive actual participation. As such, the survey of participation in resistance used in this book offers rare, fine-grained data on risky political behavior that are usually not available to scholars.

A number of prior works have also sought to document and explain Palestinian resistance by drawing on interviews with participants in such resistance (see e.g. Gordon, Gordon, and Shriteh, 2003; Collins, 2004; Hasso, 2005). As already discussed, such interviews can offer valuable new theoretical insights, as well as give voice to participant perspectives that are often absent from scholarly accounts. At the same time, interviews also have some important limitations that can limit their validity and broader generalizability. For one, because of their more in-depth nature, it is usually only possible for scholars to conduct a relatively small number of interviews. In addition, interview subjects are typically not selected using any kind of random sampling process. As a result, they may not be representative of the broader population of participants in resistance. Finally, whereas it is in principle possible to interview both participants and nonparticipants (as I do in this volume), existing works

---

[26] Previous work has focused on just five cases: the East German revolution of 1989 (Opp and Gern, 1993), Ukraine's Orange Revolution (Beissinger, 2013), the Arab Spring protests in Egypt and Tunisia (Hoffman and Jamal, 2014; Beissinger, Jamal, and Mazur, 2015), and the prodemocracy protests in Niger in 2009–10 (Mueller, 2013).

commonly interview only participants. To properly assess competing explanations, however, it is important to have a relevant counterfactual – that is, to compare participants with otherwise similar nonparticipants. To overcome these limitations, this book combines a quantitative, survey-based approach with more traditional qualitative interviews. Below, I provide an overview of each.

The Survey

This book draws on an original survey of 646 male participants and nonparticipants in unarmed resistance in the Palestinian Territories. The survey was conducted in sixty-eight localities across the West Bank, including cities, towns, villages, and refugee camps. To obtain a sample that was geographically and socioeconomically representative, the localities, neighborhoods, households, and individual respondents included in the survey were all randomly selected. Due to the necessity of sampling enough participants to make meaningful causal inferences, and given comparatively low rates of female participation in resistance, the survey targeted male respondents. However, in order to help assess the sensitivity of the book's findings to the composition of the survey sample, I also sampled a smaller number of female respondents, as well as family members of attrited respondents (e.g. due to death, imprisonment, immigration, etc.).[27] All respondents were interviewed in person by a carefully trained Palestinian interviewer. The response rate was 68 percent.[28] The resulting survey sample closely resembles the Palestinian population of the Occupied Territories in terms of geography, household composition, and socioeconomic characteristics.[29]

The survey questionnaire was carefully designed to mitigate two common types of bias afflicting survey research: social desirability bias and recall bias. Social desirability bias refers to the common desire to present oneself in a favorable light, which may lead respondents to overreport socially approved behaviors and underreport disapproved

[27] Although Palestinian women participated in resistance at unprecedented rates during the period covered by the survey, their participation rate remained much lower than that of men. See Chapter 3 and the methodological appendix for additional details.

[28] AAPOR response rate category 2. Since this response rate includes all households of unknown eligibility in the denominator, the true response rate may be higher. The response rate was calculated from a sub-sample of all household contact attempts.

[29] See the methodological appendix for a map of the sampled localities (Figure 7.1), a detailed description of the survey design and sampling procedures, and a comparison between the survey sample and the population (Table 7.2).

ones (Groves et al., 2011). In the Palestinian context, social desirability concerns could lead respondents to falsely report participation in anti-occupation protests; at the same time, it is also possible that some respondents may have feared reporting their past participation. To reduce the possibility for social desirability bias and protect respondents, all questions regarding participation in resistance were self-administered by respondents. Self-administration is the gold standard for collecting sensitive individual-level data that cannot be collected using group-level methods like list experiments (Corstange, 2009; Groves et al., 2011). Using techniques first developed by Alexandra Scacco (n.d.) and described further in the methodological appendix, the survey was administered in such a way that the interviewer could not view the respondent's answers to sensitive questions or link them to other characteristics of the respondent.

Recall bias, or the inability to accurately and completely remember past events, is also an important concern in retrospective surveys such as this one. To alleviate this bias, the survey made use of an innovative design called a life history calendar or event history calendar (LHC).[30] In contrast to traditional survey questionnaires, LHCs employ a calendar-like questionnaire design that encourages respondents to retrieve autobiographical memories through multiple pathways (e.g. both thematically and chronologically), thereby increasing the chances that they will accurately remember them (Belli, 1998). While they have not to my knowledge been used in political science until now, LHCs are widely used in sociology, public health, and other fields, where they have been shown to significantly improve the quality of survey responses. For example, in a direct experimental comparison of a life history calendar with a state-of-the-art standard survey questionnaire, the LHC yielded more complete and accurate responses on a number of questions (Belli, Shay, and Stafford, 2001). Unfortunately, conducting a similar experimental comparison on our data is not possible, as there are no comparable surveys conducted on a similar sample. However, most respondents did not find it particularly difficult to remember the information required by our survey, and excluding those who did yields similar results.[31]

---

[30] See the methodological appendix and survey questionnaires for additional details and examples.

[31] See Section A.1.5 in the online appendix [www.cambridge.org/TheRevolutionWithin] for these and other robustness checks for recall bias.

Interviews and Qualitative Sources

To leverage the distinct complementarities of qualitative and quantitative analysis, this book also draws on insights gleaned from over forty interviews. In 2009 and 2014, I conducted in-depth interviews with former participants and nonparticipants in Palestinian resistance, Palestinian political leaders and activists, teachers and students, former prisoners, and civil society members. Interviewees were generally selected using a snowball sampling approach, in which existing interviewees and informants helped me to identify prospective future interviewees. This approach not only helped me to identify interview subjects but, because I was generally referred to prospective interviewees by a trusted source, also helped me to gain subjects' confidence and cooperation.

The interviews followed a semi-structured format, and they were conducted in Arabic or English as per the interviewee's preference and language facility. The specific questions included depended on the subject's specific position or role (i.e. political leader or activist, teacher, etc.). To protect respondents and encourage their continued cooperation with the study, they did not, however, include any questions about participation in armed resistance (although some interviewees chose to raise the topic themselves). In addition, I was also careful to refrain from asking interviewees any specific questions about individuals other than themselves. In addition to raising ethical concerns, asking such questions would likely have cast suspicion on me and may have been seen by subjects as an attempt to solicit their "collaboration" in a manner akin to Israeli security service personnel. Finally, in according with the human subjects protocols for this project, all interviewees were given the option to remain anonymous, as well as to refrain from having their interviews audio-recorded. In general, these safeguards succeeded in making interviewees comfortable, and many spoke at length and in detail about their experiences. While the typical interview lasted from one to two hours, some thus lasted for several hours and/or took place over multiple interview sessions.

Finally, in addition to these interviews, this book also relies on a variety of other primary and secondary sources. Among the most useful of these sources are newspaper articles published in the weekly English-language edition of *al-Fajr* (The Dawn) newspaper over the period of interest. Founded in East Jerusalem in 1972, *al-Fajr* is a Palestinian newspaper with a nationalist and pro-PLO bent (Jamal, 2005, 38, 46). Like other Palestinian newspapers during the period under study, *al-Fajr*'s coverage was censored of the "information on tactics" and "information on numbers" that prospective protestors need in order to join impending demonstrations. Yet, while *al-Fajr* was forced to omit this type of specific information about resistance, it continued to report more general information about prior demonstrations and protests. In addition, as an English-language newspaper that many Palestinians could not read, *al-Fajr*'s weekly subsidiary was often able to print more detailed information about resistance activities than the main Arabic dailies.[32] As such, it supplements this book's other data sources and provides added insight into the determinants of individual participation in resistance.

1.8 PLAN OF THE BOOK

This book proceeds as follows. Chapter 2 traces political, social, and economic developments within the Palestinian Territories, beginning with the Israeli occupation of the Palestinian Territories in 1967 and concluding with the end of the first unarmed phase of the first intifadah in 1989. The chapter focuses on the emergence of two key conditions underlying individual participation in anti-regime resistance: an organized campaign of resistance in which it is possible to participate; and the rise of strong anti-regime sentiment. Using a variety of primary and secondary sources, it shows how a resurgence of nationalist sentiment in the mid-1970s strengthened Palestinians' will to resist and contributed to the rise of a new, more activist local leadership within the Palestinian Territories. In contrast to the traditional Palestinian elite, this new generation of leaders sought to mobilize unarmed resistance to Israeli rule in order to more forcefully challenge Israel's control over the Occupied Territories. As a result, the chapter shows, avenues for participation in protest broadened. Subsequent chapters then take these expanded avenues for participation as a starting point and ask why, given wide avenues for protest, some individuals participated in resistance whereas otherwise similar individuals did not.

Chapters 3 and 4 test the argument's main empirical implication that integration into state institutions makes individuals more likely to participate in anti-regime resistance. Chapter 3 focuses on the case of educational institutions. It demonstrates that integration into these institutions is associated with a higher probability of participation in

---

[32] Personal communication with former editor, January 10, 2017.

resistance, and that this relationship is driven by intermediate schooling. As individuals are integrated into intermediate schools outside their local communities, they expand their social networks and become more likely to begin participating in resistance than otherwise similar peers from their community. Integration into schools could promote participation in anti-regime resistance through a number of channels. In addition to reducing informational and organizational barriers to participation as this book argues, schools could also promote participation by instilling students with stronger group grievances. Using interviews with anti-regime activists and other primary sources, as well as my survey data, the chapter provides support for the institutional mechanism underlying the book's argument and against this alternative explanation. The chapter's arguments challenge conventional wisdom about who is likely to participate in anti-regime protest and suggest a new informational mechanism through which education can influence participation in political conflict.

Chapter 4 examines the book's argument within the more difficult case of disciplinary institutions. Building on prior ethnographic research on the Palestinian case, the chapter first describes how the imprisonment of a family member or friend indirectly integrates individuals into disciplinary institutions: relatives and friends of prisoners visit loved ones in jail, attend court sessions, and interact with one another within the close confines of these institutions. Consistent with the book's main argument, the chapter then goes on to demonstrate that these interactions increase the probability that previously politically inactive individuals will begin to participate in anti-regime resistance. In addition, the chapter provides original qualitative and quantitative evidence supporting the contention that integration into prisons and courts brings individuals into larger and more diverse social networks, thereby expanding their access to scarce information about protest. In contrast, the main alternative mechanism – radicalization – finds more mixed empirical support.

This book argues that, while state institutions facilitate protest in organizationally weak societies without strong civic associations, such associations are needed in order to *subsequently* link these protests into a nationwide uprising. Chapter 5 examines how state institutions interacted with independent civil society organizations and networks under Israeli occupation to produce a national protest movement. The chapter describes how, beginning in the early 1980s, autonomous Palestinian organizations emerged that joined anti-regime activists, state institutions, and local communities in a broader communications network. Drawing on original interviews, newspaper reports, and other sources, it shows how, after 1980, Palestinian activists used these associations to forge new ties within state institutions and local communities through which they could spread political information. As a result, the chapter argues, the people within these new civic networks became better able and more likely to protest, and mass protests became more coordinated and geographically widespread.

Chapter 6, the book's conclusion, summarizes the book's arguments and considers their implications for understanding the larger political conditions under which anti-regime resistance will take place. Demonstrating their broader utility beyond the Palestinian case, it also applies these arguments to explain individual participation in unarmed resistance in South Africa and Egypt and discusses their ongoing relevance in the face of technological change.

2

The Rise of Anti-regime Resistance

In the fall of 1978, Palestinian activists opposed to the Israeli occupation of the Palestinian Territories organized five large public rallies to
protest the signing of the Camp David Accords and Israeli policies in
the Palestinian Territories. On October 1, 4, 16, 18, and 20, Palestinians repeatedly gathered in defiance of Israeli restrictions on political
assembly. With diverse segments of Palestinian society in attendance –
political elites, PLO supporters, students, West Bankers, and Gazans –
the rallies were among the largest public protests held in the Occupied
Territories since 1967 (Jamal, 2005, 51; Sahliyeh, 1988, 74–5).

The staging of these unprecedented rallies in opposition to the Camp
David Accords reflected two new political developments that had taken
shape in the Palestinian Territories over the previous decade. First,
the rallies reflected the growth of an ascendant Palestinian nationalism
within the Occupied Territories. Two years earlier, in local municipal
elections conducted under Israeli occupation, Palestinians had over-
whelmingly elected new, pro-PLO nationalist elites to power. These new
leaders supplanted the Palestinian Territories' traditional elite class, who
drew their power from local, subnational identities and pledged alle-
giance to Jordan rather than to the PLO. Now, with their removal
from power, identification with more parochial village and clan identities
further gave way to the growing sense of national feeling.

Second, the rallies also represented a new, tactical shift toward the
use of organized, unarmed resistance against Israeli rule from inside the
Palestinian Territories. Throughout the first decade of occupation, opposition to Israeli rule was dominated by PLO-led armed attacks or polite
statements of protest issued by traditional Palestinian elites in the West

46

Bank and Gaza Strip (Hasso, 1998, 444). Now, as an activist local leadership came to power in these territories, replacing the traditional elite, its members sought to use more confrontational tactics. As the Camp David Accords threatened to help Israel consolidate its occupation of the Palestinian Territories, they organized rallies, demonstrations, and other forms of unarmed resistance with increasing frequency. As a result, avenues for participation in resistance among ordinary Palestinians also broadened.

This chapter traces political, social, and economic developments within the Palestinian Territories between 1967 and 1994, focusing on the rise of nationalism and organized, unarmed resistance. This book's central argument explains why, given avenues for anti-regime resistance and strong anti-regime sentiment, some individuals will participate while others abstain. However, it does not explain when and why anti-regime movements will use unarmed resistance to advance their goals, providing ordinary individuals with avenues for participation. Nor does it explain when anti-regime sentiment will become widespread among a population. This chapter traces the events, forces, and dynamics that contributed to these developments in the Palestinian case. Figure 2.1 provides a timeline of the key events of interest.

In tracing the rise of anti-regime sentiment and protest, this chapter also highlights how anti-regime resistance can emerge even without the internal organizational strength found to be important for protest in other cases. As this chapter will show, the strong autonomous institutions and networks that contributed to the first Palestinian intifadah were not yet in place when anti-regime resistance first began to increase nearly a decade earlier. Rather, these institutions developed only after, and partially in response to, the rise in mass resistance, as the Palestinian national movement sought new ways to continue mobilizing the Palestinian public under mounting repression. Thus, as growing numbers of Palestinians began participating in resistance in 1978, they did so in the absence of strong internal institutions and networks. State institutions, not independent ones, served as the initial locus for protest.

The history of the Israeli–Palestinian conflict and the Palestinian Territories begins long before this chapter's starting point of 1967 of course.[1] Palestinian nationalism, even as it gained strength in the Palestinian Territories in the late 1970s, traces its roots to the early twentieth century (see

---

[1] For an authoritative history of the Israeli–Palestinian conflict that also covers this earlier period, see Tessler (1994).

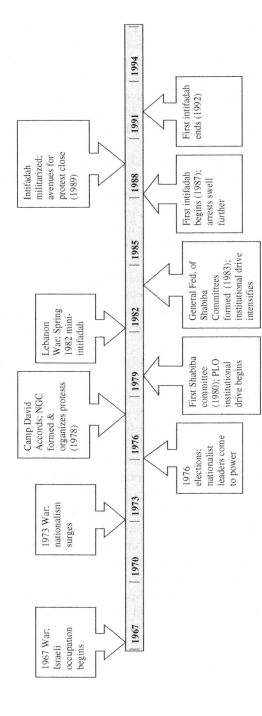

FIGURE 2.1 Timeline of key events, 1967–1994

e.g. Khalidi, 2010). As this book focuses on the drivers of participation in resistance against Israeli rule in the Palestinian Territories, however, the initiation of this rule provides a logical starting point. This starting point is the 1967 War and the beginning of the Israeli military occupation of the West Bank and Gaza Strip.

2.1 THE 1967 WAR AND PALESTINIAN SOCIETY UNDER OCCUPATION

On June 8, 1967, the map of the Middle East was fundamentally redrawn. Following six days of war with its Arab neighbors, Israel assumed control over the Palestinian Territories. As Jordanian tanks retreated eastward back to Amman, Israel began putting in place a military government to administer the West Bank. The Gaza Strip, formerly under Egyptian rule, was also placed under military administration. East Jerusalem, annexed along with the West Bank by Jordan in 1948, was now annexed by Israel and placed under Israeli law.

In the wake of the war, there was little in the way of mass resistance to Israeli rule. The PLO and its distinct brand of Palestinian nationalism had not yet become ascendant among Palestinians, either inside or outside the Palestinian Territories. Inside the Territories, Palestinians also lacked an indigenous national leadership that was willing and able to challenge Israeli authority and organize mass resistance. Nor did the rural and fragmented structure of Palestinian domestic society favor such resistance. Social networks within the Palestinian Territories tended to be narrow and parochial, and there were few civil society organizations or other autonomous institutions to bridge such social divisions. Overall, then, the prospects for Palestinians to take collective action against the Israeli occupation of the Palestinian Territories were quite limited.

Formed only three years earlier, the Palestinian Liberation Organization (PLO) was not yet a dominant force in 1967. Established in Cairo by the Arab League to serve Egyptian interests and aspirations, it initially commanded little real political influence or popular support among Palestinians, either inside the Palestinian Territories or in the organization's bases of operation outside them. While the PLO was ostensibly formed to organize "the Palestinian people and [enable] them to play their role in the liberation of their country and their self-determination," the organization's actual purpose was, in fact, to restrain the growing Palestinian resistance movement and prevent it from drawing Egypt and other Arab states into another war with Israel

(Tessler, 1994, 373–4). Rather than representing and organizing Palestinians, it sought to coopt and contain them. Fatah, the Palestinian nationalist political-military faction that would come to lead the PLO and transform it into a guerrilla organization, was also not yet an important player.[2] In the heyday of Arab nationalism, its "Palestine first" ideology did not yet have broad appeal, and its small group of militants had not yet established a significant political or social presence anywhere.

Palestinians in the newly occupied territories also lacked an indigenous national leadership that was motivated and able to confront Israeli authorities and mobilize mass resistance. Under Jordanian and Egyptian rule, the key powerholders were local "notables": urban, landowning elites that had first gained in prominence under the Ottoman Empire. Since that time, these notables had acted as intermediaries between the local Palestinian population and successive foreign governments. For ordinary Palestinians, access to state services depended on ties to these local notables. For the notables themselves, political relevance depended, in large part, on their continued ability to deliver state services. As a result, in the wake of the 1967 War, the Palestinian notable class largely sought a quick return to Arab sovereignty and, with it, the privileged status they commanded. Wary of radical change and divided along local lines, its members were neither willing nor able to unite Palestinians in defiance to Israeli occupation. As a result, local identities and networks remained strong (Robinson, 1997, 3–11; Migdal, 2014). Much as they had before, Palestinian social relations continued to revolve largely around the three frameworks of agriculture, village, and the extended family (Migdal, 2014, 56).

This localist orientation facilitated Israeli control and inhibited mass resistance. In the West Bank, Israel assumed control over a predominantly rural and fragmented society. Seventy percent of West Bankers still lived in small, rural villages dominated by a few large, extended families or clans (*hamulas*) (Gordon, 2008, 111). Familial and local identities formed the backbone of this rural social structure. Most Palestinians continued to live in their ancestral villages, work on family and village

---

[2] In February 1969, Palestinian guerrilla factions gained a majority of seats on the PLO's executive committee, effectively capturing the organization. Of these factions, Fatah gained the largest number of seats, and its leader, Yasser Arafat, was elected as chairman, solidifying its leadership over the organization as a whole (Tessler, 1994, 428–29; Sayigh, 1997, 220–21).

farms, and socialize, and even marry, within their extended families (Migdal, 2014, 56). Discouraged by Jordanian policies that sought to limit the development of wider social cohesion and mobilization, ties between villages and districts – which had begun to grow during the British colonial period – were also weak. As a result, few connections existed across villages, limiting the prospects for wider collective action.

Despite its much higher population density, social fragmentation also limited the prospects for mass mobilization in the Gaza Strip. On the eve of the Israeli occupation of the Gaza Strip, over half of Gaza'a large refugee population still lived within dense, crowded refugee camps.[3] Yet, within the camps, organizational and social life still centered around the extended family and village. Families and neighbors from the same pre-1948 villages lived in their own district quarters with their own mukhtars or village leaders, preserving the original village social structure (Roy, 1995, 19). Refugees "turned inwards," clinging to "traditional forms of social organization and authority relations" (Roy, 1995, 24). Thus, while Gaza's high population density provided fertile ground for resistance against Israeli occupation, social fragmentation also limited the prospects for wider collective action.

This social fragmentation was compounded by the absence of independent institutions that could bring Palestinians together across local and familial lines. Palestinian civil society was weak in the wake of the 1967 War. Under Jordanian and Egyptian rule before the war, Palestinian civil society organizations had been subject to strict limits on freedom of association. For example, until 1967, not a single charity existed in the Gaza Strip (Lavine, n.d., 158). Labor union organizing was also completely banned until 1956 and faced resistance from both the Egyptian government and Gaza elites until 1963 (Brand, 1991, 86–89).

Similarly, in the Jordanian-ruled West Bank, political parties and trade unions were banned until the early 1950s. Social organizations were allowed to operate, but the Jordanian regime viewed any organization made up predominantly of Palestinians as threatening to its rule. While some charitable organizations were allowed to operate in the West Bank, they were required to obtain a permit from the Jordanian government and remain strictly apolitical (Brand, 1991, 164; Salem, 2012). After 1953, trade union activity was legalized in Jordan,

---

[3] Approximately 750,000 Palestinians were expelled or fled from their homes in the 1948 (Arab-Israeli) War, becoming stateless refugees. For a detailed account, see Tessler (1994).

and, particularly under the liberal Nabulsi government of 1956–57, the number of union members multiplied. Yet, with the coup attempt of 1957, the government again cracked down on organized civil society activity (Brand, 1991, 188–91). Political parties and many civil society associations were banned, and trade unions faced increasing repression. As a result, the total number of unions declined, as did union membership. In the immediate wake of the Israeli occupation, there were thus just twenty-four unions throughout the entire Palestinian Territories, and only eleven of them were located outside Israeli-annexed East Jerusalem (Hiltermann, 1993, 62).

In this limited institutional environment, schools were some of the only institutions to bring Palestinians of different backgrounds together. After the primary level, these schools tended to be located in large towns and cities rather than the rural villages where the majority of Palestinians lived (Benvenisti and Khayat, 1988, 124–37). As a result, the growing number of rural students attending intermediate and higher-level schools did so alongside urban youth from the cities and towns. For those Palestinians who went on to attend these schools, integration into educational institutions thus brought them into new, wider social networks, which spanned existing social and geographic boundaries. For those youth who went to work instead, however, there were few comparable equivalents. Under Jordanian rule, the West Bank had been an "economic backwater," supplying agricultural produce to Jordan's more industrialized East Bank (Gordon, 2008, 111). The Gaza Strip was even less industrialized. With only a few small workshops in the West Bank and "no industrial sector at all" in Gaza (Hiltermann, 1993, 18), there were thus very few large factories or firms that could serve as a similar basis for mass mobilization.

Under these difficult conditions, the imposition of Israeli occupation did not at first meet with mass resistance. Initial local resistance to Israeli occupation mainly took the form of polite protest by local notables in the Palestinian Territories, as well as isolated attacks by small cells of Palestinian militants. In the first few months of occupation, Palestinian elites issued a series of statements condemning Israel's annexation of the city and reasserting its Arab and Islamic character (Sahliyeh, 1988, 22). Urban elites also sought to create institutions that could "give political expression to the interests of the local populace" (Sahliyeh, 1988, 23). Yet, with the exception of strikes mounted by the lawyers' and teachers' unions during this time, early forms of civic disobedience were dominated by Palestinian elites, particularly the traditional notable class.

For the most part, ordinary Palestinians did not participate in protest (Interview 17, Fatah activist, Tulkarm, October 29, 2009). Reflecting this elite orientation, initial demands centered primarily on reunifying Jerusalem and the West Bank with Jordan and restoring them to Jordanian sovereignty. Rejecting both the PLO's calls for the "total liberation of all of Palestine" and those of some local Palestinian figures for an independent Palestinian state in the Occupied Territories, they emphasized a return to the prewar status quo over Palestinian nationalist aspirations (Jamal, 2005, 34–35; Sahliyeh, 1988, 24–25).

In addition to elite opposition, Palestinian militants also carried out armed attacks against Israeli targets. In the months following the 1967 War, Yasser Arafat and a group of Fatah militants infiltrated the Israeli-occupied West Bank in an attempt to start an insurgency. The Fatah cofounder, who would go on to assume the leadership of the PLO and the Palestinian national movement, traveled through the West Bank organizing small armed cells and roving guerrilla bands known as *dawiyyat al-mutarada* (fugitive patrols) (Sayigh, 1997, 162). Yet, the Fatah leader's vision of sparking a broader "popular liberation war" never materialized. Aided by captured Jordanian intelligence files left behind in the war, Israel's formidable security apparatus rounded up hundreds of guerrillas, who lacked the kind of deep support networks in the West Bank that might have helped them evade capture. Resoundingly pro-Jordanian, local elites had little interest in risking their lives and livelihoods to aid the radical PLO (Tessler, 1994, 424–25, 472), and the guerrillas also lacked broader popular backing (Pearlman, 2011, 95). With little elite or mass support behind it, the rebellion thus fizzled. While small cells of militants would continue to carry out sporadic attacks for the next two years, these too were, eventually, largely eliminated (Sahliyeh, 1988, 33–34).

Armed resistance was more intense in the Gaza Strip but, there too, there was little unarmed protest. Less than a year after the 1967 War and the beginning of Israeli occupation, the Palestinian Liberation Army (PLA) launched armed operations inside the Gaza Strip. Established as the official military force of the PLO, PLA fighters were armed and trained by Egypt for conventional warfare, and many had seen combat during the 1967 War. Now, in the war's aftermath, PLA fighters based in Gaza's overcrowded refugee camps fought a guerrilla war against Israeli targets inside the Strip (Roy, 1995, 104). By 1970, they challenged Israeli control over the territory by night, prompting Israel to crack down on them and their supporters. Under the command of Israeli General Ariel Sharon, the military launched a campaign to take back control of Gaza's refugee camps, displacing over thirteen thousand residents from their homes. Twelve thousand family members of suspected militants were also sent to detention camps in the Sinai Peninsula (Roy, 1995, 104–5; Tessler, 1994, 472). With the refugee camps thus cleared of many of their inhabitants, Israeli forces killed large numbers of Palestinian fighters in gun battles in the camps (Tessler, 1994, 472). After more than a year and a half of violence, all that remained of the rebellion was "the festering resentment of the people of Gaza" (Halabi, 1985, 82).[4]

Thus, in the wake of the 1967 War, there was little broad-based resistance to the Israeli occupation of the Palestinian Territories. Local Palestinian elites in the West Bank remained loyal to Jordan and limited their opposition to issuing public statements and other forms of "polite protest." The PLO, controlled by Egypt, had also not yet gained ascendancy, and Fatah, the main Palestinian nationalist faction, was committed to "armed struggle" – not mass mobilization. Moreover, with most Palestinian elites still backing Jordan and limited popular support for the Fatah movement, its efforts to spark an insurgency in the West Bank faltered. In the Gaza Strip, armed resistance was more successful, but, by 1971, it had also been snuffed out. For the first decade of Israeli occupation, avenues for political participation by ordinary Palestinians thus remained limited.

2.2 MILITARY RULE, MASS IMPRISONMENT, AND CENSORSHIP

With the imposition of Israeli military rule, the prospects for mass protests in the Palestinian Territories – already limited by social fragmentation – waned further. While granting some autonomy at the local level, the military administration erected by Israel following the 1967 War severely restricted Palestinian political rights. Israeli military orders, the new law of the land, tightly circumscribed all forms of public political participation. These orders also censored the media and school curriculum, limiting the information available to ordinary Palestinians and hindering their ability to resist Israeli rule. Those who violated the orders risked arrest and imprisonment within the new Israeli military court system. As a result, during the first decade of occupation, any form of mass resistance to Israeli rule remained very limited.

Upon first taking control of the Palestinian Territories, Israel sought to preserve the existing, notable-led social order and minimize local

---

4 See also Tessler (1994, 473).

opposition to its rule. Crafted by then Israeli Minister of Defense Moshe Dayan, initial Israeli policy centered on three principles: "nonpresence," "noninterference," and "open bridges." Israeli authorities initially sought to leave a light footprint, minimizing visible signs of their presence so as to reduce tensions with the Palestinian population. In a manner akin to indirect colonial rule, they placed as much responsibility for economic and administrative activities as permitted by the imperatives of occupation in local hands. In addition, they maintained "open bridges" between the Palestinian Territories and the wider Arab world (Rekhess, 1975).[5] Israeli authorities also maintained an open border between Israel and the Palestinian Territories, allowing Palestinians to visit and work in Israel. By permitting Palestinians to work in higher-paying jobs in Israel, they hoped to mitigate grievances among the local population and prevent them from supporting Palestinian guerrilla fighters (Hiltermann, 1993, 18). Beginning in 1968, tens of thousands of Palestinians, primarily rural villagers, crossed the Green Line daily to work in construction and service jobs inside Israel.[6]

To administer the Palestinian Territories, Israel established a military government ("military administration"). The military administration was actually two regional administrations, one based in the West Bank and the other in the Gaza Strip. A military commander, who served as both the executive and legislative authority for the region, headed each administration. The military commander governed by decrees called military orders that had the force of law. Since 1967, Israeli military commanders have issued over 2,500 military orders regulating military, judicial, administrative, and fiscal affairs (Gordon, 2008, 27). These military orders form part of a complex patchwork of laws applied to the Palestinian Territories, including Ottoman, British, Jordanian, and Egyptian law. In accordance with the Hague Convention, which specifies that occupying powers should recognize the laws in place before occupation, these previous bodies of law were kept in place. However, they could be canceled or changed by military order, allowing Israel to choose between laws in accordance with its own political objectives (Gordon, 2008, 26–28).

Palestinians charged with violating Israeli military orders were arrested and tried by the new military court system. As the number of

---

[5] See also Hiltermann (1993, 19) and Tessler (1994, 473).
[6] The Green Line refers to the pre-1967 border separating Israel from East Jerusalem, the West Bank, and the Gaza Strip.

Palestinians within the system multiplied, prisoners and their families would gain unexpected informational and organizational advantages for collective action, rendering them better able to protest. The military court system was established in the first decade of Israeli occupation in order to prosecute Palestinians charged with committing "security offenses," defined by Israeli authorities to include a wide range of violent and nonviolent offenses (Hajjar, 2005, 3). In this early phase of the occupation, those arrested were primarily members of the PLO or other illegal, political-military groups, political activists, and those suspected of contact with activists, who were typically detained for only short periods. However, in the early 1980s, the use of imprisonment as a tactic widened (Rosenfeld, 2004, 223–24, 232–37). Reflecting the centrality of schools to protest, preparatory and secondary school students increasingly became the target of arrests, and many were subjected to repeated, intermittent arrests and interrogations (Rosenfeld, 2004, 233). As a result, state prisons and courts came to resemble a broad cross section of Palestinian society. Due to their social interactions within these increasingly diverse institutions, Palestinian prisoners and their families went on to form a vibrant prisoners' movement within the broader Palestinian national movement against Israeli occupation.

The military court system was part of a more extensive Israeli military administration, consisting of two branches: a security branch and a civil branch, with the latter overseeing schools and other civil institutions in the newly occupied Palestinian Territories. In keeping with the Israeli policies of "non-presence" and "non-interference," the civil branch and its institutions were largely staffed by Palestinians. Making up over 90 percent of military government employees, Palestinians remained in charge of the day-to-day operations of public schools, hospitals, post offices, and even police stations (Gordon, 2008, 30). However, because Israeli military officials headed these institutions and retained actual control over them, these personnel had little ability to shape institutional policy or culture. For example, as they had under Jordanian and Egyptian rule, Palestinian educators continued to staff all state schools in the Palestinian Territories. But while Palestinian teachers and principals retained their positions, they were expected to hew closely to the official curriculum imposed by Israeli authorities and faced stiff penalties if they did not. As a result, Palestinian schools taught little in the way of nationalist or political content that could inspire Palestinian youth to protest.

Palestinians also continued to exercise some political autonomy at the local level, reinforcing local identities and networks and limiting the influence of national and transnational PLO leaders. In the West Bank, Israel maintained the structure of local leadership in place under Jordan. As they had under Jordanian rule, village mukhtars – village leaders or chiefs from the traditional notable class – continued to rule in rural areas. In towns and cities, mayors and municipal councillors from the notable class also governed. While their authority was much reduced (Gordon, 2008, 96–100), these local notables continued to play an important, intermediary role between central authorities and ordinary Palestinians. In Hebron, for example, the longtime mayor "passed easily from being the vital link of the Jordanians to the population to playing the same role for the Israelis" (Migdal, 2014, 49; Levi, 1982).[7] Thus, local identities and networks remained strong, and local notables loyal to Jordan and Egypt and wary of the radical change sought by the PLO continued to command power and influence at the local level (Tessler, 1994, 473).

While local officials remained in power and Palestinians retained some autonomy in day-to-day matters, they lacked basic political rights – particularly the right to assembly. Rather than an elected legislature, the Israeli military commander held legislative power. Military decrees issued by the military commander were the law of the land. These decrees restricted any form of public political participation or expression. For example, Israeli military order 101, issued in the first year of occupation and still in force today, rendered it "forbidden to conduct a protest march or meeting (grouping of ten or more where the subject concerns or is related to politics) without permission from the Military Commander. It is also forbidden to raise flags or other symbols, to distribute or publish a political article and pictures with political connotations. No attempt should be made to influence public opinion in a way which would be detrimental to public order/security" (IMO 101, in Rabah and Fairweather, 1993). With its broad and undefined provisions, this order limited not only protests but also political seminars, discussions, and even private gatherings. Violations of the order were punishable by a maximum of ten years' imprisonment or a heavy fine.[8] With permits nearly impossible to obtain, participation in unauthorized political gatherings thus involved high risks.

[7] See also Gordon (2008, 98).
[8] www.btselem.org/demonstrations/military_order_101 (accessed September 26, 2016).

Additional orders and regulations also censored the information available to Palestinians, hindering their capacity for protest. Censorship was based on the 1945 British Emergency Regulations. Promulgated by the British mandatory authorities and subsequently revived by Israel, these regulations stated that "the censor may by order prohibit the importation or expropriation or the printing or publishing of any publication... which in his opinion would be or [is] likely to become, prejudicial for the defense of Palestine or to the public safety or public order" (Falloon, 1986, 5). Israeli military order 50 from July 1967 reiterated these regulations, prohibiting the publication or distribution of "newspapers" without a permit issued by the Israeli military administration. Because newspapers were defined broadly to include "any pamphlet containing news, information, events, occurrences, or explanations relating to news items, stories, or any other item of public interest," the regulations rendered virtually all Palestinian publications subject to Israeli approval (Gordon, 2008, 36–37).

Those newspapers that received permits to operate from the Israeli military authorities were also subject to strict censorship (Gordon, 2008, 36–37). Palestinian newspapers were required to carry their galley sheets – including even advertisements, weather forecasts, sports reports, and obituaries – to the military censor's office in West Jerusalem to be approved, partially censored, or banned (Najjar, 2015, 1236–38). News articles reporting on protests or other forms of resistance to Israeli occupation were typically reduced to a single paragraph reporting that an event took place; details such as the number of participants were excised (Gordon, 2008, 37). More general information about the Palestinian national movement and the PLO was also often expunged. The PLO was designated by Israel as a terrorist organization, making it illegal for newspapers to publish "words of praise or sympathy for, or an appeal for aid or support of" the PLO or, eventually, to contact, interview, or quote activists and supporters.[9] Rather than draw on local PLO sources, Palestinian newspapers were thus forced to draw verbatim from the organization's wire service dispatches from outside the Palestinian Territories (Kuttab, 1998). During politically tense periods, they were often forced to cease circulation altogether (see e.g. Friedman, 1983, 93, 98; Gordon, 2008, 109).

---

[9] In 1986, contacting an official of a "terrorist organization" was also made illegal, making it difficult for newspapers to contact PLO sources (Najjar, 2015, 1236–38).

As a result, Palestinians in the Occupied Territories could not turn to newspapers for information about the PLO or resistance to Israeli occupation. While the Palestinian press did report on protests, strikes, and other political events inside the Occupied Territories, these reports were heavily censored and lacked the "information on numbers" that is important for participation. And even these reports often reached Palestinians late, after first being published in the Israeli or foreign press and translated back into Arabic.[10] Thus, during periods of confrontation such as the first Palestinian intifadah, "the Palestinian press was the last place anyone would turn to in order to find out what was happening" (Kuttab, 1998).

In addition to the news media, Israeli authorities also censored the curriculum taught in schools of any kind of nationalist or political content. Initially, as they had done in Palestinian schools inside Israel's 1948 borders, Israeli authorities tried to impose the Israeli curriculum in the Occupied Territories. When this proposal met with opposition, however, the Israeli military administration reinstated the existing Jordanian and Egyptian curricula.[11] These curricula, intended to foster Jordanian and Egyptian (and in the Egyptian case also pan-Arab) national pride, did not mention Palestinian identity. In Jordan, which had annexed the West Bank and sought to assimilate its Palestinian population, the word "Palestine" was banned from schoolbooks as it was in any official document or correspondence (Sayigh, 1997, 42). In Egypt as well, Palestinian and other subnational identities that could serve as sources of division or dissent were simply omitted from the curriculum (Brand, 2014*b*, 37–66).

Under Israeli occupation, the Palestinian educational system was further stripped of any national content. Within only a couple of months of the 1967 War, Israeli authorities banned the use of fifty-five textbooks outright. Other books were radically altered (Shehadeh and Kuttāb, 1980). All references to the land, history, geography, people, literature, and even poetry of Palestine were removed, expunging words, paragraphs, and entire chapters. Borders were also erased from maps, which now showed Israel, the West Bank, and the Gaza Strip as part of a single

---

[10] Rather than "break" news stories that could not be published, Palestinian journalists would pass them on to their Israeli or foreign counterparts for publication, after which the story, translated back into Arabic, would sometimes be allowed to run in the local Palestinian press (Kuttab, 1998).

[11] Opposition was led by the teachers' union, which initiated a general strike in September 1967.

"Greater Israel" (Gordon, 2008, 58; Alzaroo and Hunt, 2003, 6). Thus, in contrast to postcolonial schools elsewhere in the Arab world, which sought to engender and reinforce national identity, the school system put in place by Israeli authorities sought to suppress it. When protests eventually emerged in schools, then, it would be in spite of, rather than because of, the formal curriculum.

In sum, while granting some autonomy at the local level, the military administration erected by Israel following the 1967 War severely circumscribed Palestinian political rights. Public political participation was nearly all but prohibited. Military authorities used censorship to prevent students and other Palestinians from becoming politicized and limit their access to political information, hampering their ability to participate in unarmed resistance. Yet Palestinian teachers and civil servants continued to staff public institutions, and local officials continued to govern within their respective communities. In the West Bank, local notables loyal to Jordan and wary of the nationalist PLO continued to serve as mayors and mukhtars much as they had under Jordanian rule. Assured of the cooperation of the traditional political elite and seeking to legitimize its occupation, Israel thus moved to hold new municipal elections in the West Bank in spring of 1972.

2.3 THE RESURGENCE OF PALESTINIAN NATIONALISM AND DEEPENING NATIONALIST GRIEVANCES

As Israel moved to hold elections and consolidate its control over the Palestinian Territories in the spring of 1972, Palestinians faced limited opportunities to participate in organized protests against Israeli rule. Local leaders hesitant to challenge Israeli authorities too forcefully remained in power, and public opinion had also not yet united behind the PLO and its Palestinian nationalist ideology. While anti-regime sentiment had begun to simmer, support for an independent Palestinian state was still far from universal. However, within the next five years, a renewed nationalist spirit would surge through the Palestinian Territories, ushering in a new, more confrontational political leadership and, with it, new avenues for participation in protest.

In spring of 1972, as the occupation was entering its fifth year, Israel moved to further consolidate its control over the Palestinian Territories. Assured of the cooperation of the traditional notable class that held local office, Israeli authorities sought to bolster its power by holding municipal elections in the West Bank. In holding elections, Israeli authorities hoped to "strengthen the mandate of the municipal councils and their leaders," allowing them "to co-operate with the military administration more closely" (Gazit, 2003, 167–68). For their part, local leaders saw the elections as an opportunity for Palestinians to exercise greater control over their own affairs (Tessler, 1994, 473). For this reason, the PLO strongly opposed the elections. Seeing the emergence of a stronger local leadership in the West Bank as a threat to the unity of the Palestinian national movement and its own political leadership, it called on eligible voters in the West Bank to boycott the polls (Gordon, 2008, 100).[12] In spite of the PLO's appeals, Palestinian voters – limited to male property owners – turned out in large numbers to support traditional candidates (Tessler, 1994, 473–74). Thus, consistent with Israel's goal of preserving the existing social order, the elections served to reinforce the role of local identities and divisions within Palestinian social life. Yet, over the next few years, developments both inside and outside the Palestinian Territories would dramatically change this state of affairs.

For the present, however, the PLO and its brand of Palestinian nationalism did not yet attract widespread support in the Palestinian Territories. After Fatah's aborted insurgency in the West Bank, the PLO's rebel factions had turned their attention to building a political and military base of operations in Jordan. With the center of its activity in Jordan, the organization devoted little time or attention to mobilization inside the Palestinian Territories (Sayigh, 1997, 345). As a result, it had only weak support among West Bank inhabitants (Sahliyeh, 1988, 34). Moreover, as the PLO's growing assertiveness brought it into direct conflict with the Jordanian regime during the "Black September" of 1970, its support in the West Bank waned further. Expelled from Jordan, lacking access to the West Bank, and facing collapse, the organization's support and influence plummeted (Sahliyeh, 1988, 34). Thus, when municipal elections were held in the West Bank a year later, few voters heeded the PLO's appeals for a boycott.

Yet the organization was not without important allies in the Occupied Territories. In the years following the 1972 elections, a new generation of pro-PLO activists from inside the territories sought to mobilize Palestinian national identity and support for the PLO, paving the way for the emergence of mass resistance to Israeli occupation (Sahliyeh, 1988, 54–63). In 1973, local, pro-PLO activists formed the Palestinian National

---

[12] Under Jordanian law still in force, only male property owners were eligible to vote in the elections (Gordon, 2008, 101).

Front (PNF). The PNF was a coalition consisting of activists from the main PLO factions (with the exception of the PFLP, which did not participate), the Communist Party, and independent political figures. Its mission was to reassert a distinct Palestinian national identity and to mobilize public opinion in favor of the PLO and its positions (Hiltermann, 1993, 44; Sahliyeh, 1988, 53, 62).[13] At the same time, the PNF also acted as a kind of pressure group, lobbying the PLO to be more responsive to the interests of Palestinians living inside the Palestinian Territories and to accept a territorially delimited Palestinian state within its boundaries. While the PNF ultimately collapsed in 1977 due to internal fragmentation and Israeli repression, it was important in mobilizing support for the PLO and shifting the organization's focus more squarely toward the Palestinian Territories (Sahliyeh, 1988, 54–63).

The PNF's efforts were strengthened by developments occurring both inside and outside the Palestinian Territories, which shifted power from conservative traditional leaders to a new nationalist elite. Inside the Palestinian Territories, the notable class, which had held onto its status in the 1972 municipal elections, was beginning to lose its standing. With their power circumscribed by the Israeli authorities, they could not deliver the same benefits to the population as they had under Jordanian rule. Broad socioeconomic forces, put into motion by Israeli policies in the Occupied Territories, also eroded their influence. As a result of Israel's policy of open borders between Israel and the Palestinian Territories, tens of thousands of Palestinians – primarily rural peasants – were crossing the Green Line to work in Israel for higher wages every day. All of a sudden, a Palestinian peasant or *fellah* could earn a better livelihood than the landowner whose lands he had formerly farmed. These changes did not diminish the overall importance of the village in Palestinian social life: Palestinian workers typically returned to their village every night, and recruitment into and work in Israel took place along familial and local lines. However, *within* the village, they challenged the long-standing village hierarchy with landowning notables at its top (Tamari, 1981).

Outside the Palestinian Territories, renewed conflict between Israel and the Arab World also bolstered the PNF's efforts to mobilize nationalist and pro-PLO sentiment. On October 6, 1973, the date of the Jewish holy day of Yom Kippur, Egypt and Syria launched a surprise attack on Israeli positions in the Sinai Peninsula and Golan Heights. While Israel

---

[13] The Popular Front for the Liberation of Palestine (PFLP) is a Marxist-Leninist and nationalist faction belonging to the PLO.

defeated Egyptian and Syrian forces in less than a month, its victory was hard fought (Tessler, 1994, 476–77). Israel's unexpected military troubles contributed to the rising nationalist and pro-PLO feeling inside the Palestinian Territories. Although Egyptian and Syrian forces were defeated militarily, Palestinians and Arabs widely hailed the war as a relative victory that restored the balance of power between Israel and its Arab neighbors. By shattering the perception of Israeli invincibility, the war thus strengthened the position of the PLO and the PNF in the Occupied Territories.

As a result of these developments, a renewed nationalist spirit swept through the Palestinian Territories. Reflecting the growing nationalist mood, a survey conducted after the war by Israel's *Ma'ariv* newspaper found that support for the PLO was growing rapidly. A large percentage of the population now favored establishing an independent Palestinian state. The shift in public opinion, the newspaper claimed, was "extensive and alarming" (Gordon, 2008, 102).

With the popularity and influence of the PLO rapidly eclipsing that of traditional elites, Israeli leaders sought to promote an alternative indigenous leadership with which it could do business. In 1976, they again permitted municipal elections – scheduled under Jordanian laws still in force – to be held in the West Bank. While this decision is puzzling in retrospect, Israeli authorities likely hoped that, as they had in 1972, elections would bolster the declining standing of the traditional elite and act as a counterweight to the growing strength of the PLO (Gordon, 2008). Elections may also have been intended to staunch the building international and local criticism of Israel's occupation of the Palestinian Territories (Tessler, 1994, 491). This reasoning may have also underlain Israel's decision, taken before the elections, to extend the franchise to women and those not owning property, thereby nearly tripling the number of eligible voters (Sahliyeh, 1988, 104; Gordon, 2008, 64).

These calculations proved wrong, however. Rather than buttressing Israeli occupation, the 1976 elections – unlike the 1972 elections – would dramatically undermine it. On April 12 of that year, Palestinians in twenty-two of the largest West Bank towns went to the polls. With its popularity peaking, the PLO did not urge a boycott. Seeing the elections as an opportunity for pro-PLO activists to come to power, the mainstream PLO factions tacitly consented to the elections and approved the participation of pro-PLO candidates (Sahliyeh, 1988, 66). Their gambit proved correct, as the elections resulted in a resounding victory for

nationalist and pro-PLO forces in the West Bank. New political figures, many of them nationalists, assumed roughly three-quarters of the
municipal council seats and one-half of the mayoralties (Gordon, 2008,
104–5).

Upon assuming office, these leaders adopted a new strategy of organizing unarmed resistance to Israeli occupation, providing ordinary
Palestinians with new avenues for political participation. Within weeks
of the elections, protests and demonstrations began occurring in scat-
tered cities throughout the Palestinian Territories. After a demonstration
commemorating the 1948 Palestinian *nakbah* (catastrophe) in which two
Palestinian teenagers were killed, the newly elected nationalist mayors
spearheaded a series of protests and demonstrations in the West Bank
(Gordon, 2008, 105). Throughout the next few years, they worked with
municipal councillors and other members of the new nationalist elite to
initiate strikes, demonstrations, and sit-ins throughout the Palestinian
Territories (Sahliyeh, 1988, 69). In addition, they cooperated with each
other to issue unified statements against Israeli (and sometimes Arab)
policies and actions, helping to coordinate public opposition around
them (Sahliyeh, 1988, 68–69; Gordon, 2008, 106).

Organized resistance to Israeli rule increased further after the surprising victory of the Likud party in Israeli elections held the following year.
On May 17, 1977, Israeli voters elected the right-wing Likud Union
party to power, ending nearly forty years of Labor Party rule. Unlike
the left-wing Labor Party, the Likud party viewed the West Bank and
the Gaza Strip as part of the historic, biblical land of Israel and favored
permanently retaining these lands rather than exchanging them for peace
(Tessler, 1994, 477, 500). Once in power, the Likud government quickly
set about implementing this territorially maximalist vision. Almost immediately, it began building and expanding Jewish settlements in the West
Bank and Gaza Strip (Gordon, 2008, 125; Tessler, 1994, 506). To
accommodate the new settlements, land expropriation also intensified,
accelerating the pattern of Palestinian labor migration into Israel and the
decline of the traditional rural landholding class (Hiltermann, 1993, 19).
These dynamics, in turn, further eroded the importance of local identities and affiliations and contributed to the growing wave of nationalist
feeling.

Thus, by 1977, two key conditions for the emergence of mass resistance to Israeli rule were in place. First, a renewed nationalist spirit had
taken hold in the Palestinian Territories. As the 1976 municipal elections
made clear, Palestinian public opinion was now firmly united behind the

PLO and its Palestinian nationalist ideology. Second, a local leadership now existed that could channel this resurgent nationalist spirit. Unlike the PLO leadership based outside the Palestinian Territories, this local leadership sought to organize unarmed resistance to Israeli rule, presenting ordinary Palestinians with new avenues for participation. By the end of 1977, Palestinians therefore had both new opportunities for participation in resistance and a renewed determination to resist. Yet, at the same time, they lacked a third condition that is often theorized to be necessary for protest to emerge: internal organizational strength.

2.4 THE INITIAL WEAKNESS OF PALESTINIAN CIVIL SOCIETY

As the Israeli occupation entered its second decade, Palestinian civil society remained weak. Hobbled first by authoritarian Egyptian and Jordanian rule and subsequently by the pressures of Israeli occupation, Palestinian civil society organizations were unable to provide prospective dissidents with meaningful resources for protest. Upon first occupying the Palestinian Territories in 1967, Israel had suspended all organized societal activity (Muslih, 1993, 63). In the Gaza Strip, all trade union activity was banned until 1979, and even then it remained limited in scope. In the West Bank, trade unions remained legal under Israeli occupation. However, much as it had under Jordanian rule, constant repression by Israeli authorities severely hampered their ability to operate (Hiltermann, 1993, 61–62). Making the matter worse, after 1979 Israel stopped granting licenses to new unions, forcing the majority of unions to operate illegally without a license (Hiltermann, 1993, 68). Such restrictions were not imposed on unions alone: in general, Palestinian associations were required to register with the Israeli authorities, and licenses for new associations were difficult to obtain. As a result, in the wake of the Israeli occupation of the Palestinian Territories, the civic landscape consisted of a small number of mostly urban civil society associations with little penetration into or participation from society at large.

In the early 1970s, West Bank members of the Jordanian Communist Party (JCP) began the first limited forays into reviving civic life in the Occupied Territories. Drawing on their experiences working underground during Jordanian rule, Communist Party activists defied Israeli repression to reconstitute dormant trade unions and establish new ones (Taraki, 1984; Hiltermann, 1993). During this time, activists associated with the Communist Party also began forming voluntary working committees (VWCs), which combined volunteer work with political socialization (Interview 4, PNF activist, Jerusalem, October 26, 2009).[14] Yet, in a rural, conservative society, the Communist Party held little appeal among the general population. In addition, its activists rarely ventured outside the party's urban strongholds (Hiltermann, 1993, 56). As such, while the JCP played a pioneering role in rebuilding civic life in the West Bank, its unions and organizations had only a limited constituency.

In contrast to the Communist Party, the more popular PLO showed little interest in building institutions in the Palestinian Territories at this time. Throughout the 1960s and 1970s, Fatah and the PLO were committed to liberating all of historic Palestine though military resistance. As a result, they devoted little attention to the Palestinian Territories and building institutions there (Robinson, 1997, 20). Beginning in the late 1970s, Marxist-Leninist factions inside the PLO did begin giving greater lip service to the importance of building "mass organizations" in the Occupied Territories. Yet, these factions did not take any meaningful steps to translate these words into action for at least several more years (Sayigh, 1997, 471–73; Jamal, 2005, 57–61). As Yezid Sayigh observed of the DFLP, the PLO faction arguably most committed to institution-building, "For all its stress on political mobilization or mass action and interest in labor unions, the DFLP had not fundamentally altered its methods or devoted major resources to social mobilization by the time its second general conference reconvened [in May 1981]" (Sayigh, 1997, 471).

Despite having strong nationalist grievances and new avenues for participation in resistance, Palestinians thus nonetheless lacked the strong autonomous institutions widely believed to be necessary for protest. Until the late 1970s, no civil society associations "of any size or influence" existed at all (Hiltermann, 1993, 14). Trade unions remained small in size and were confined to the six largest Palestinian cities (Hiltermann, 1993, 64). Consequently, unionization rates also remained low. As a result, even after a resurgence of union activity in the early 1980s, relatively few Palestinian workers were organized into unions (i.e. 5.4–10 percent in 1982) (Sahliyeh, 1988, 104; Sayigh, 1997, 476). And, even among those that were organized, not all were union members in any meaningful sense of the term. Rather, as PLO factions began competing with one another to organize workers into faction-based unions in the

---

[14] See also Hiltermann (1993, 41–42).

early 1980s, union membership was often little more than a label. As one former union member recalled:

All of us were registered in the [truck] drivers' union, everybody. All of us registered but for nothing. They didn't do anything for us, what can they do anyway?! And they won't do anything for us, we never paid anything and they never gave us anything. Registration was just a name (Interview 20, Nablus, March (n.d.) 2014)

Other types of civil society organizations were also weak, particularly in rural areas. In the villages where the majority of West Bank Palestinians lived, a 1981 survey found only ninety-one civil society associations: sixty-one charitable societies and thirty social clubs.[15] Of the 409 villages in the West Bank, only 25 percent had any civic institutions other than the local municipality.[16] For example, in the northern village of Anabta, "there were no institutions other than the municipality and a women's association [before 1980] because everything was forbidden and needed a license from the military government and it was difficult to get a license" (Interview 11, Fatah/Shabiba activist, Anabta, March 17, 2014). Thus, particularly in the rural villages where the vast majority of Palestinians lived, few associations existed that could serve as "mobilizing structures" for resistance.

Thus, when the Camp David Accords were signed between Egypt and Israel in 1978, mass resistance seemed unlikely. Despite the rising nationalist and pro-PLO feeling in the Palestinian Territories and an activist local leadership that sought to channel this feeling into organized resistance to Israeli occupation, Palestinians lacked the internal organizational strength that is often theorized to be necessary for unarmed protest. Yet, even in the absence of strong independent institutions and organizations, the signing of the Camp David Accords would begin a decade of growing popular protest against Israeli rule.

2.5 THE CAMP DAVID ACCORDS AND NEW AVENUES FOR POLITICAL PARTICIPATION

On September 17, 1978, Egypt and Israel signed the Camp David Accords, establishing peace between the two countries. Yet, while the

---

[15] Calculated from survey on "Public services in villages of the West Bank and Gaza Strip" (al-Shaᶜabani and Khadr, 1982).

[16] This figure includes charitable societies and social clubs; it does not include religious institutions, which were not counted in al-Sha'bani and Khadr (1982). In some cases, childcare centers may also indicate the presence of civil society associations. If these are also counted, 40 percent of villages had any civil society associations at this time.

Accords ushered in peace between Egypt and Israel, they set off a new era of unrest inside the Palestinian Territories. The Accords capped off nearly a year of American-sponsored diplomacy under the aegis of US President Jimmy Carter. At a historic summit meeting at Camp David sponsored by Carter, Egyptian President Anwar Sadat and Israeli President Menachem Begin signed the "Framework for the Conclusion of a Peace Treaty between Egypt and Israel," which would serve as the basis for a final peace treaty concluded in March 1979. Under this treaty, Israel would withdraw from the Sinai Peninsula, which it had occupied during the 1967 War, and return it to Egyptian sovereignty. In exchange, it would gain full and normal diplomatic relations with Egypt, ending thirty years of war between the two countries. The status of the Palestinian Territories – also captured from Egypt and Jordan in the 1967 War – was, however, left much less clear.

In addition to the framework agreement, the Camp David Accords also included a second agreement concerning the Palestinian dimension of the conflict, which most Palestinians staunchly opposed. This agreement called for an elected "Self-Governing Authority" to be established in the West Bank and Gaza Strip, followed by negotiations over the final status of these territories between Egypt, Israel, Jordan, and local elected representatives (but, notably, not the PLO). These negotiations would be based on United Nations Resolution 242, which calls for the withdrawal of Israeli armed forces from "territories occupied" in the 1967 War and forms the legal basis for the two-state solution. However, while this second framework agreement could be viewed as an important first step toward the end of Israeli occupation and the achievement of Palestinian self-determination in the Palestinian Territories (as, indeed it was, by Egypt), it did not bind the parties to such an outcome. Unlike the first Egyptian–Israeli agreement, the document was vague and did not contain any meaningful enforcement mechanisms (Tessler, 1994, 514). Moreover, even as negotiations toward a final Egyptian–Israeli agreement were proceeding, Israel's Likud-led government made it clear that it did not intend to withdraw from the Palestinian Territories (Tessler, 1994, 516–19). For these reasons, the Accords were opposed by the vast majority of Palestinians inside and outside the Palestinian Territories, as well as much of the wider Arab world.

The signing of the Camp David Accords thus set off a wave of protests inside the Palestinian Territories, initiating a decade of unarmed resistance to Israeli rule. Two weeks after the historic summit at Camp David, a large public rally was held in Jerusalem. Its main goal was to generate a common strategy to prevent the implementation of the "autonomy plan" proposed under the Camp David Accords, which it rejected in "form and substance" (Jamal, 2005, 51–52). Organized by Ibrahim Dakkak, a prominent, politically independent political figure and one of the driving forces behind the PNF, it was attended by an ideologically diverse group of political leaders and activists from throughout the Palestinian Territories.

Toward the goal of reaching a common strategy, rally attendees recommended the formation of a committee to organize opposition to the Accords in the West Bank. From its formation in November of 1978 until its collapse four years later, this committee – the National Guidance Committee (NGC) – would play an instrumental role in organizing unarmed resistance to Israeli rule throughout the Palestinian Territories. The NGC was a coalition of newly empowered nationalist elites who were united by their opposition to the Camp David Accords and support for the PLO. In addition to eight of the new nationalist mayors of the West Bank, it included representatives from the Gaza Strip, leaders of those nascent civil society organizations already operating in the Palestinian Territories, and journalists, business people, and other urban professionals (Sahliyeh, 1988, 73). Soon after the formation of this group, the NGC organized four additional rallies to protest the signing of the Camp David Accords and Israeli policies in the Occupied Territories (Sahliyeh, 1988, 74). Over the next year, demonstrations and other "public disturbances" recorded by the IDF would multiply from five hundred in 1977–78 to one thousand in 1979–80 (Frisch, 1996, 8).[17]

As they had since the early 1970s, students played a leading role in these protests and demonstrations (Jamal, 2005, 51; Taraki, 1984, 454). Reflecting the centrality of student protest to the broader movement against Israeli occupation, the NGC coordinated with student representatives, and several of its rallies were held on university campuses (Jamal, 2005, 52; Sahliyeh, 1988, 74). University students, for their part, worked in tandem with lower school students to organize street demonstrations and strikes against Israeli practices and express their support for the PLO (Sahliyeh, 1988, 125). This period also saw the continuation of the concerted demonstrations around prisoners' issues, occurring simultaneously

---

[17] These data are for the West Bank. In the Gaza Strip, the absolute number of demonstrations was lower, but they increased at an even greater rate (i.e. from thirty-five to ninety in the same period).

in the prisons and the streets, which had begun several years earlier (Nashif, 2008, 58).

Despite this growing cooperation between the NGC and student leaders, however, most protests remained relatively uncoordinated. As a primarily urban, elite organization with its basis in the main West Bank cities and towns, the NGC lacked wide roots in Palestinian society at large (see e.g. Sahliyeh, 1988; Frisch, 1993). In addition, as a centralized political structure, the committee would prove to be highly vulnerable to Israeli repression (see e.g. Taraki, 1984). As a result, while the NGC provided Palestinians with new opportunities for participation in mass protest, it was increasingly unable to play a broader coordinating role. With the NGC thus circumscribed and few civil society organizations inside or outside the committee to connect far-flung schools to one another, students protested "largely as an unorganized body lacking discipline and political direction" (Taraki, 1984, 454). While school-based social networks connected some schools to the NGC and made their students better able to participate in organized nationalist activity, most student protests lacked such a national scope. More generally, until the 1982 "mini-intifadah," most protests against the occupation tended to be "sporadic and uncoordinated, lacking either a central authority or clearly unified political objective" (Peretz, 1990, 389).

Meanwhile, outside the Palestinian Territories, the PLO and Jordan also sought to counteract the impact of the Camp David Accords by forming the Palestinian-Jordanian Coordinating Committee. The Committee sought to thwart Israeli plans for "administrative autonomy" by funneling financial aid from the Arab League to the Palestinian Territories. Yet, rather than building new civic organizations that could channel and support protest, most of the committee's funds went to support traditional, conservative social sectors. The committee consisted of representatives from the PLO (dominated by Fatah) and the Jordanian government, which temporarily set aside its rivalry with the PLO for influence in the Occupied Territories to participate. However, Fatah opposed letting the NGC control the allocation of funds. Instead, under its control, the committee concentrated on "the pre-1967 traditional sectors" that would not pose a challenge to Fatah's political dominance: municipalities, housing, and the expanding Palestinian university system (Jamal, 2005, 65–66).

Frustrated by the indifference of the external Fatah and PLO leadership to mass mobilization in the Palestinian Territories, some local activists sought to build independent institutions that could better channel Palestinian resistance to the ongoing Israeli occupation. In 1980, young Fatah activists from the northern West Bank village of Anabta formed the first Shabiba (youth) committee in the Occupied Territories. The Shabiba committees marked Fatah's first serious attempt at political mobilization inside the Occupied Territories (Frisch, 1996, 5). For most of its history, the Fatah-led PLO had sought to achieve its goal of liberating Palestine through military resistance from outside the Occupied Territories. While PLO factions, particularly those on the left, had for some years called for political resistance inside the Occupied Territories, they had done little to translate these calls into action (Sayigh, 1997, 471–73; Jamal, 2005, 57–61). Beginning in 1981, however, this began to change as the PLO's factions increasingly sought to organize Palestinians into youth groups, trade unions, and other "mass organizations" (Jamal, 2005, 57–62; Taraki, 1984, 448).[18]

Similarly to the voluntary working committees previously formed by the Communist Party, the Shabiba committees organized Palestinian students and youth to take part in social welfare projects and political socialization activities. Through their voluntarism in schools, charity toward prisoners' families, and social welfare provision in local communities, the committee's young members forged a nationwide network of contacts and supporters and brought new coherence and coordination to the growing movement against Israeli occupation. By 1983, there were over one hundred local Shabiba committees as well as a new body, the General Federation of Youth Committees for Social Work, that had formed to coordinate between them (Jamal, 2005, 74–82). This rapid growth came about, in part, because of growing Israeli pressure on the PLO both inside and outside the Palestinian Territories, necessitating the organization to adopt a comprehensive change of tactics.

2.6 REPRESSION, INSTITUTION-BUILDING, AND THE GROWING COORDINATION OF PROTEST

As resistance to Israeli occupation intensified in the late 1970s, Israel sought to curtail the influence of the new nationalist leadership inside the Palestinian Territories. Yet its hard-line strategy would have unintended consequences. With the nationalist leadership weakened and repression on the rise, the PLO only intensified its institution-building drive. Seeking

---

[18] See also Hiltermann (1993, 49–51) and Robinson (1997, 20–21).

a way to spread and sustain protests under mounting repression, PLO activists formed a new diffuse network of local civil society organizations that could better withstand Israeli pressures. As a result, as evidenced in the "mini-intifadah" of spring 1982, mass protests also became more coordinated and intense.

The introduction of more repressive measures against local nationalist leaders began as early as spring 1980. After a PLO-inspired attack on Jewish settlers in Hebron, Israel deported the mayors of Hebron and the nearby town of Halhoul. Three days later, Israeli television announced that the government had authorized the implementation of new, more restrictive measures against NGC members. Later that summer, it placed seven of the NGC's more active members under town arrest, prohibiting them from leaving their towns of residence without prior approval from the Israeli military government. They were also barred from making political statements and attending political rallies, and their telephone lines were cut (Sahliyeh, 1988, 83–84).

Repression of the political leadership tightened further in the summer of 1981, with the election of a second, even more hard-line, Likud government. Under the first Likud government (1977–1981), the cabinet had been roughly divided between proponents of a relatively more permissive approach toward the Palestinian political leadership and advocates of more hard-line tactics. Members of the "liberal" camp, notably Ezer Weizman, saw the new Palestinian leadership as prospective partners in negotiations about the future status of the Occupied Territories. This position stood in contrast to that of the hard-liners, who regarded the Palestinian leadership as subservient to the PLO and, therefore, as unsuitable partners for any future autonomy talks (Sahliyeh, 1988, 81–83).

With the resignation of the relatively more liberal government ministers and the reelection of the second Likud government, the hard-liners prevailed. Israeli tolerance for any kind of independent political activity diminished, and an "iron-fist" approach took hold. As part of this approach, Israel moved to implement its own limited vision of autonomy for Palestinians in the Occupied Territories. On November 8, 1981, Israel established the Civilian Administration to replace the military government in the Occupied Territories. The Civilian Administration assumed the management of all of the civil branches formerly under the control of the military government, formally separating civil affairs from the military (Gordon, 2008, 107; Tessler, 1994, 548). Informally, however, the military retained control. Legislative authority remained with the military, and military officers continued to staff many positions within the civil administration. Moreover, all decisions made by the civilian administration could be reversed by the military and the General Security Service (i.e. the GSS or "Shabak"). Thus, while the Civil Administration was presented as a transfer of power from the military to an autonomous civilian body, the military retained its primacy (Gordon, 2008, 107–8).

The Likud government also sought to weaken the nationalist mayors and councillors and replace them with more compliant local leaders (Gordon, 2008; Robinson, 1997; Sahliyeh, 1988). To this end, it disbanded many elected municipal and village councils and replaced them with Village Leagues – alternative local governments whose Palestinian members, unlike the popularly elected mayors and municipal councils, were appointed and funded by Israel (Tessler, 1994, 548–49). Much like the traditional notables before them, the Leagues' members were given the power to distribute various forms of state patronage: League members facilitated the process of obtaining traveling permits to Jordan, made recommendations on family reunification requests and the release of political prisoners, and helped determine appointments to public positions (Gordon, 2008, 112). At the same time, Israel also banned the transfer of funds from Arab states to the Palestinian Territories, effectively shutting down the Joint Committee and depriving the municipalities of other sources of funding (Gordon, 2008, 109). In this way, Israel attempted to create an alternative leadership class that was more willing to cooperate with its rule and restore the political arrangement in place before the nationalist-dominated elections of 1976.

With the nationalist mayors and municipalities thus weakened and repression on the rise, the PLO intensified its institution-building drive inside the Palestinian Territories. Under increasing pressure from the Israeli authorities, Lisa Taraki argues, the movement's activists were left with two choices: return to clandestine action and sacrifice their growing mass base of support or develop new institutions that would be better capable of spreading and sustaining protest under repression (Taraki, 1984, 442). A network of local civil society organizations would be more diffuse and difficult to destroy than a centralized structure like the NGC and provided the PLO's illegal underground factions with a communication channel for spreading information about protest. Thus, as public protest met with increasing repression and activists were targeted with harsher measures, Palestinian activists formed new civil society organizations that could better facilitate communication and coordination under repression. Consequently, after 1982, unions, student groups, and other civil society organizations replaced municipalities as important "arenas for political competition and mobilization" (Graham-Brown, 1984, in Hiltermann (1993, 51)).

As a result of this development, the "spring uprising" of 1982 saw the most intense, coordinated, and sustained resistance in the fifteen years since Israel had assumed control of the Palestinian Territories (Peretz, 1990, 389; Tessler, 1994, 562). Between April 1, 1981, and September 31, 1982, the IDF recorded twelve hundred "public disturbances" – strikes, demonstrations, and other forms of unarmed resistance – an increase of over 25 percent from the previous year (Frisch, 1996, 8). For the first time, demonstrations, marches, strikes, and incidents of stone-throwing occurred simultaneously through the West Bank (Peretz, 1990, 389). Student protests, previously unorganized and "lacking in direction" (Taraki, 1984), showed evidence of new coordination. For example, in just a single day in April, *al-Fajr* reported student demonstrations in the city of Tulkarm and the nearby village of Anabta, in Jenin and four nearby villages, and in several towns and villages in Hebron. Students were also reported injured in the Bethlehem area and the Gaza Strip.[19] To prevent further unrest, and as a means of collective punishment, Israeli authorities closed dozens of Palestinian schools for multiple weeks at a time (Gordon, 2008, 110).

In response to the protests, Israel intensified its repression of the new nationalist elite. However, this repression did little to staunch the growing tide of public support for the PLO. On March 11, 1982, Israel banned the NGC (Tessler, 1994, 565), whose more active members had already been under "town arrest" since August of 1980 (Sahliyeh, 1988, 83). Shortly after, it removed the more activist of the mayors and municipal councillors who had come to power in the municipal elections of 1976 (Gordon, 2008, 109; Tessler, 1994, 565–66). In spite of these repressive measures, however, the Palestinian public remained fervent in its support for the PLO. As demonstrations and clashes intensified, two separate polls taken by *Time* magazine and al-Najah University showed wide public support for an independent Palestinian state under the organization's leadership. In the *Time* poll, 98 percent of Palestinians surveyed favored a Palestinian state, and 86 percent believed that state should be governed by the PLO; in contrast, only 0.2 percent expressed support for Village League leader Mustafa Doudin. Similarly, the al-Najah poll found that 86 percent of Palestinians considered themselves to be represented by the

---

[19] *Al-Fajr* Jerusalem, April 23–29, 1982, in Tessler (1994, 562–63).

PLO and an additional 17 percent by the PLO and Jordan jointly (Tessler, 1994, 567).

With support for the PLO and resistance to Israeli occupation at a historic high, Israel sought to restore order by striking at what it saw as the source of the unrest: the external PLO leadership based in Lebanon (Tessler, 1994, 568–69). With this goal in mind, Israeli troops invaded Lebanon on June 6, 1982. They quickly achieved the limited objectives – the establishment of a 40-mile security zone north of the Israeli–Lebanon border – that had been approved by the Israeli cabinet and communicated in discussions with American officials. Yet, upon achieving these initial objectives, Israel expanded its campaign. Israeli troops, backed by Israel's air force and navy, pressed northwards toward Beirut, encircling the city. Led by then Israeli Defense Minister Ariel Sharon, Israeli officials now articulated a much broader rationale for the war: eliminating the PLO as a political military threat and installing a friendly, Christian-dominated, Lebanese government in Beirut. To achieve this end, the Israeli military intensified its assault on Beirut, bombing and shelling PLO positions, including the densely populated Palestinian refugee camps on the city's outskirts (Tessler, 1994).[20]

By August 1982, the PLO was defeated and had no choice but to negotiate a retreat. Yet, contrary to Israeli plans, the PLO's defeat did not spell the collapse of resistance in the Occupied Territories. Under the terms of an American-brokered evacuation plan, the PLO had agreed to withdraw from Lebanon and disperse to various Arab capitals. With the destruction of their state-within-a-state in Lebanon, the newly exiled PLO leadership only intensified its focus on building institutions and mobilizing the population in the Occupied Territories (Robinson, 1997, 17; Sahliyeh, 1988, 165; Brown, 2003, 149). As PLO attention and resources became exclusively fixed on the Palestinian Territories, unarmed resistance to Israeli rule continued to increase throughout the 1980s (Robinson, 1997, 17; Frisch, 1996, 8; Sayigh, 1997, 608). This resistance reached new heights in the winter of 1987, with the beginning of the first Palestinian intifadah.

---

[20] While figures on the number of fatalities vary widely, the count of Palestinians and Lebanese killed in the entire campaign numbers in the thousands, with many more displaced in the fighting. Among those killed were hundreds of Palestinian civilians massacred inside the Sabra and Shatila refugee camps by Lebanese Christian Phalangist militamen, with the knowledge and possible approval of Israeli authorities (Tessler, 1994).

2.7 THE FIRST INTIFADAH AND ITS AFTERMATH

Reaping the benefits of the PLO's institutional drive, the first Palestinian intifadah was a unified nationwide uprising against the Israeli occupation of the Palestinian Territories. Academic and journalistic accounts of the first intifadah tend to treat it as an "eruption" – a sudden, spontaneous, and unexpected outpouring of simmering tensions and resentments. Yet, from the beginning, the intifadah's protests were highly coordinated. Aided by a new nationwide network of civil society organizations, PLO activists linked students, the growing prisoners' movement, and rural villagers in a massive and unified protest campaign. Faced with this unprecedented wave of protests, Israel ramped up arrests, bringing more and more Palestinian families into activist networks. Yet, by 1989, this repression would take its toll. With the leadership of the uprising decimated, violent attacks began to replace mass protests, choking off opportunities for participation by ordinary Palestinians.

The first intifadah began on December 8, 1987, in the Jabaliya refugee camp inside the Gaza Strip. Earlier that day, an Israeli truck driver had driven his semitrailer into two vans at the Gaza Strip border checkpoint with Israel, killing four Palestinian workers and injuring nine others. To many Gazans, this incident was not merely a tragic accident. Two days earlier, an Israeli salesman had been killed in the Gaza Strip, and, to Gazans, the truck driver's actions seemed like a deliberate act of revenge. That night, four thousand Jabliya residents attended the funeral for the four dead workers. The next day, hundreds of people demonstrated and threw stones at Israeli soldiers inside the camp.[21]

But while Gazans may have responded with unexpected anger to the deaths, their protests were not uncoordinated or unplanned. Drawing on the network of civil society organizations they had built up over the previous decade, activists mobilized Gaza's students to take to the streets in a unified show of dissent. As Tawfik Abu Khousa, a Shabiba leader in the Gaza Strip, reported: "We [Shabiba] had nine youth committees in Jebalia [Jabaliya] Refugee Camp. On the evening of December 8, we told the leader of those nine committees, Suheil El Tuloli, that on the next day all the high school students and all other youths should come to the funeral of the people from Jebalia who were killed in the truck accident and stage a mass demonstration against the Israelis. We also

---

[21] "Demonstrations Sweep Occupied Territories, Many Killed and Wounded." 1987, December 13. *Jerusalem Dawn Palestinian Weekly* 8(395), 1, 3.

got the high school and university students affiliated with us to join the demonstration" (quoted in Gordon, Gordon, and Shriteh, 2003, 59).

From Jabaliya, the protests spread outward to cities throughout the Occupied Territories. On December 12, a total commercial strike was called in East Jerusalem and the West Bank cities of Ramallah and Nablus. The same day, *al-Fajr* reported, Israeli soldiers came "under attack from demonstrators" in the West Bank cities of Hebron, Nablus, Ramallah, and al-Bireh, as well as in several refugee camps. Israeli authorities responded to the unrest with repression, sending in military reinforcements to back up the regular army and firing at demonstrators with live ammunition. By December 13, less than a week into the uprising, eight Palestinians had been killed and over one hundred injured.[22]

As the protests began to spread, Israeli authorities moved to contain the uprising by limiting information about the mounting protests. On December 11, just three days into the uprising, they banned the distribution of the Arabic edition of *al-Fajr* in the Palestinian Territories for a period of ten days. The newspaper was alleged to have published "pictures and news about demonstrations in the Gaza Strip" that had not been submitted to and approved by the Israeli censor.[23] Thus, "as the intifada was raging, and the world press was focusing on the Palestinian conflict," wrote the veteran Palestinian journalist Daoud Kuttab, "the Palestinian press was the last place anyone would turn to in order to find out what was happening" (Kuttab, 1998). To acquire the information needed to participate in protests, Palestinians thus instead turned to their new civic networks.

Aided by these organizational networks, protestors defied Israeli censorship to demonstrate throughout the month of December. For the first time, they were joined by an increasingly large number of town and village dwellers outside of the main cities – particularly students – with whom they now shared social ties. On December 19, students and citizens from the town of Arrabeh, a relatively large town of 10,000 located 13 kilometers southwest of Jenin, joined the uprising. School students marched through the town chanting "O our people, join us, for the martyr has sacrificed with his blood," taking "the first concrete

---

[22] "Demonstrations Sweep Occupied Territories, Many Killed and Wounded." 1987, December 13. *Jerusalem Dawn Palestinian Weekly* 8(395), 1, 3–4.
[23] Nuseibeh, Reem. 1987, December 12. "Israel Bans al Fajr Arabic." *Jerusalem Dawn Palestinian Weekly* 8(395), 1, 3–4.

step in mobilizing the rest of town" (FACTS Information Committee, 1990c, 65). On December 20, Idna, a large town of 15,000 located near Hebron in the southern West Bank, also joined when a large group of "young people" erected barricades to stop Israeli soldiers from conducting their daily rounds inside the village (FACTS Information Committee, 1990c, 90). On the next day, Peace Day, a general strike was declared in the Palestinian Territories and among Palestinians in Israel. That day, protests were also recorded in the Jenin Refugee Camp in the northern West Bank, the southern West Bank town of Yatta, and the small Palestinian village of Arroura near Ramallah (FACTS Information Committee, 1990c). For perhaps the first time since the beginning of Israeli occupation, the villages, where the vast majority of Palestinians lived, were resisting.

As the uprising continued into its second month, a unified leadership – the United National Leadership of the Uprising (UNLU) – emerged to direct the mounting protests. The UNLU was an underground, anonymous body made up of representatives of the main political factions in the Palestinian Territories: Fatah, the PFLP, the DFLP, the Communist Party, and the Islamist factions outside the PLO (i.e. Islamic Jihad). Its members, who rotated seats on a fifteen-member committee in order to shield the organization from Israeli repression, determined the general goals, strategies, and tactics of the uprising. This leadership would prove to be instrumental in planning a nationwide campaign of resistance to Israeli occupation. On January 4, 1988, the UNLU issued its first underground communiqué, calling on Palestinians to "observe scrupulously the call for a general strike from January 11, 1988 until Wednesday evening, January 13, 1988" (quoted in Mishal and Aharoni, 1994). Over the next two years, it would issue dozens of such leaflets or *bayanat* calling on Palestinians to participate in demonstrations and marches, clashes, strikes, boycotts, and acts of solidarity and support for the uprising.

Yet without the civic networks put into place over the previous decade, the UNLU's appeals would likely have been much less successful. Pro-PLO civil society activists disseminated the UNLU's communiqués through their civic networks and translated their general directives into common, concrete blueprints for action. Shabiba (youth) activists coordinated with politically active school students to turn school students out to demonstrate (Collins, 2004, 148; Interview 11, Fatah/Shabiba activist, Anabta, March 17, 2014). Trade union activists formed local committees charged with disseminating news and information from house to house and encouraging residents to protest (Hiltermann, 1993, 194). Activists also spread information about the uprising's tactics using graffiti or, sometimes, via announcements made on the loudspeakers of the local mosque. Yet, for news of the intifadah's progress, the strength of protests, and Israeli countermeasures against them, Palestinians relied principally on their social networks. Without the civic ties forged during the previous decade, the UNLU's directives may thus never have reached many Palestinians. Protests, now synchronized, would have remained more diffuse and uncoordinated.

With Palestinian villages, cities, and refugee camps newly united in protest, Israel stepped up its repression. In an effort to prevent mass demonstrations, and possibly also as a form of collective punishment, Israeli authorities shuttered Palestinian schools and universities for weeks at a time (Tessler, 1994, 700). When demonstrations persisted in spite of the closings, security forces used harsher tactics. After the use of live ammunition against protestors drew wide international and domestic condemnation, Israeli Defense Minister Yitzhak Rabin encouraged Israeli soldiers to "break Palestinians' bones" instead. Under the new "force, might and beatings" policy, Israeli troops were issued clubs, which they often used indiscriminately against fleeing protestors (Pearlman, 2011, 114; Tessler, 1994, 699). These new procedures dramatically increased the risks of participation in protest, deterring some Palestinians from participating directly in the uprising. One participant who was not deterred remembered: "Of course, there was fear – from getting beaten up, not from going to prison for eighteen days [the length of administrative detention]. Even if it was two or three months, if you were in prison, no one beat you. The real problem was if the soldiers caught you. They can beat you up and break your bones. That was the fear" (Interview 18, Nablus, March 2, 2014).

Imprisonment was also used more frequently and for longer periods, bringing ordinary people and their families into the prison system and its networks and, in turn, into political activism. Arrests swelled, tripling the Palestinian prisoner population from 5,000 before the uprising to 14,000 in 1989 – one of the highest incarceration rates in the world. Suspected activists were systematically targeted, but some arrests were essentially random. Responding to the ongoing demonstrations, Israeli soldiers on street patrols randomly grabbed young men off the street, hauled them off to base, and charged them with spurious offenses (Ron, 2000, 455). Even being in the vicinity of a demonstration rendered one vulnerable to arrest, making it difficult for prospective participants to gauge the crowd's size and strength before joining. As a result of this expansion of arrest and incarceration, and its widening to include less politically active Palestinians, previously politically inactive families and friends of prisoners were exposed to the state's disciplinary structures for the first time, rendering them more likely to protest.

In addition to this ramping up of everyday repression, Israel also targeted the leadership of the uprising – inadvertently bringing more militant leaders to the fore and narrowing opportunities for participation by ordinary people. Seeking to undermine the uprising, Israeli authorities arrested and imprisoned successive coalitions of UNLU activists, who rotated their membership in the UNLU in order to defuse the impact of this repression on the organization. In contravention of the Fourth Geneva Convention, Israeli officials also deported thirty-five suspected leaders in the first year of the uprising (Tessler, 1994, 700). Among them were seasoned and disciplined leaders, who had honed their strategies and tactics over the last decade. Now, with their removal, younger and more militant leaders gained in prominence. By 1990, repression weakened the UNLU to the point that it no longer functioned as a coherent entity (Pearlman, 2011, 117; Tessler, 1994, 691). As a result, competition between Palestinian political factions, contained during the first two years of the uprising, resumed with greater intensity (Pearlman, 2011, 116–17). Without a unifying leadership to guide strategy and help discipline participants, nonviolent protest increasingly gave way to more violent tactics (Pearlman, 2011). Shooting incidents, while still relatively rare, increased from a mere 0.16 of all incidents recorded in 1988 to 0.84 of all incidents in 1991 (Pearlman, 2011, 106).

This constant repression and militarization increased the risks of participating in the intifadah, closing off avenues for participation by ordinary people. As the intifadah entered its third year, "strike forces" of armed, masked young men replaced the crowds of unarmed demonstrators that had characterized the early years of the uprising (Pearlman, 2011, 118). As men with kaffiyehs and Kalashnikovs took over the streets, avenues for participation by ordinary Palestinians, in turn, narrowed. After over a decade in which Palestinians had sustained wide opportunities to participate in unarmed resistance, violent resistance again came to the fore, choking off these opportunities. Thus, even before the first intifadah was over, its mass character had ended.

2.8 CONCLUSIONS

The first intifadah was the culmination of a nearly decade-long increase in organized unarmed resistance in the Palestinian Territories. As a result of developments both inside and outside the Palestinian Territories in the early 1970s, a revived nationalist spirit took hold in the Territories. In 1976, this resurgence of nationalist feeling manifested itself in the election of a new nationalist and activist leadership in the West Bank, which adopted an alternative strategy of unarmed resistance against the Israeli occupation. With the Likud victory in Israel and, particularly, the signing of the Camp David Accords between Israel and Egypt, organized unarmed opposition to Israeli rule increased. With this tactical shift, opportunities for participation by ordinary Palestinians also broadened. Driven by a resurgent sense of Palestinian nationalism and support for the PLO, more and more Palestinians began to avail themselves of these opportunities. Mass protests, rare before 1978, became a more and more commonplace occurrence.

Yet, despite vast public support for the PLO and its goal of establishing an independent Palestinian state, only a minority of Palestinians directly challenged Israeli rule. Under a Likud government that took a tougher line against dissent than its predecessors, protestors faced mounting risks of arrest, imprisonment, and injury. And, since the Israeli government sought to staunch the growing tide of protest by further restricting the Palestinian media, ordinary Palestinians lacked access to critical information about protest that further limited their participation. Under these conditions, most Palestinians continued to refrain from resistance even as they increasingly supported it.

Against this backdrop, Palestinian schools became key nodes for resistance against Israeli occupation, with middle and high school students playing a leading role in the protests. These students did not necessarily hold more intense nationalist grievances than nonstudent youth: the PLO commanded broad support among both students and non-students, as it did among the population more broadly, and the Israeli-controlled Palestinian educational system was designed to suppress national identity rather than stimulate it. Nor were Palestinian schools "zones of autonomy," where students could organize free of Israeli interference (see e.g. LeBas, 2013). In the next chapter, I demonstrate how and why, despite strict Israeli control over the school system, Palestinian students came to play a leading role in resisting Israeli rule through unarmed means.

3

Educational Institutions and Participation in Resistance

3.1 INTRODUCTION

Palestinian schools were unlikely incubators for protest. Strictly controlled by the Israeli authorities, they were meant to depoliticize students – not mobilize them. In contrast to most modern educational systems, which sought to engender and reinforce national identity, the system put into place by Israeli authorities sought to suppress it. Schoolbooks that referred to Palestinian identity, history, or geography were censored or banned outright. Teaching from supplementary materials was strictly prohibited, and teachers who violated this injunction were punished.

Yet, as an organized resistance to Israeli rule began to stir, demonstrations and stone-throwing became "part of a tradition" in schools (Kuttab, 1988): a "regular part of the formal educational experience" (Collins, 2004, 151). On "national days" – days of national significance in Palestinian history such as the anniversaries of the Balfour Declaration, the UN Partition Plan, or "Nakba Day" – school students would take to the streets and protest en masse. Some participated even more regularly, throwing stones at Israel soldiers and settlers every day after school. While not every school student chose to participate in demonstrations or clashes, by the 1980s, middle and high school students were among the leading participants in resistance against the ongoing Israeli occupation of the Palestinian Territories.

This book argues that, when groups have high anti-regime sentiment and low organizational strength, integration into state institutions makes individuals more likely to participate in anti-regime protest. This chapter advances and tests this argument in the case of state educational institutions or schools. It demonstrates how, as state-controlled mass institutions, schools provided Palestinian youth with informational and organizational advantages that made them better able to participate in protest. As some Palestinian youth were integrated into intermediate-level "preparatory" schools, they joined wider and more information-rich social networks, could better communicate and coordinate with their peers, and faced lower risks of protest. All else equal, these students thus had greater access to information about anti-regime resistance and were better able to resist than their nonstudent peers. As a result, they were more likely to begin participating in resistance than were otherwise similar youth outside the school setting. These early experiences of protest during their "impressionable years" in turn forged lasting habits of participation, which persisted beyond the school environment and into adulthood.

Consistent with this argument, this chapter demonstrates that integration into educational institutions has a curvilinear effect on protest participation, which rises with intermediate schooling and subsequently diminishes. Drawing on an original large-scale survey of Palestinian participants and nonparticipants in unarmed resistance between 1978 and 1989, it shows that individuals who were integrated into intermediate-level preparatory schools – i.e. grades 7–9 – were significantly more likely to participate than otherwise similar individuals who were not.[1] However, because participation is "sticky," additional schooling beyond the preparatory level did not have any added effect on the probability of participation. Importantly, while preparatory school was compulsory in the Palestinian Territories, approximately half of all youth did not complete preparatory school and, therefore, constitute a useful "control group" for comparison.[2]

In keeping with this book's overall emphasis, this chapter's findings help explain how mobilization and participation occur among organizationally weak groups often thought to lack the capacity for protest. Internal organizational strength – the presence of strong autonomous

[1] See the introduction for more information on case selection, including this periodization.
[2] In 1986, 50 percent of Palestinian students dropped out by the time they reached ninth grade, with the majority dropping out between the seventh and tenth grades (Roy, 1995, 276). These statistics are comparable to those in our own survey sample, in which 37 percent of respondents had not completed preparatory school by the same year. This lower rate is likely due in large part to my male sample, as Palestinian men typically attained higher levels of education than women (Rosenfeld, 2004, 122).

institutions, organizations, and networks – is often seen as necessary for groups to protest (McAdam, 2010; Tilly and Tarrow, 2007; Nepstad, 2011, 6).[3] Yet, as shown in the previous chapter, Palestinians living in the Occupied Territories initially lacked these kinds of supportive structures and networks. Civil society associations were largely confined to the main Palestinian cities and, therefore, were limited in their size and influence. In the absence of such "mobilizing structures," integration into Israeli-controlled schools thus made young Palestinians better able, and therefore more likely, to participate in protests against Israeli rule.

In addition, the chapter's findings have important implications for understanding two topics of wide interest to political scientists and policy makers. First, these findings provide novel insights into the ongoing debate about the relationship between education and participation in political conflict and violence (see also Zeira, 2019). In contrast to prevailing perspectives on anti-regime protest, which point to the role of higher education in fostering dissent, it finds that integration into higher educational institutions does not increase individuals' propensity to protest (Campante and Chor, 2012; Hoffman and Jamal, 2014; Beissinger, Jamal, and Mazur, 2015). Even among individuals with high levels of education and poor economic outcomes, who may experience "relative deprivation," higher education does not uniformly increase the probability of protest (see e.g. Gurr, 1970; Kepel, 1985; Gelvin, 2012). However, in contrast to most existing research on armed resistance – which sees participants as disproportionately poor, uneducated, and marginalized – moderately educated individuals are more likely to resist than their less educated peers (Paige, 1978; Scott, 1976; Collier and Hoeffler, 2004; Humphreys and Weinstein, 2008).[4] These findings suggest that the impact of education on participation in political conflict is likely to vary with the type of resistance and contextual factors, necessitating further comparative research.

Second, the chapter's conclusions also raise questions about the importance of formal educational curriculums for shaping individual political orientations.[5] Current debates about "incitement" and "radicalization" in Palestine and the larger Muslim world are often waged over the educational curriculum and whether or not it promotes extremism. For

---

[3] See also Diani and McAdam's review of this literature (2003).
[4] For recent work that questions the link between poverty and violence, see also Berman et al. (2011); Shapiro and Fair (2010).
[5] See Brown (2003) for a similar critique.

example, upon reviewing the claims that the Palestinian curriculum foments hate, an Israeli politician charged, "It is no wonder that the calls to disturbances, riots and violence found attentive ears among the Palestinian youth this week since they grew up in an atmosphere of anti-Zionism and anti-Semitism" (Livnat, quoted in Brown, 2003, 287n1). In contrast to this view, this chapter shows that, even in a tightly controlled educational system that contained little if any nationalist or political content, schools were important sites of mobilization and participation in anti-regime resistance. This suggests that the formal educational curriculum offers at best only a partial explanation for students' participation in such resistance. Consequently, educational reforms such as introducing new textbooks may have a weaker effect on students' political behavior than is sometimes supposed.

3.2 THE PRIMACY OF PALESTINIAN SCHOOLS IN RESISTANCE

Schools were at the epicenter of resistance to the Israeli occupation of the Palestinian Territories. Drawing on interviews, community diaries, and other primary sources, this section describes the pivotal role played by Palestinian students and schools in resisting Israeli rule in these territories. As these sources will show, in the face of deepening national grievances and few other institutions that could serve as a basis for mobilization, a tradition of protest became firmly entrenched within Palestinian schools. As a result, when the first intifadah broke out in 1987, school students were at the forefront of the uprising.

As opposition to continued Israeli occupation began to mount in the late 1970s, Palestinian schools became hubs of resistance. On days of national significance in Palestinian history, school students would abandon their classrooms and take to the streets, where they would demonstrate as a group. In some cases, students instigated spontaneous protests at or near schools. In other cases, they joined planned demonstrations organized by political factions. For example, former Birzeit University student body president and Shabiba youth group leader Hassan Shteiwi recalled how he and his classmates would gather after school on national occasions to attend demonstrations while he was in school:[6]

---

[6] As previously described, the Shabiba movement is the youth movement affiliated with the Palestinian Fatah party and the largest youth movement in the Occupied Territories during the period of study.

In Nablus, I attended the Jahath [sic] School. We students from the school were protesting against the Israeli occupation in Nablus. After the last class of the day, we would gather ourselves and go [to demonstrations]. On the occasion of Nakba Day and other national days (the Naksa, the Partition Plan), we would go in the morning for the whole day. (Interview, H. Shteiwi, Ramallah, February 20, 2014)

When school students joined organized demonstrations, they tended to do so as a group rather than as individuals. With few other institutions that could serve as a basis for mobilization, students would assemble at schools before taking to the streets in protest, even when they seemingly had no intention of attending classes. As a former student and protestor interviewed by John Collins in his book *Occupied by Memory* recounted:

On certain occasions, like Land Day, for example, *it was known that the students would go to the schools, but wouldn't go into the classroom.* Then they would leave the school – practically the whole school would go out – and they would burn tires. (Collins, 2004, 151; my emphasis)

Students also initiated spontaneous protests in reaction to immediate events at the national or local level. "I remember one time when we were sitting in the class, when the teacher was giving a lecture, and suddenly we heard bullets everywhere and everyone was screaming, so we went out [to make a demonstration]," remembered one former student and participant (Collins, 2004, 151). Similarly, political activist Tahani Abu Daqa recalled, "When I was sixteen years old, after a student was killed by Israeli soldiers, I urged my classmates to go out and protest against the occupation" (Gordon, Gordon, and Shriteh, 2003, 32).

As a renewed wave of nationalist sentiment swept over the Palestinian Territories in the late 1970s, demonstrations and stone-throwing became "part of a tradition" in schools (Kuttab, 1988): a "regular part of the formal educational experience" (Collins, 2004, 151). Some students participated in demonstrations almost as an extracurricular activity, meeting after school every day to throw stones at soldiers, police, or passing settlers. For example, "Adel," a former protestor who attended the al-Hashimiyya School in Ramallah in 1979 and 1980, recounted: "Every day, after school, we would throw stones at the military police station" (Interview 10, "Adel," Ramallah, March 6, 2014).[7] Israeli authorities subsequently relocated the Hashimiyya School from the center of Ramallah to a new building in Jabal Tawil, 3 kilometers east of the city center. Yet, the protests did not abate. In December 1983, an opening ceremony at the new school organized by the Israeli civil administration

---

7 All names in quotation marks are pseudonyms used to protect respondents' anonymity.

was postponed due to clashes between students and Israeli soldiers. In an attempt to prevent the ceremony from taking place, about three hundred students – approximately 85 percent of the school's total enrollment – blocked entrances to the school with stones and burning tires and threw stones at the soldiers.[8]

When the first Palestinian intifadah broke out in December 1987, school students were at the forefront of the uprising. School-age students were often the "first movers" in a given town or refugee camp, taking the lead in organizing and attending the initial protests (Lawrence, 2017). For example, on December 19, 1987, ten days after the start of the uprising, school students organized and participated in the first mass demonstration in Arrabeh, a town near the northern city of Jenin. According to the Arrabeh "community diary" published by the FACTS Information Committee:

Arrabeh joined the rest of the occupied territories in the intifada [on December 19, 1987]. A demonstration of male and female school students marched through Arrabeh chanting "O our people join for the martyr has sacrificed with his blood." The demonstration lasted for hours and although the Israeli troops kept away, it was important since hundreds of youths had rallied together and taken the first concrete step in mobilizing the rest of the town. (FACTS Information Committee, 1988, 79)

School students also played a leading role in organizing and attending demonstrations in other settings. In Jenin Camp, a refugee camp located west of the city of Jenin, the community diary reported that "School children started a huge demonstration which was attacked by the troops, who used tear gas, rubber bullets, live ammunition as well as batons. Dozens of male and female school children were poisoned from tear gas and others were injured from rubber bullets. Ten youths were seriously injured with live bullets. A number of soldiers were hit with stones from the demonstrators. Another curfew was imposed, which lasted until the morning of Tuesday 9th February" (FACTS Information Committee, 1988, 63).

Similarly, in the Christian town of Bethlehem, one of a trio of towns known for their pioneering methods of nonviolent resistance, students also played an important role. As the intifadah entered its second year in January 1989, the local FACTS Committee reported that secondary school students planned a peaceful march to protest the killing

---

[8] "Bireh Secondary School Students Clash With Soldiers." 1983, December 30. *Jerusalem Dawn Palestinian Weekly* 2.

of Nabil Mohammed Abu Leban from the nearby Dheisheh [Refugee] Camp, which was joined by hundreds of students from the local boys' preparatory school. According to the committee's report:

At 7:45 that morning, students from the school met and agreed to protest the killing of Nabil Mohammed Abu Leban from the nearby Dheisheh Camp and the curfew subsequently imposed on the camp, which had prohibited a number of their classmates from reaching school that day. Some of the girls proposed a sit-in at the school, while others feared this would only offer the soldiers an excuse to raid the school, beat students, and close down the school. Because the students reasoned that the soldiers were looking for such an excuse, they rejected this proposal. Others proposed a demonstration, but this was also rejected for fear that the school would be closed. In the end, the students decided to hold a peaceful march to the center of town, so they could express their national feelings outside the school and thus avoid jeopardizing its continued operation.

In the meantime, several groups of local citizens were confronting soldiers in various parts of the town... On al-Anatra Street, a large student demonstration took place and in the Fawaghra and Madbasa neighborhoods, women and masked youth burned tires and erected blockades in the streets. The march planned by Bethlehem students from the secondary school began and, before it reached the intersection near the Education Office near the main road between Jerusalem and Hebron, hundreds of students from the preparatory boys school joined them. (FACTS Information Committee, 1990c, 213–14)

These narratives suggest that school students were among the principal players in unarmed resistance and that schools served as key sites of mobilization and protest against Israeli occupation. This book's theory provides an explanation for why this was the case. It argues that, as state-controlled mass institutions, schools provide youth with important informational and organizational advantages for collective action. In the next section, I trace the ways in which schools provided Palestinian students with such advantages and, as anti-regime activity mounted, made them better able to participate in the growing protests around them.

3.3 CAUSAL MECHANISMS

Prospective participants in anti-regime protest face formidable informational and organizational barriers to protest that often deter them from participating. As outlined in Chapter 1, integration into educational institutions lowers these barriers through at least three interrelated causal mechanisms: by joining individuals in wider, more information-rich social networks; by facilitating communication and coordination; and by reducing uncertainty about the risks of protest. This section traces these mechanisms using qualitative evidence from the Palestinian case before, in the following sections, systematically testing them via statistical analysis.

3.3.1 Wide Social Networks

Qualitative evidence suggests that integration into educational institutions connected Palestinian youth in wider and more information-rich social networks. As I will elaborate, with access to education limited outside of urban areas, the growing numbers of Palestinian youth attending intermediate-level schools did so outside of their own communities. There they were exposed to other young people from diverse geographic and social backgrounds and gained access to new sources of political information. As civil society organizations began to expand in the early 1980s and their members made inroads into schools, students also became linked into new civic networks rich in political information. In contrast, nonstudents remained locked in more narrow and parochial social networks. As a result, school students were better able, and more likely, to begin participating in unarmed resistance than their nonstudent peers and, consequently, to develop lasting habits of participation.

As avenues for protest widened in the 1970s and 1980s, schools served as some of the only institutions or organizations connecting local Palestinian communities to one another. As described in Chapter 2, during the 1970s and 1980s, Palestinian society was predominantly rural and fragmented along local and familial lines. The majority of Palestinians continued to live in small villages, and social relations continued to revolve around the village and the *hamula*: the Palestinian extended family or clan. With few civil society organizations to connect them, ties between local communities remained weak. Palestinian society was thus divided along local, village, and familial lines, with few frameworks for communication and coordination across these cleavages.

Within this fragmented society, schools served as the "primary source of social interaction" beyond the extended family for many young people (FACTS Information Committee, 1990b, 337). Within schools, urban youth came to know rural youth from the outlying villages where the majority of Palestinians still lived, and rural youth also came together across family and village boundaries. With the majority of villages lacking any schools beyond the primary level, most preparatory and secondary schools were located in cities and large towns. For example, a survey conducted by the Birzeit University Office for Literacy and Adult Education between 1979 and 1981 found that 210 of 265 Palestinian villages – 79 percent of the total – did not have any schools beyond the primary level (years 1–6). As late as 1987, the first year of the intifadah, nearly half of all Palestinian villages still lacked any upper-level preparatory or secondary schools (Benvenisti and Khayat, 1988, 124–37). As a result of these deficits – common across the developing world – schools became an important space for social connection, the exchange of information, and wider collective action.

The experience of students from Anabta, a rural village in the northern West Bank, illustrates this associational role of schools in Palestinian society. With no upper-level schools in Anabta, village youth attended secondary school in the nearby city of Tulkarm, where they often participated in demonstrations alongside the city's students. As a former student and activist who studied in Tulkarm in the late 1970s recalled: "The youth who were studying from outside Tulkarm, they also used to participate. The school was located beside the street, so when the students see the first group [of Israeli settlers] crossing the street, they go out from their classes and go 'welcoming' them [by throwing stones]" (Interview 11, Fatah/Shabiba activist, Anabta, March 17, 2014).

In contrast to students like those from Anabta, Palestinian youth who did not attain additional schooling tended to have narrow, more parochial social networks rooted in the extended family or village. With low levels of industrialization in the Palestinian Territories, those young Palestinians who did not pursue additional schooling typically worked in small, often family-owned, farms, shops, and workshops. For example, "Bashir," a young Palestinian man from Nablus with only a primary school education, was apprenticed to a metalworker until the age of sixteen and subsequently went to work in a small machinery repair shop. Although Bashir was interested in politics, he did not know of any civil society associations present in Nablus until the first intifadah, and he did not participate in the uprising either directly or indirectly (Interview 21, "Bashir," Nablus, March (n.d.) 2014). With few contacts outside of his family, shop, and neighborhood, he remained relatively cut off from more politicized networks and the information they carried about protest.

For the growing number of Palestinian youth seeking employment across the border in Israel over additional schooling, work also reproduced and reinforced the importance of local and familial networks with limited informational value. Due to the physical proximity of Palestinian communities to Israeli work centers, many workers returned to their villages every night and participated fully in the social life of the village. Patterns of recruitment into the Israeli labor market also followed local and familial lines: most workers obtained their job through a brother, cousin, or other relative, and almost all work teams consisted of workers from the same village. As Palestinian sociologist Salim Tamari wrote in 1981, "Social relations continued to revolve around the extended family and the village: this constant interaction with, and dependence on, his kin, reinforces the worker's village identity" (Tamari, 1981, 60). As a result, even those villagers who worked in Israel continued to interact within narrow local and familial networks with little informational value. With their access to political information thus circumscribed, they were therefore also less likely to participate in resistance.

Civic Networks

Integration into educational institutions also brought Palestinian youth into burgeoning *civic networks*: social networks linking youth to fledgling civil society associations and their politicized members. As this section will show, the same informational and organizational advantages that benefited students also made them attractive targets for mobilization by Palestinian activists. Using the new, quasi-legal civil society associations, these activists reached into schools to spread information about demonstrations and mobilize students to participate. As a result, students had greater access to scarce information about protest than other youth, rendering them better able and more likely to participate.

Just as the school environment allows students to access novel sources of information, communicate and coordinate with one another more easily, and participate in protests at lower risk, this environment also offers important advantages for political activists. As described in Chapter 1, because schools concentrate large numbers of young people in a single place, they allow activists to spread their message more quickly and easily. In contacting only a few students, they can potentially reach many more. In other words, as a result of the school environment, activists can draw on "bloc recruitment"-style tactics (Oberschall, 1973). Rather than recruiting one student at a time, they can communicate with and organize thousands of students more or less simultaneously.

These informational and organizational advantages made schools attractive targets of mobilization to Palestinian nationalist activists. With the growth of Palestinian civil society organizations such as student and youth groups in the early 1980s, Palestinian activists used these more open structures to forge new social ties to school students. These newly formed civic networks would become important conduits for spreading information about protest. In the lead-up to a demonstration or protest, activists belonging to both a particular PLO faction and its affiliated civic organizations would contact politically active students within schools – typically younger members of the same student or youth group – to inform them about the protest and the role that students should play.[9] These students would then spread this information among the wider student body.

For example, the local Shabiba committee in Anabta, one of the first such committees in the West Bank, assigned its members responsibility for mobilizing particular schools. Asked how he would prepare for a demonstration, a former Fatah member and founding member of the committee said: "On the day of the demonstration, we used to divide the work, saying to someone, 'You go to this school.' You want to hear how a big demonstration used to be organized, is that right? For instance, if someone became a martyr, we automatically meet and divide the work, we say [name] and [name] go to this X school in X area." (Interview 23, Anabta, March 17, 2014).

Similarly, another founding member of the Anabta Shabiba committee described contacting students known to him from Shabiba's voluntary work activities to spread information about protests in schools. These students, typically Shabiba members or supporters who were not formally affiliated with Fatah, served as informal "liaisons" connecting Fatah/Shabiba activists to the wider student population. Describing this process, he said:

When demonstrations used to happen, all the schools participated in it. Shabiba would make the students exit the school and join the protest. We are part of the school students and they are part of us, *we communicate with them through voluntary work and the organizational work* [my emphasis], and even with some of the girls' schools at that time... *Within the schools, we have connections with older students who we trusted and could give to him [sic] the information so he [sic] can spread it inside the school* [my emphasis]. We agreed amongst each other who is responsible for what so, for instance, I took responsibility for the girls' school; I used to communicate with one girl from the school who spread the information about the next event. (Interview 11, Fatah/Shabiba activist Anabta, March 17, 2014)

---

9 These activists were typically older, upper secondary or university students or graduates. Membership in student and youth groups was open to a relatively wide age range; for example, individuals up to thirty-four years old were eligible to join Fatah's Shabiba committees (Interview 12, Fatah/Shabiba activist Shuafat Camp, Jerusalem, March 7, 2014).

Activists in Nablus' Balata refugee camp interviewed by John Collins in *Occupied by Memory* provide similar accounts to these. For example, "Ayman," a secondary school student responsible for mobilizing students in the local preparatory school, described a hypothetical seventh grader who is arrested and subsequently returns to become a political leader within the school:

He will coordinate with a group outside the school, or with those [activists] responsible for the school [such as Ayman], and they will decide to make a suspension [*taliq*] of classes – without the knowledge of the teachers or the headmaster. And the students would go out... The positive thing is that the young people are more enthusiastic than the teacher or other older people. They will go out to make a protest [*ihtijaj*], and the teacher will say "Why are you protesting" because maybe he is afraid for the students... But the student wants to go out and lead the demonstration. (Collins, 2004, 148)

These accounts highlight the importance of schools as conduits into new, wider, and more information-rich social networks. As some Palestinian youth began attending large intermediate schools located outside their communities, they met young people from different clans, villages, and neighborhoods and gained access to novel sources of information. With the revival of Palestinian civil society in the early 1980s, these students were also incorporated into new civic networks saturated with political information. These new, more information-rich networks helped young Palestinians overcome the limitations of a fragmented rural society and join together in collective resistance to Israeli occupation. Yet, just as important as these informational networks was the ease with which information could be shared within the school environment.

3.3.2 Communication and Coordination

Attending educational institutions also made Palestinian students better able to participate in anti-regime resistance by facilitating communication and coordination. Like other state institutions, schools gathered hundreds and sometimes thousands of often like-minded youth in a single geographic location. This "ecological concentration" allowed for information to flow rapidly and reduced organizational and transaction costs (Lichbach, 1998*b*). When a trigger event for protest such as the death of a "martyr" would occur, students would hear about it more quickly than nonstudents. As a result, they were better able, and more likely, to participate in protest than nonstudents were.

The crowded conditions inside most Palestinian schools further compounded these informational and organizational advantages. With a growing school-age population and little Israeli investment in educational infrastructure, the vast majority of Palestinian schools were overcrowded. In the minority of schools administered by the United Nations Relief and Works Agency (UNRWA), average class sizes reached nearly forty-four students per classroom in the West Bank and fifty students per classroom in the Gaza Strip (Rosenfeld, 2004, 116). No official figures are available for the government schools attended by the majority of Palestinian students. However, crowding in government schools was reported to be even more severe than in the UNRWA ones (Graham-Brown, 1984, 65), and some teachers I interviewed reported student-teacher ratios of 60:1 or more (Interview 1, Abu Dis, February 8, 2014).

While detrimental for learning, these conditions were beneficial for collective action. With hundreds of students gathered in the same school, information traveled fast, and there were fewer organizational and transaction costs of collective action. Echoing Lipset's observation that "it is relatively easy to reach students: leaflets handed out at the campus gate will usually do the job" (Lipset, 1964, 35), a former student activist described how, with just a small number of leaflets, he reached over one thousand students:

Using carbon paper, a group of us high school students would write and copy leaflets with declarations condemning the Israeli occupation. One of our first leaflets was before the second anniversary of Land Day [in 1977]; in the leaflet, we condemned the Israelis for confiscating the land that belonged to the Palestinians. We did not sign the leaflets. *We put four leaflets in each classroom, and I believe that our message reached most of the 1700 students in Palestine High School.* (Gordon, Gordon, and Shriteh, 2003, 50; my emphasis)

The concentration of large numbers of students inside schools also allowed students to mobilize rapidly in response to events on the ground. Aided by their numbers and crowded conditions, news of killings or abuses traveled quickly among students, and they were able to organize themselves quickly and efficiently in response. According to a student leader active in this time period, "Maybe, if there is an event – let's say the occupation killed somebody – the students will join in and organize themselves to join in a protest... It happened without anyone planning it. When the students used to hear about a martyr, they used to gather each other to go to a protest... The biggest [societal] section to mobilize was the students" (Interview, T. Abu Afifeh, Jerusalem, February 26,

2014). In contrast, nonstudent youth would join in protests only more occasionally and arbitrarily. Reflecting on their role, Abu Afifeh further recalled, "Yes, of course, if they happened to be there at the same time of the protest and hear about it, they would go out... If he [a nonstudent] was nearby, he would go, but, if he was far away, how would he know about it?!" (Ibid.).

As these examples illustrate, schools facilitated communication and coordination about political occasions and protests. As legal sites of assembly, they held a unique organizational role in Palestinian society, and overcrowding helped information reach thousands of students quickly. Students could coordinate among themselves quickly and spontaneously in response to such information, and student activists could also spread messages about more organized protests with only a few leaflets. Such communications conveyed information about the timing and location of protests and, as we will see, they also provided vital information about the risks of participation.

3.3.3 Safety in Numbers and the Risks of Protest

The third and final way in which integration into educational institutions makes individuals better able to participate in anti-regime resistance is by affecting their calculations about the risks of protest. As elsewhere, such calculations were very important in influencing Palestinians' decisions about protest participation. As described in Chapter 2, Israeli military law prohibited political gatherings except with the express permission of the Military Commander. With such permission all but impossible to obtain, participation in unauthorized demonstrations, marches, and protests involved high risks. Protestors who violated the Israeli military order barring political meetings and gatherings faced a maximum of ten years' imprisonment or a heavy fine.[10] While ordinary participants were typically detained for much shorter periods, most did not escape arrest or beating.

As a result, before the vast protest marches of the first intifadah, few people participated in demonstrations as individuals. Only those having the safety in numbers provided within state institutions or other large groups tended to participate. As one former union activist explained:

[10] www.btselem.org/demonstrations/military_order_101 (accessed September 26, 2016).

The percentage of [people participating] "as individuals" is very small. Except when it came to the first intifada. The first intifada, individual involvement was maybe as much as the organized involvement. But, before that, no, only those who are organized [in schools] and in organizations with a political [faction] or union are more involved. Rarely you will find individuals. (Interview 28, "Samer," Nablus, March 17, 2014)

School students participated in the earlier smaller, and more risky, protests before the intifadah because of their relative safety in numbers compared with other groups. In a context in which assembly was restricted, schools were "the natural place for a demonstration to begin because of the large number of children gathered in one place" (Kuttab, 1988, 16). School students knew that, in a protest, they would be one of many. In contrast, nonstudent youth did not have the benefit of this knowledge. Uncertain about the size of the crowd and afraid to be one of a vulnerable few, many chose not to participate. As one former student participant described:

The people who were participating were the school students, the university students... Workers, they were individuals. There was no school or university or organize them. Because the students would gather themselves and they would all say, "Let's go, let's go!" There were a lot of them. *But the worker, he would just go alone* [my emphasis].[11]

Attesting to students' "power in numbers," Israeli authorities attempted to contain demonstrations by breaking up large schools and sometimes closing them altogether. In September 1983, *al-Fajr English* edition reported on a large protest at the Fashiyeh [sic] Secondary School (in the Jabiliya refugee camp) against the Israeli authorities' decision to transfer four hundred of the school's students to a more remote school. According to *al-Fajr*'s report, Israeli officials informed the students that the transfer was intended to ameliorate the crowded conditions inside the school. However, *al-Fajr*'s reporter added, "students believe that the transfer is aimed at dispersing them to make protest activities more vulnerable to Israeli soldiers."[12] While it is impossible to discern the Israeli authorities' true motives, the students' account is consistent with the argument that crowded schools provided "safety in numbers" for student protestors.

---

[11] Interview 10, "Adel," Ramallah, March 6, 2014.
[12] "School Transfers Spark Protest." 1983, September 9. *Jerusalem Dawn Palestinian Weekly*, 4.

Along with wider, more diverse social networks and rapid communication and coordination, integration into educational institutions thus reduced uncertainty about the risks of protest. Schools offered students relative safety in numbers, as well as made it easier to acquire information about the size and strength of protests. As a result, students were more likely to begin participating in anti-regime protest than nonstudent youth and, through these early experiences, to develop enduring habits of participation. In the sections that follow, I further develop the main empirical implications of this argument and describe the data and measures that I use to test it.

3.4 HYPOTHESES

The preceding arguments suggest four testable hypotheses. The main hypothesis is that integration in educational institutions will have a positive and curvilinear effect on the likelihood that individuals will participate in anti-regime resistance (H1). Specifically, individuals who are integrated into intermediate schools beyond the primary level should be more likely to participate in resistance than their peers with less schooling. However, due to the persistence of participation, integration into higher-level schools should not further increase their prospects of participation, producing a curvilinear relationship.

To illustrate why this is the case, consider how different levels of schooling affect the probability of participation in anti-regime resistance. At low levels of schooling (i.e. primary school), children are generally too young to participate in resistance. Regardless of their level of schooling, their probability of participation is low.[13] As children enter adolescence, however, those who continue on to preparatory schools are integrated into an institutional environment that facilitates collective action: they are joined in wider and more information-rich social networks, can more easily communicate and coordinate with one another, and face lower risks of protest. As a result, they are more likely to begin participating in protest than youth who do not continue their schooling and are not exposed to this institutional environment.

Once youth begin participating in anti-regime activities, they are likely to continue. Whether or not they pursue higher-level schooling, youth who complete preparatory school remain connected to one another in

---

[13] As mentioned in Chapter 1, primary school students may also be less likely to participate in resistance because, as local institutions, primary schools do not engender the same kind of wide and information-rich social networks that intermediate and higher-level schools do.

the wider social networks formed during their school days and, as the introduction describes, they are also likely to be socialized into ongoing participation in other ways. As a result, youth who continue on to still higher levels of schooling should not be significantly more likely to participate than those who complete preparatory school alone. This produces a curvilinear relationship, with the probability of participation rising with intermediate schooling and diminishing with additional higher levels of schooling. In contrast, if participation did not persist, then the probability of participation should continue to rise with additional higher levels of schooling rather than flattening in this manner.[14]

To further illustrate, consider the stylized example of two young Palestinian men, whom I will call Hisham and Mahmoud. Hisham and Mahmoud both attained additional schooling beyond the primary level, attending and completing preparatory school together (i.e. grades 7–9). While attending preparatory school, they both began to participate in nationalist demonstrations, where they heard anti-regime speeches, discussed politics with other student protestors, and met anti-occupation activists.[15] After completing preparatory school, Hisham continued on to secondary school while Mahmoud became apprenticed to a local mechanic. Yet, the two former school friends remained in close touch, meeting often to exchange news and talk about political happenings in the Occupied Territories and the wider Arab world. As a result of these continuing contacts, as well as the socializing experience of their initial participation, both Hisham and Mahmoud remained active in politics. While Hisham went on to higher levels of schooling and Mahmoud did not, both continued to participate in anti-occupation protests. Generalizing from this example, if this book's argument is correct *and* participation is persistent, higher levels of schooling beyond preparatory school should not further increase the likelihood of participation in anti-regime resistance. As a result, integration in educational institutions should have a positive and curvilinear effect on the probability of participation in resistance, which rises with preparatory schooling and subsequently diminishes.

Importantly, these arguments do not imply that individuals who pursue still higher levels of schooling do not participate in anti-regime

---

[14] While a curvilinear relationship is consistent with this argument, it is also consistent with a number of other explanations. For a more direct test of the claim that participation is persistent, see Table A.9 and the accompanying discussion in the online appendix [www.cambridge.org/TheRevolutionWithin].

[15] These details draw from Doug McAdam (1986).

resistance. As observers of the Palestinian case know, university students were active participants in protests against Israeli rule. Rather, I argue that, while university students did participate in resistance, their participation was not due to their university education but, rather, to their earlier, pre-university integration into schools and their mobilizing environment. Similarly, Kam and Palmer show that, in the United States, university education does not affect political participation after accounting for pre-adult experiences and influences in place during high school (Kam and Palmer, 2008).

In addition to this main hypothesis, these arguments suggest three additional testable hypotheses. First, in contrast to the main alternative mechanisms, they suggest that integration into educational institutions should make individuals more likely to participate in some forms of resistance than others. In particular, schooling should be associated with both more risky and more collective forms of protest (H2 and H3). Schooling should promote participation in more risky forms of protest because, as previously discussed, it lowers the relative risks of protest participation. As one of many, students face lower risks of identification and punishment than members of other groups, and they can more easily obtain "information on numbers." As a result, they are better able to participate in high-risk collective action than otherwise similar youth outside schools.

In addition, schooling should also increase participation in more collective forms of protest or what Granovetter terms *crowd collective action*: that is, collective action in which members of a group are face-to-face, such as demonstrations and marches (Granovetter, 1978). Crowd collective action may be distinguished both from individual acts of resistance, such as writing graffiti, and from mass collective action in which physical proximity is not necessary, such as joining boycotts or signing petitions. Unlike participants in these other types of resistance, participants in crowd collective action benefit from "safety in numbers." As the number of other participants around them grow and they gain "power in numbers," they face lower risks of participation. Because students in schools enjoy such power in numbers, they should thus be more likely to participate in crowd collective action than in other types of resistance. In contrast, the main alternative mechanisms suggest that schooling should have an equal impact on different types of resistance. For example, if schooling promotes participation in protest by strengthening national grievances, it should make individuals as likely to write nationalist graffiti as to participate in nationalist demonstrations.

Finally, intermediate schooling should also be associated with larger and more diverse social networks (H4). As argued earlier, integration into intermediate-level schools tends to connect youth in wider, more heterogeneous social networks, which provide students with greater access to information about protest and render them better able to participate than their nonstudent peers. Similarly, because schools' advantages for collective action also make them attractive targets for activists, intermediate schooling may also bring youth into politicized civic networks.[16] Thus, in addition to its impact on protest, intermediate schooling should also be associated with changes in an individual's social networks.

3.5 SURVEY DESIGN

The remainder of this chapter systematically tests the relationship between integration into educational institutions and participation in anti-regime resistance. To do so, it draws on an original large-scale survey of former participants and nonparticipants in unarmed resistance in the Palestinian Territories conducted in 2011. The survey took place in sixty-eight localities across the West Bank, including Palestinian cities, towns, villages, and refugee camps.[17] All respondents were interviewed in person by a carefully trained Palestinian interviewer from their own geographic region. The response rate was 68 percent.[18]

To obtain a sample that was geographically and socioeconomically representative, randomization was used at every level of sample selection from the locality to the individual respondent. Survey sampling was conducted using a multistage cluster sampling procedure, in which the number of clusters assigned to each locality was proportional to its population size.[19] Within each locality, households and individual respondents were also randomly selected. Because a simple random sample of respondents would likely not have produced a large enough sample of participants, however, the survey was limited to males who were in the

---

[16] For a similar argument, albeit via a different mechanism, see Lee (2011).

[17] See the methodological appendix for a map of the surveyed localities, a detailed description of the survey design and sampling procedures, and a comparison between the survey sample and overall population.

[18] AAPOR response rate category 2. Since this response rate includes all households of unknown eligibility in the denominator, the true response rate may be higher. The response rate was estimated based on a subsample of all household contact attempts.

[19] For a similar methodology, see also Humphreys and Weinstein (2008).

appropriate age range for participation during the time period studied.[20] The resulting sample thus includes 646 male Palestinian participants and nonparticipants in unarmed resistance.[21] As shown in the methodological appendix, this sample closely resembles the overall population in terms of its geography, household composition, and socioeconomic characteristics (see Table 7.2).

Data was collected on each individual bi-yearly (i.e. every two years) from 1978 to 1989 and aggregated into two-year periods for analysis.[22] As described in the methodological appendix, data on the independent variables was collected on every even-numbered year beginning with 1978, and data on the dependent variables was collected on every odd-numbered year beginning with 1979. By collecting biyearly rather than yearly data, I was able to cover the entire time period of interest without making the survey overly long and thereby depressing completion rates. In addition, by collecting data on the independent and dependent variables in alternating years, I was able to analyze the impact of each independent variable in a given year (i.e. at time t) on the dependent variable in the following year (i.e. at time $t + 1$). This, in turn, allowed me to better establish the sequence of events and account for the possibility of simple reverse causality without losing data due to lagging the independent variables.

The resulting dataset thus includes six observations on 646 respondents for a total of 3876 complete observations, with the unit of analysis being the individual-period. By collecting and analyzing data on each individual over multiple time periods, I am able to compare not only each individual to other individuals but also each individual to himself at a different point of time. Individuals differ from each other in many observed and unobserved ways that statistical analysis cannot always fully account for. By comparing individuals to themselves over time and not only to other individuals, I am thus better able to control for such differences

---

[20] Despite the unprecedented nature of women's participation within conservative Palestinian society and the considerable attention given to women's participation, female participation rates remained low. Compared with the overall participation rate of 35 percent, the survey data indicate that fewer than 10 percent of women participated.

[21] In addition, I also sampled a smaller number of female respondents, as well as family members of sampled respondents who were missing (e.g. due to death, imprisonment, immigration, etc.) These groups were also sampled in order to help assess the sensitivity of the book's findings to the composition of the survey sample.

[22] The results that follow are also robust to grouping the data into wider, four-year periods, which allow respondents more room for error in recalling the timing of their participation. See Table A.8 in the online appendix [www.cambridge.org/TheRevolutionWithin].

between individuals and, therefore, also better able to identify the causal relationships of interest in this study.

3.5.1   Mitigating Bias in Survey Research

The survey was designed to mitigate two types of biases that can affect survey research: recall bias and social desirability bias. Given the retrospective nature of the survey, an important concern was that respondents would not accurately recall the answers to the survey questions. As time passes, respondents may be unable to retrieve information stored in their long-term memory or may add potentially inaccurate details from outside their firsthand experience (e.g. from other people's memories). Such memory problems are generally less severe for distinctive and emotionally salient events such as protest events. In addition, research shows that, while memory drops off quite rapidly at first, it subsequently levels off. Thus, a retrospective survey that is conducted twenty years after the events of interest may not suffer from worse recall bias than one conducted merely two years afterward (Groves et al., 2011, 213–18). Nonetheless, to mitigate such memory problems, my survey made use of an innovative questionnaire design shown to improve recall in retrospective surveys.

The survey was designed using a unique format called a life history calendar (LHC) or event history calendar.[23] This approach uses a calendar-like questionnaire design to improve recall in retrospective surveys. Life history calendars improve recall by better reflecting the processes people use to retrieve autobiographical memory. Whereas traditional survey questionnaires encourage respondents to retrieve autobiographical memory through only one of three possible pathways, LHCs encourage respondents to remember such information through all three possible pathways through which people access autobiographical memory (Belli, 1998). For example, both LHCs and standard survey questionnaires encourage respondents to remember past events through "top-down retrieval," in which more general memories cue the retrieval of more specific memories.[24] However, because of their calendar-like design, LHCs also encourage respondents to remember

---

[23] See the methodological appendix and survey questionnaires for additional details and examples.

[24] To borrow an example from Belli (1998), more general memories about "living with X" can cue the retrieval of memories about "holiday in Italy with X" and "dinner with X on our last night in Rome."

events chronologically, mirroring the way in which many people actually remember past events. Because LHCs cue people to remember past events through multiple pathways, they increase the chance that they will accurately and completely remember them.

While they have not, to the best of my knowledge, been used in political science before now, life history calendars have been demonstrated to significantly improve the reliability of respondents' answers in retrospective surveys. In a direct experimental comparison of a life history calendar with a state-of-the-art standard survey questionnaire, the LHC yielded more complete and better-quality reports on a number of social and economic variables (Belli, Shay, and Stafford, 2001). Unfortunately, with no comparable surveys conducted on a similar sample, it is not possible to conduct such an experimental comparison with my data. However, most respondents did not find it particularly difficult to remember the information required by the survey, and excluding those who did yields similar results.[25] In addition to the demonstrated efficacy of the life history calendar approach, this result gives me further confidence in the reliability of the survey data.

The survey was also designed to mitigate social desirability bias. Social desirability bias refers to the common desire to present oneself in a favorable light. As a result of this desire, survey respondents tend to overreport socially approved behaviors like voting (in the US context) and underreport socially disapproved ones like using illegal drugs (Groves et al., 2011). In the Palestinian context, social desirability bias could potentially lead respondents to overreport their participation in resistance, particularly during the first intifadah. Given the presence of a "powerful public discourse of heroic, unified national resistance" during the uprising (Collins, 2004, 153–54), survey respondents may have felt social pressure to self-identify as former participants even if they were not. At the same time, although the risks of identifying as a participant are relatively low today, it is also possible that some respondents may nonetheless have been afraid to report their participation.

To reduce the possibility for social desirability bias, as well as to protect respondents, all questions regarding participation were self-administered by the respondent. Self-administration is the gold standard for collecting sensitive individual-level data that cannot be collected using group-level methods like list experiments (Corstange, 2009).

---

[25] See Section A.1.5 in the online appendix: www.cambridge.org/TheRevolutionWithin

By removing the "social presence" of the interviewer from the process of survey administration, self-administration reduces the pressure on survey respondents to conform to social norms and allays concerns about punishment or retaliation (Groves et al., 2011, 270). For example, in a study of illegal drug use in the United States, respondents were almost two and a half times more likely to admit to using cocaine when the questions were self-administered rather than administered by an interviewer (Groves et al., 2011, 155–58). For these reasons, all sensitive questions on the survey were self-administered by the respondent. Using techniques pioneered by Scacco and described further in the methodological appendix, the survey was administered in such a way that the interviewer could not view any of the respondent's answers to sensitive questions or link them to other characteristics of the respondent (Scacco, n.d.).

While self-administration improves the accuracy of respondents' answers to sensitive questions, it does not completely eliminate social desirability concerns. While these concerns may still persist, however, they are not expected to unduly bias this analysis for at least two reasons. First, while respondents may feel some social pressure to identify as participants, this social pressure should be as strong for individuals who were formerly integrated into state institutions as those who were not. As such, while it may inflate this book's estimate of the overall participation rate, it should not bias its findings about the relationship between integration into state institutions and protest participation. Second, as already described, this social pressure also runs both ways – there is pressure for respondents both to overreport a socially approved behavior in Palestinian society and underreport an illegal behavior under Israeli law. As such, with regard to the overall participation rate, these competing imperatives may cancel each other out.

3.6 MAIN SURVEY MEASURES

3.6.1 Participation in Anti-regime Resistance

This study's main dependent variable is participation in anti-regime resistance, defined as regular participation in risky unarmed collective action targeted against repressive regimes. As described in Chapter 2, from 1978 to 1989, domestic PLO activists were the primary organizers of such resistance in the Palestinian Territories. Following the Oslo

TABLE 3.1 *Participants in survey sample*

	Frequency in Sample	Proportions
Participants	229	0.35
Nonparticipants	295	0.46
Missing	122	0.19
Total	646	1.00

Accords and the establishment of the Palestinian Authority, the PLO's political-military factions became political parties and are today widely referred to as such. Participation was thus coded based on the following survey question.

In year [1979], did you support any political parties, where by support I mean regularly participating in party activities such as [illegal] cultural and political seminars, demonstrations, sit-ins, mass funerals or prison visits?

Respondents were coded as participants in a given year if they selected any of the following response options in that year: (1) "Yes"; (2) "I was participating in such activities, but they were not organized by a party"; or (3) "I was participating in such activities but from all parties/not for any particular party." Respondents who selected "No" were coded as nonparticipants.

Table 3.1 presents the distribution of participants and non-participants in the survey sample. In all, 229 respondents – 35 percent of the survey sample – reported participating in anti-regime resistance.[26] Nearly three hundred respondents, making up 46 percent of the sample, reported never participating in resistance. Information on participation is missing for 19 percent of the sample, primarily due to failure to finish the entire survey. As will be further discussed, this book's core findings about state institutions are robust to very minimal assumptions about the distribution of participants and nonparticipants among these missing respondents.

---

[26] This figure is similar to the participation rate reported in the NAVCO dataset, whereas presumably it should be higher (i.e. as the participation rate among most likely participants). This may be because the NAVCO dataset estimates participation in a campaign's peak event, which is likely to be a higher figure than the overall participation rate. Consistent with this idea, the participation rate in 1988–1989, the peak year of participation in my survey, is 43 percent.

Participants in anti-occupation resistance in the Palestinian Territories took part in demonstrations, strikes, boycotts, tax refusals, and other acts of defiance and dissent. Resistance also encompassed participation in other culturally specific "repertoires of contention" such as mass funerals (often followed directly by marches and tense demonstrations), organized visits to prisoners, "martyrs," and their families, and illegal Palestinian cultural and political seminars. While many forms of resistance were nonviolent in nature, Palestinians also faced off in clashes with Israeli soldiers in which they threw stones or other homemade weapons, burned tires, and blocked roads. Figure 3.1 shows the percentage of participant-years in which participants engaged in each of these types of activities. As seen in Figure 3.1, the most common types of resistance in which respondents participated were "demonstrations and mass funerals" (henceforth "demonstrations"), followed by strikes, then boycotts, and finally clashes, respectively.[27]

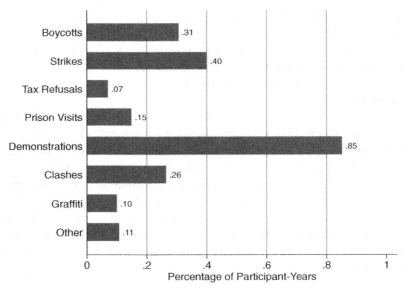

FIGURE 3.1 Percentage of participant-years per type of resistance
Note: Percentage of participant-years in which participants engaged in each type of resistance. N=622 participant-years total.

---

[27] A follow-up question added halfway through survey administration asked respondents to identify the specific activities they participated in. As a result, these data are available for the 133 participants out of 335 total respondents who were asked this question.

3.6.2 Measuring and Modeling Integration into Educational Institutions

To capture the curvilinear relationship between integration into educational institutions and participation in protest, integration into educational institutions is measured as a series of binary variables indicating the highest level of schooling completed in each year.[28] The highest level of schooling completed by a respondent captures the full effect of exposure to a given level of schooling and integration into the school's institutional environment. As will be further discussed, my main results are also robust to using an alternate measure of integration into educational institutions, which uses a series of indicators for the highest level of schooling attended rather than completed. In both cases, the indicators used correspond to the structure of the Palestinian school system. *Primary* indicates completion of primary school, which is equivalent to six years of schooling. *Preparatory* indicates completion of preparatory school, which is equivalent to nine years of schooling. *Secondary* indicates completing secondary school (twelve years of schooling), and *University* indicates completing university or higher (sixteen years or more of schooling).[29]

To model the curvilinear relationship between integration into educational institutions and participation, the indicators for *Preparatory*, *Secondary*, and *University* are included in the model simultaneously, with *Primary* serving as the baseline category (i.e. the excluded category). Including an indicator for each level of schooling completed allows for each level to have a distinct effect and, thus, for the overall relationship between schooling and protest participation to be nonlinear. However, unlike using a polynomial model to model this nonlinear relationship, this approach also allows for estimating the added effect of each subsequent level of schooling and, thus, identifying *which* level(s) account for the overall relationship between schooling and participation in resistance. All results are also robust to the use of data visualization as well as multiple alternative ways of modeling the relationship between schooling

---

[28] All variables used in the book are also described in the codebook; the text of all survey questions used to construct these variables is in the survey questionnaires.

[29] Individuals who have some schooling at, but did not complete, any given level are coded as not having completed that level. For example, individuals with eleven years of schooling are coded as having completed preparatory school but not secondary school. *Preparatory* thus captures the effect of having at least nine and no more than eleven years of schooling.

TABLE 3.2 *The effect of schooling on participation in anti-regime resistance*

Participation	Baseline Model	Generational Effects Model
Age	0.08***	0.05***
	(0.01)	(0.02)
Preparatory	1.07***	0.87***
	(0.17)	(0.19)
Secondary	0.01	−0.04
	(0.18)	(0.20)
University	−0.01	−0.01
	(0.21)	(0.25)
Household Amenities	0.21***	0.00
	(0.04)	(0.04)
Father's Education	−0.66***	−0.66***
	(0.17)	(0.20)
Constant	−2.63***	−2.23***
	(0.27)	(0.39)
Observations	2874	2874

Multilevel logit coefficients and standard errors reported.
All models include cubic splines.
$^*p<0.10$ $^{**}p<0.05$ $^{***}p<0.01$

and protest participation, including a polynomial model with a quadratic term for years of schooling and an alternative series of indicators measuring levels of schooling attended. Finally, consistent with the theory, a binary indicator of student status and a continuous measure of years of schooling also yield positive and statistically significant results.[30]

3.7   RESULTS

Supporting this chapter's main hypothesis, this section shows that integration into educational institutions has a positive and curvilinear effect on participation in anti-regime resistance. As seen in Table 3.2, individuals who completed preparatory school were significantly more likely to go on to participate in resistance than individuals who completed primary school or no school at all (p<0.01). This impact of preparatory schooling on participation is substantial. As Figure 3.2 shows, preparatory schooling is associated with a 7 percentage point (generational effects model) to 13 percentage point (baseline model) average increase in

---

[30] See Section A.1.7 in the online appendix for the results of these robustness checks: www.cambridge.org/TheRevolutionWithin

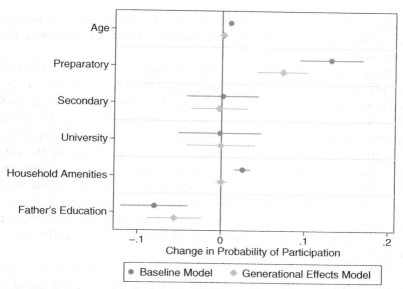

FIGURE 3.2 The marginal effect of schooling on participation in anti-regime
resistance
*Note: Marginal effects from multilevel regression models with varying intercepts by
locality (i.e. locality-level random effects). Additional control variables not shown include
period dummies, generational effects, and cubic splines. N=2874.*

the probability of participating in protest. For a typical individual in the
sample, preparatory schooling raises the predicted probability of participation from 30 percent to as much as 44 percent.[31] This effect is larger
than or comparable to the within-sample effects of other key variables
theorized to determine participation in political conflict, such as other
aspects of socioeconomic status and membership in social networks (Collier and Hoeffler, 2004; McAdam, 1986; Petersen, 2001; Laitin, 1995).

In contrast to this effect of preparatory schooling, however, higher
levels of schooling do not appear to have any additional impact on
the likelihood of participation in anti-regime resistance. Both secondary
schooling and university education have only a small effect on this likelihood, and neither variable is statistically significant. Thus, consistent
with this chapter's main hypothesis, the relationship between integration into educational institutions and participation in resistance appears

---

[31] This change in the predicted probability of participation was calculated using the
baseline model. All continuous independent variables were set at their means, and all
categorical variables were set at their modal values.

to be a curvilinear one. Data visualization and the results of a polynomial model, included in the online appendix to this book, also indicate a curvilinear relationship.

These results are based on a multilevel logistic regression model with varying intercepts by locality. An overview of the model is presented here, and interested readers can find a more technical discussion of all modeling choices in Section 3.7.1. As previously described, the dependent variable in this model is a binary measure of participation in anti-regime resistance, and the main independent variables are three binary variables indicating completion of preparatory school, secondary school, and university or higher. Logistic regression is the standard way of modeling binary dependent variables. Because participation in resistance is measured as a binary dependent variable – individuals may either participate or not participate – a logistic regression model is thus the correct choice.

To better model the individual determinants of participation in anti-regime resistance, this book uses a generalization of the standard logistic regression model – a multilevel logistic regression – in which the model's intercepts vary by locality.[32] As described in more detail below, this model helps to identify the individual-level characteristics that drive participation in resistance and better rule out alternative locality-level explanations. As also described later in this chapter, the results that follow are also robust to alternative approaches to accounting for differences between localities that could otherwise confound the results.

In addition, the model also controls for three potentially confounding variables: age, wealth, and family status. Wealth is measured as a binary variable indicating the number of "amenities" owned by the household (e.g. refrigerator, radio, etc.), which is a better measure of wealth than income in Palestine and many developing countries. Family status is measured as a binary variable indicating whether or not an individual's father completed primary school, a relatively high level of education for this generation. Family status and parental education are among the most important determinants of an individual's educational attainment (see e.g. Jencks et al., 1972). Since these factors may also influence participation in anti-regime protest, I control for them in the analysis; however, the results are also robust to excluding them (see Table A.16 in the online

---

[32] For additional information on this approach, see Gelman (2007, 237–47).

appendix) (see e.g. Jencks et al., 1972).[33] Like the schooling indicators, all control variables in the model are lagged by one year to minimize the possibility of reverse causality, and additional robustness checks for reverse causality are also reported and discussed in Section A.1.1 in the online appendix. Finally, as further discussed in Section 3.7.1, the model also accounts for the statistical problem of duration dependence in panel survey data by including three equally spaced cubic splines.

As seen in Table 3.2, this baseline model is also robust to controlling for generational effects on participation in anti-regime resistance. Controlling for generational effects is important because opportunities for participation are likely to vary with both age and time. For example, individuals who came of age during the first intifadah should be more likely to participate in protest than individuals who came of age during the previous, less intense period of anti-regime dissent. To account for these generational effects, the alternative model not only controls for age (as does the baseline model) but also includes time period dummies and controls for the interaction between age and time period.[34]

These findings provide support for this chapter's arguments and challenge influential perspectives about participation in political conflict and violence. Contrary to perspectives that view participants in political conflict as poor, uneducated, and marginalized (Paige, 1978; Scott, 1976; Collier and Hoeffler, 2004; Humphreys and Weinstein, 2008), individuals who completed preparatory school – the median level of education – were significantly more likely to participate in resistance than those with less schooling.[35] However, contrary to another popular view of dissidents as well educated, underemployed, and disaffected (Gurr, 1970; Kepel, 1985; Gelvin, 2012), individuals who completed secondary school or university were no more likely to participate in protest than those who completed preparatory school alone.[36] Further, as I demonstrate below, this relationship between schooling and protest

33 Father's education may influence participation negatively because, in the Palestinian context, fathers were educated before protest was widespread and thus were not socialized to participate. As such, more educated elites often sought to dissuade their sons from participating.
34 Including time period dummies also controls for any secular trends in school completion rates and protest participation.
35 Note that, while these perspectives stem from the literature on armed conflict, their theoretical logic is not particular to violent conflict.
36 See also Campante and Chor (2012); Hoffman and Jamal (2014); Beissinger, Jamal, and Mazur (2015).

participation is not contingent on individuals' economic status or situation. Before doing so, however, I elaborate on the modeling choices made in the statistical analysis.

3.7.1 Details of Statistical Models

As previously mentioned, this book's analyses use a generalization of the basic logistic regression model – a multilevel logistic regression – in which the model's intercepts vary by locality.[37] Multilevel models are useful for modeling clustered or "nested" data such as individual survey data, in which individual respondents are clustered within geographic localities. Multilevel models with varying intercepts are identical to regression models with locality-level random effects and similar to models with locality-level fixed effects. Like including locality-level random or fixed effects, allowing intercepts to vary by locality accounts for the fact that different localities will have varying participation rates and that individuals residing in the same locality are thus likely to have similar propensities for participation (i.e. they are not statistically independent observations). For example, urban localities may, on average, have higher rates of participation than rural localities. In addition, different localities may vary from each other in other ways that we cannot easily observe. By allowing intercepts to vary by locality, the model takes into account such observed and unobserved differences between localities. Consequently, it can better identify the individual-level characteristics that determine participation in resistance and rule out alternative locality-level explanations.

These results are also robust to including locality-level fixed effects in the regression model, which adds a separate intercept for each locality rather than a random draw from a locality-level probability distribution.[38] This approach compares each individual only to other individuals in the same locality and, therefore, completely rules out the possibility that the results are driven by locality-level differences rather than individual-level ones. However, because fixed effects models are relatively inefficient from a statistical perspective, I use the multilevel model described here as the baseline and then test the robustness of this model to the inclusion of fixed effects.

---

[37] See Gelman (2007, 237–47) for additional information on this approach.
[38] See Section A.1.7 in the online appendix for the results of the fixed effects model: www.cambridge.org/TheRevolutionWithin

As previously mentioned, the model also accounts for the statistical problem of duration dependence in panel survey data, which have multiple observations on the same individual over time. Due to their structure, panel survey data often exhibit duration dependence, meaning that the probability of an event of interest in a given period depends on the time passed since the last such event. In the case of our survey data, duration dependence may arise if the probability of participation in anti-regime resistance were dependent on the time passed since the previous instance of participation. In this not unlikely case, these data would violate the assumption of statistical independence of observations in the ordinary logit model and, if this problem were not addressed, could lead to misleading results. To prevent this problem, the model thus includes three equally spaced cubic splines, which is the recommended solution for panel data with a binary dependent variable such as ours (Beck, Katz, and Tucker, 1998). These results are also robust to an alternative approach to correcting temporal dependence using robust clustered standard errors.[39]

In addition to these main tests, the results are also robust to multiple ways of specifying the statistical model and other key robustness checks. In particular, as the next section will show, they are not due to selection bias caused by missing data on participation in anti-regime resistance.

3.7.2 Accounting for Missing Data and Selection Bias

As previously mentioned, information on participation in anti-regime resistance is missing for 19 percent of the survey sample. These data are missing primarily due to respondents' failure to complete the entire survey rather than their failure to complete specific survey questions or items (i.e. "item non-response"). However, if respondents' propensity to complete the survey is associated with their integration into state institutions or with other key personal characteristics, this could potentially bias the findings.[40]

To address this possibility, I conduct a series of bounding analyses based on Manski's extreme bounds (1995). I estimate the effect of integration into educational institutions on the probability of participation

---

[39] See Section A.1.7 in the online appendix: www.cambridge.org/TheRevolutionWithin
[40] There is some evidence that socioeconomic status is associated with survey completion rates: while education is only weakly correlated with survey completion ($r = 0.05$), there is a moderately strong correlation between wealth and survey completion ($r = 0.20$).

TABLE 3.3 *Bounding analysis*

Participation	Baseline Model (with Missing Data)	Upper Bound	Lower Bound
Age	0.08***	0.07***	0.08***
	(0.01)	(0.01)	(0.01)
Preparatory	1.07***	0.77***	1.12***
	(0.17)	(0.13)	(0.16)
Secondary	0.01	−0.07	0.03
	(0.18)	(0.15)	(0.17)
University	−0.01	−0.15	0.18
	(0.21)	(0.17)	(0.19)
Household Amenities	0.21***	0.18***	0.21***
	(0.04)	(0.03)	(0.04)
Father's Education	−0.66***	−0.30**	−0.83***
	(0.17)	(0.13)	(0.16)
Constant	−2.63***	−1.62***	−3.11***
	(0.27)	(0.20)	(0.28)
Observations	2874	3581	3581

Multilevel logit coefficients and standard errors reported.
All models include cubic splines.
*$p<0.10$ **$p<0.05$ ***$p<0.01$

in anti-regime resistance under two extreme assumptions: (1) the missing respondents are all participants (i.e. upper bound on participation); and (2) the missing respondents are all nonparticipants (i.e. lower bound on participation). The true effect of integration into educational institutions on the probability of participation lies between its effect under these lower and upper bounds. Because it is extremely unlikely that the missing respondents would be either all participants or all nonparticipants, this is a very difficult test of the robustness of the results to missing data.

Table 3.3 presents the results of the bounding analysis for the baseline model shown in Table 3.2. As seen in the table, the results hold regardless of the distribution of participants and nonparticipants among the missing respondents. That is, integration into educational institutions has the same effect on participation in resistance regardless of whether we assume the missing respondents are all participants or all nonparticipants. Likewise, the effects of all other variables in the model are also consistent with my previous findings.[41] Overall, these results should give us confidence that the observed relationship between integration into

---

[41] As in the baseline model, wealth increases the likelihood of participation; however, as in Table 3.2, this effect disappears with the inclusion of generational effects in the model.

these institutions and participation in resistance is not biased due to missing data on the dependent variable. Section A.1 of the online appendix shows that the results for disciplinary institutions are also robust to bounding analysis and provides additional information and tests.

3.7.3 Additional Robustness Checks

This chapter's findings are also robust to three additional robustness checks, which are reported in Section A.1 of the online appendix. First, I examine whether reverse causality could be driving the observed relationship between integration into educational institutions and participation in anti-regime resistance; that is, I test whether participation in resistance could be shaping the level of schooling completed rather than the other way around. To do so, I estimate the effect of schooling in a given period on the probability that a previously politically inactive individual begins to participate in anti-regime resistance in later periods. The dependent variable in this analysis is thus the initial onset of participation in resistance (among previous nonparticipants). The results are similar to the previous findings.

Second, I account for the possibility of selection bias stemming from the self-selection of likely participants in anti-regime resistance into higher levels of schooling. That is, I account for the possibility that individuals are self-selecting or being selected into preparatory schooling on the basis of characteristics that also predict participation in resistance. Qualitative interviews with students and teachers indicate that the main determinants of Palestinian males' level of schooling in the time period of interest is their household socioeconomic status and their personal characteristics, namely their academic aptitude and performance.[42] As mentioned before, the preceding analysis already controls for household socioeconomic status using household wealth and father's educational attainment. To account for academic aptitude and success, I now include a measure of individuals' conscientiousness as a control variable in the model. Conscientiousness is one of the most important predictors of academic achievement and success, with some studies suggesting its effect rivals that of intelligence (Poropat, 2009). Importantly, as Kam and Palmer note (2008, 615), conscientiousness may also influence political participation, making it an important variable to control for.[43]

---

[42] See e.g. Interview 1, Abu Dis, February 8, 2014; Interview 20, Nablus, March (n.d.) 2014.

[43] Drawing on the wider academic literature on personality traits in politics, Kam and Palmer propose that "personality traits that manifest during or prior to adolescence (e.g.

As expected, conscientiousness is positively correlated with preparatory schooling in the survey data ($r = 0.17$). However, it is only weakly correlated with participation in anti-regime resistance ($r = 0.08$), and its inclusion in the model does not change the core results as we would expect if self-selection were at work in the manner already described. Thus, the effect of schooling on participation in resistance does not appear to be due to selection on the basis of either socioeconomic factors or broader personality traits. See Section A.1.3 in the online appendix for the full results and additional details.

Finally, in addition to the mentioned variables, the effect of schooling is also robust to controlling for a variety of other possible confounding variables, including biographical availability, refugee status, exposure to violence, religious activity, and land ownership in mandatory Palestine.

3.8 TESTING THE CAUSAL MECHANISMS

Supporting this book's overall arguments, this chapter has demonstrated that integration into educational institutions is associated with a higher probability of participation in anti-regime resistance. This section assesses the main informational and organizational mechanisms argued to account for this relationship. In particular, it evaluates two additional empirical implications of the theoretical argument. First, it examines whether integration into educational institutions brought individuals into larger, more diverse social networks, providing them with greater access to political information. Second, it considers the implications of the argument's logic for the types of unarmed resistance in which individuals engage.

How does integration into educational institutions affect the breadth of an individual's social networks and, in turn, their propensity for protest? Consistent with this chapter's argument, Table 3.4 shows that integration into these institutions is associated with an increase in the size of an individual's *extra-local social networks*, meaning social ties outside one's family and community.[44] Also consistent with the argument,

---

sense of duty, efficaciousness, and willingness to delay gratification) may also be causal factors that propel both educational attainment and political participation" (Kam and Palmer, 2008, 615).

44 The size of an individual's extra-local social networks is measured as the number of communities in which an individual was in regular contact with someone outside the family in a given year. This measure is coded as a five-level categorical variable, with

TABLE 3.4 *The effect of schooling on social network size*

Social Networks	Extra-local Networks	Civic Networks
Age	0.04***	0.02***
	(0.00)	(0.00)
Preparatory	0.28**	0.27**
	(0.10)	(0.11)
Secondary	0.25**	−0.04
	(0.11)	(0.12)
University	0.21*	0.33**
	(0.11)	(0.14)
Household Amenities	0.11***	0.09***
	(0.02)	(0.03)
Father's Education	−0.08	−0.16
	(0.11)	(0.10)
Constant	−0.37	−0.15
	(0.33)	(0.36)
Observations	3124	2738

OLS coefficients and standard errors reported
All models include locality fixed effects and robust clustered standard errors (on individual).
*$p<0.10$ **$p<0.05$ ***$p<0.01$

preparatory schooling has the largest impact on an individual's extra-local networks of any other level of schooling, increasing their size by 0.28 on a five-point scale or approximately 0.25 standard deviations ($p<0.05$). In contrast, higher levels of schooling appear to have a slightly smaller and weaker, additive effect on extra-local ties.

Schooling also has a similar impact on incorporation into politicized civic networks.[45] In line with this chapter's argument, preparatory school completion is associated with a 0.27 standard deviation increase in the size of these networks ($p<0.05$).[46] In contrast, higher levels of schooling have a mixed effect on network size: secondary school completion is not associated with an additional increase in the size of an individual's civic networks but, for students who also complete university, network size further increases.

higher values indicating a larger number of communities in which the individual is in regular contact with someone.

[45] Civic networks is measured as a four-level categorical variable indicating the number of civil society associations in which the respondent personally knew a member in each year, ranging from "0" (no associations) to "3" (three or more associations).

[46] The standard deviation of the civic networks variable is 1, such that the coefficient also equals the effect size.

These patterns are consistent with the argument that integration into educational institutions widens an individual's social networks, providing them with new sources of information and rendering them better able to participate in protest. Preparatory school completion is associated with increases in extra-local ties that can provide information from outside an individual's immediate social circles, as well as with larger civic networks. Additional schooling may further increase the size of these networks, but it has a diminishing effect. Moreover, if participation tends to persist once started, such additional increases in the size of an individual's social networks should not significantly affect an individual's propensity for protest. Individuals who are better integrated into the movement's social networks may intensify their involvement in anti-regime resistance, devoting more time to resistance or engaging in riskier acts. However, they should not be significantly more likely to participate in anti-regime resistance, which is my main outcome of interest.

3.8.1   The Impact of Schooling on the Type of Resistance

This book's arguments also imply that integration into educational institutions should have a greater impact on some forms of unarmed resistance than others. As Section 3.4 described, it should make individuals more likely to participate in more risky and more collective forms of protest as compared with less risky and individual acts of dissent. In contrast, grievance-based and expressive mechanisms such as national identity, relative deprivation, or political interest imply that integration into schools should affect participation in different types of protest equally.

Table 3.5 shows the effect of schooling on different types of unarmed collective action. Participation in high-risk collective action is measured as participation in "demonstrations and mass funerals" and/or clashes; participation in crowd collective action includes these two categories as well as a third category – strikes – which often involve mass walkouts in which group members are face-to-face.[47] Conditional on any participation, individuals who completed preparatory school were

---

[47] Participation in boycotts, prison visits, and the writing of graffiti were all coded as less risky and individual acts of resistance. To evaluate whether schooling makes individuals more likely to participate in these forms of protest, individuals who did not participate at all were excluded. The results are also robust to coding participation in strikes as individual acts of resistance, as well as including non-participants and comparing participants in crowd collective action to both participants in individual acts of resistance and nonparticipants.

TABLE 3.5 *The effect of schooling on resistance type*

Types of Resistance	High-Risk Collective Action	Crowd Collective Action
Age	0.00	−0.03
	(0.03)	(0.03)
Preparatory	1.41**	1.32**
	(0.57)	(0.58)
Secondary	−0.56	−0.43
	(0.56)	(0.57)
University	1.26*	0.97
	(0.68)	(0.63)
Household Amenities	0.21*	0.27**
	(0.13)	(0.13)
Father's Education	−0.71	−0.80
	(0.53)	(0.53)
Constant	2.10**	3.03***
	(0.91)	(0.99)
Observations	580	580

Multilevel logit coefficients and standard errors reported.
All models include cubic splines.
*p<0.10 **p<0.05 ***p<0.01

significantly more likely to participate in high-risk collective action than in relatively less risky resistance ($p<0.01$). In substantive terms, they were 10 percentage points more likely to participate in more risky forms of protest than less risky types of dissent.[48] Similarly, preparatory school graduates were also between 4 and 11 percentage points more likely to participate in crowd collective action than in individual acts of resistance ($p<0.05$).[49] While not conclusive, these findings suggest that schooling affects participation in anti-regime resistance through institutional properties that affect more risky and collective forms of protest in particular rather than alternative mechanisms that affect all anti-regime protest equally.

3.9 ALTERNATIVE EXPLANATIONS

This chapter has shown that integration into educational institutions is associated with an increased probability of participation in anti-regime resistance. Within a given locality and time period, Palestinians who

[48] Note that conditioning on participation restricts the sample to participants only, decreasing the sample size in this analysis. As such, it would be useful to replicate these findings on a larger sample size.
[49] When adding generational effects, the estimated effect increases to 11 percentage points.

were integrated into preparatory schools were significantly more likely to protest against Israeli occupation than those who were not. In addition, conditional on having participated in some form of unarmed resistance, individuals who were integrated into preparatory schools were particularly likely to participate in both more risky and more collective forms of protest. These results suggest that the structure of educational institutions – which gather large numbers of youth in a single location and reduce their risks of participation – accounts for their effects.

Alternative expressive and grievance-based explanations for these findings point to the content of education rather than its structure. Rather than making individuals more able to participate in anti-regime resistance, these explanations hold that it makes them more *willing* to do so. Integration into educational institutions could make individuals more willing to participate in resistance in at least three ways. First, as modern "institutions of power," integration into these institutions could instill citizens with a stronger sense of national identity and grievances (Andersen, 1983; Darden, 2013). Second, integration into these institutions could also impart greater political interest, awareness, or civic feeling (Wolfinger, 1980; Brady, Verba, and Schlozman, 1995; Campbell, 1980). Finally, integration into educational institutions could also give rise to high expectations that may not be met, fostering feelings of relative deprivation that could lead individuals to protest (Gurr, 1970). In this section, I explore these alternative explanations.

3.9.1 National Identity and Grievances

Instead of improving individuals' capacity for protest, integration into educational institutions could make individuals more willing to protest by strengthening national identity or grievances. Foundational theories of nationalism identify modern educational systems as "institutions of power" that transmit national identity to citizens (Andersen, 1983). More recently, Keith Darden has argued that the national identities promoted in schools at the time of mass literacy explain subsequent patterns of resistance to foreign occupation (Darden, 2013). These works suggest that schooling may have made Palestinian students more likely to resist Israeli occupation by instilling them with a stronger sense of national identity or more deeply felt national grievances.

National identity and grievances offer unlikely explanations for the effect of educational institutions on participation in resistance in Palestine, however. Subject to successive foreign administrations – first

Ottoman and British, then Egyptian and Jordanian, and, finally, Israeli – Palestinian schools did not come under domestic political control until 1994. Under these successive foreign regimes, Palestinian national identity was absent from the curriculum. Before the advent of Israeli occupation in 1967, Egyptian and Jordanian authorities used schooling as a political tool with which to build their own national identities, as well as, in the Egyptian case, to foster pan-Arab feeling. Subnational identities such as Palestinian identity, which threatened this unifying project, were deliberately undermined (Brand, 2014a, 37–66). Thus, as Nathan Brown has written, "Palestinian students devoted greater attention to Pharaonic Egypt and the Hashemite [Jordanian] leadership of the Arab revolt than to their [own] particular history" (Brown, 2003, 198).

Under Israeli military administration, the Palestinian educational system was further stripped of any national content. Military censors inspected all schoolbooks and teaching materials and removed any references to the land, history, geography, people, or literature of Palestine. Maps were changed to show the new "Greater Israel," encompassing both Israel within its pre-1967 borders and the newly occupied Palestinian Territories (Alzaroo and Hunt, 2003, 6). Adherence to this new curriculum was strictly enforced. Teaching any supplementary material was prohibited, and teachers were cautioned to confine themselves to the approved textbooks and to refrain from using any outside sources (Shehadeh and Kuttāb, 1980, 90).

These restrictions had a chilling effect on teachers, who lacked the "safety in numbers" afforded to students. Unlike student protestors, teachers who taught nationalist subjects and/or from a nationalist perspective were highly visible and identifiable. With students sometimes acting as informers for the Shin Bet [Israel's domestic intelligence agency], most teachers hewed closely to the approved curriculum and avoided political topics or discussion. The few teachers who did not were penalized severely, deterring others from following suit. As one such nationalist teacher recalled:

In the school in Beit Hanina, we had twelve teachers and only two were national – me and my friend. Most other teachers were scared to tell the students anything that was not in the textbook... The Shin Bet [Israel's domestic intelligence agency] used students as informers, and of course there were also informers outside the school.[50]

---

[50] Interview 1, Abu Dis, February 28, 2014. See also Interview, R. Sabbah, Ramallah, February 27, 2014; Interviews 5, 18, and 26, March 2014.

Similarly, a former teacher who was very active in the profession described how only a small minority of teachers dared to venture outside the official Israeli-approved curriculum. Concerned about their jobs and salaries, as well as staying out of jail, the vast majority of teachers were simply unwilling to take the risks:

Look, the teachers as a sector, they are *"jubana"* – cowards. Because they always... underneath they are conservative, they are afraid about their salaries, about their positions, and it was very [dangerous]... If you are a teacher before the first intifadah, it means you are in a very good position because the salary came from two sides – the Israelis and the Jordanians. [There were] maybe 95 percent who didn't do it and 5 percent who did [teach any national or political material]. (Interview, R. Sabbah, Ramallah, February 27, 2014)

Consistent with teachers' perspectives, most students also reported hearing little nationalist or political content in the classroom. For example, asked whether he learned about Palestinian history, geography, or literature in school, a young man who was completing preparatory school when the first intifadah began in 1987 replied:

It wasn't in the curriculum, because curriculums were produced by the civil administration in those days. Israel was responsible for everything, it was an occupation. Nowadays, the Palestinian Authority, as it is supposed to, [is the one who] teaches the new generation about Palestine. Therefore, our generation, or the generation that didn't have [the teachings about Palestine in its curriculum], I think, it depended upon its own knowledge. (Interview 5, Nablus, March 10, 2014)

The tight control exercised over the educational system by Israel and the resulting atmosphere of fear cast doubt on national identity and grievances as the operative causal mechanism. However, is it possible that the stark contrast between the depoliticized educational curriculum and the highly politicized reality of daily life under occupation developed a sense of national identity organically among school students (Gordon, 2008)? While this possibility cannot be dismissed, no interviewee described such a process. Indeed, the extensive efforts by Palestinian nationalist activists to provide informal nationalist education outside schools suggest that national awareness was not an organic response to the official curriculum (see e.g. Hiltermann, 1993).

3.9.2   Political Interest and Awareness

Integration into educational institutions could also promote participation in anti-regime resistance by transmitting political interest, general political knowledge, or civic responsibility. Classic studies of participation in democratic politics argue that education develops political interest and awareness that are important for political participation, and recent studies suggest that these factors could also play an important role in determining participation in non-institutionalized political conflict (Wolfinger, 1980; Brady, Verba, and Schlozman, 1995; Lee, 2011). Other studies argue that education confers civic skills or a sense of civic duty that fosters political participation (Brady, Verba, and Schlozman, 1995; Campbell, 1980). As with grievance-based theories, these arguments suggest that it is not the structure of schooling but the content that matters.

Political interest and awareness offer unlikely explanations for the patterns of participation in resistance that we observe in Palestine, however. As described previously, it is unlikely that depoliticized readings, lectures, and discussions generated political interest among students or that relevant information about Palestinian politics was transmitted in the classroom. Similarly, it is difficult to imagine how an educational system intended to depoliticize students could foster meaningful civic skills or a sense of duty to participate in anti-regime protest.

The survey evidence also casts some doubt on the idea that integration into educational institutions makes individuals more likely to participate in anti-regime resistance by increasing political interest and awareness. If this idea were to be born out, we should expect individuals with greater interest in politics to display higher rates of protest participation than less interested ones. We can test this hypothesis using the frequency of newspaper readership as a proxy for political interest. Newspaper readership makes a useful proxy for political interest because, while Palestinian newspapers were censored, they nonetheless took a nationalist line. Although they could not print detailed information about protests, they continued to print more general information about resistance, political editorials, and death notices of "martyrs" (although usually not without penalty) (see e.g. Friedman, 1983, 93–96). Some categories of news, such as information about the West, were also typically spared from censorship (Friedman, 1983, 99). Thus, even as politically aware Palestinians looked elsewhere for specific information about resistance, they continued to read Palestinian newspapers for their general nationalist bent.

Contrary to the political interest and awareness hypothesis, however, there seems to be only a weak relationship between political interest and participation in anti-regime resistance. Table 3.6 shows that newspaper

TABLE 3.6 *The effect of political interest on participation in anti-regime resistance*

Participation	Coefficient (SE)
Age	0.08***
	(0.01)
Preparatory	1.17***
	(0.17)
Secondary	0.08
	(0.19)
University	−0.01
	(0.21)
Household Amenities	0.22***
	(0.04)
Father's Education	−0.66***
	(0.17)
News Readership	−0.31**
	(0.14)
Constant	−2.67***
	(0.27)
Observations	2838

Multi-level logit coefficients and standard errors reported.
All models include cubic splines.
*p<0.10 **p<0.05 ***p<0.01

readership has a small *negative* association with future participation in resistance rather than a positive one; moreover, its inclusion in the baseline model does not diminish the effect of preparatory schooling as would be expected if political interest were the operative causal mechanism linking schooling to resistance. While a more conclusive test of the political interest and awareness mechanism would require additional, more fine-grained measures of these variables, this initial exploration thus suggests that these mechanisms are probably not at work. However, I cannot dismiss the possibility that integration into educational institutions augments human capital in other ways that could foster participation in resistance.

3.9.3   Relative Deprivation

Finally, integration into educational institutions could also make individuals more willing to participate in anti-regime resistance by fostering subjective economic grievances and feelings of deprivation. According to relative deprivation theory, individuals choose to rebel due to frustration stemming from a gap between their aspirations and their material conditions. Schooling, in this theory, is a social force that gives rise to high expectations; when these expectations are not satisfied, they lead to frustration and rebellion (Gurr, 1970). This logic has often been invoked to explain participation in anti-regime resistance in the Middle East, including Islamic activism and the recent Arab uprisings (Kepel, 1985; Gelvin, 2012).

The relative deprivation mechanism implies that there is an interactive effect between schooling and economic conditions. Poor individuals with more schooling, it predicts, will become frustrated with their circumstances and rebel. Wealthy individuals with more schooling, in contrast, will stay on the sidelines. We can test this implication by estimating the marginal effect of schooling conditional on wealth. If the relative deprivation explanation is correct, schooling should significantly increase the likelihood of participation in resistance for poorer individuals but have no significant effect on participation for wealthier ones.

Table 3.7 estimates the marginal effect of preparatory schooling on participation conditional on wealth.[51] For ease of interpretation, wealth is measured as a binary variable indicating whether the number of household amenities is above or below the sample median of three amenities. Household amenities is an appropriate measure for dependent youth as well as independent adults because family wealth exerts a strong influence on youths' current and future economic outcomes. In any case, measuring youths' economic conditions independently of their families' status is very difficult if not impossible. An alternative measure of socioeconomic status based on father's education yields similar results (see Table A.17).

As Table 3.7 shows, schooling increases the likelihood of participation in anti-regime resistance among poor individuals by 15 percentage points. However, it also increases the likelihood of participation in resistance among wealthy individuals by a very similar and even slightly greater amount. Thus, based on the evidence at hand, relative deprivation does not seem to explain the effect of schooling on participation in resistance.

[51] The model estimated is the baseline model (Table 3.2, Model 1). Marginal effects are estimated holding continuous variables at their means and categorical variables at their modal values. All results are also robust to estimating the generational effects model in Table 3.2.

TABLE 3.7 *The marginal effect of schooling on participation by household wealth*

	Wealth – Above Median	Wealth – Median or Below
Preparatory Schooling	0.16***	0.15***
	(0.03)	(0.03)
Observations	1066	1688

Note: Marginal effects from multilevel logit regression model with varying intercepts by locality (baseline model in Table 3.2). Additional variables not shown include additional schooling indicators, age, wealth/household amenities, father's education, and cubic splines. Marginal effects estimated by holding continuous variables at their means and categorical variables at their modal values.
*p<0.10 **p<0.05 ***p<0.01

3.10 CONCLUSIONS

This chapter has shown that integration into educational institutions is associated with a higher probability of participation in anti-regime resistance. Otherwise similar Palestinians living in the same city, town, or village at the same time were significantly more likely to participate in resistance if they had been integrated into preparatory schools. However, in contrast to existing perspectives that portray participants in resistance as highly educated and underemployed, they were no less likely to participate than their peers with additional higher-level schooling.

Integration into educational institutions made Palestinians better able to participate in anti-regime resistance by lowering informational and organizational barriers to collective action. Unable to learn about resistance to Israeli rule in the Palestinian media or other widely available sources, Palestinians relied on their social networks to gain information about dissent. Yet, for the many Palestinians joined in parochial family and village-based networks, access to such sensitive political information was limited. Integration into schools resolved this information problem. As demonstrated in the chapter, integration into schools connected students into larger and more diverse extra-local and civic networks, providing them with access to scarce information about protest. Schools also made students better able to protest by facilitating communication and coordination and by reducing uncertainty about the risks of protest.

Schools are not the only institutions to provide these informational and organizational advantages, however. Under repressive regimes with high incarceration rates, prisons, courts, and other disciplinary institutions may also share these collective action-enhancing properties. At the same time, integration into disciplinary institutions represents a hard test of this book's argument about the mobilizing power of state institutions. Even more than schools, integration into prisons and courts subjects individuals to control by the state, potentially deterring them from resisting. Moreover, because prisoners' family members and friends are only indirectly integrated into prisons and courts, it is possible that exposure to these institutions would not affect them at all. In the next chapter, I turn to examining the impact of integration into state institutions in this more difficult case.

4

Disciplinary Institutions and Participation in Resistance

4.1 INTRODUCTION

On December 17, 1982, approximately 750 relatives of Palestinian prisoners held in Israel's Beer Sheba prison held an impromptu demonstration. The demonstration reportedly began when, during a family visit to the prison, a prison guard insulted the family of one of the prisoners. As prisoners and prison guards started clashing inside the jail, the visiting families were forced outside. There, they gathered and chanted support for their imprisoned relatives until they were forcibly dispersed by border guard reinforcements with batons and tear gas.[1] Following the clashes and demonstration on December 17, a hundred relatives of prisoners held a sit-in at the headquarters of the International Committee of the Red Cross (ICRC) in Jerusalem. The sit-in was at least the second such strike in December alone.[2]

Along with students, prisoners' families such as the Beer Sheba protestors were among the most active participants in unarmed resistance to the Israeli military occupation of the Palestinian Territories. This chapter provides a novel explanation for the high rates of activism among this group that focuses on the advantages that integration into prisons and courts – like integration into other types of state institutions – offers for collective action. As the demonstration at Beer Sheba prison shows, the imprisonment of a relative or friend integrates individuals

---

[1] "Guards Beat up Beer Sheba Inmates." 1982, December 31. *Jerusalem Dawn Palestinian Weekly* 3(139), 1.

[2] "Women Sit-in to Protest Nafha, Beer Sheba Conditions." 1982, December 31. *Jerusalem Dawn Palestinian Weekly* 3(139), 1.

into the state's disciplinary apparatus: when a loved one is imprisoned, his relatives and friends visit prison, attend court, and otherwise interact within state disciplinary institutions. Extending this book's general theory to such institutions, this chapter argues that integration into prisons and courts joined prisoners' relatives and friends in broader, more information-rich social networks and fostered communication and coordination between them. Integration into prisons and courts may also have provided safety in numbers and decreased uncertainty about the risks of protest, although, because these institutions generally gathered fewer people together than schools, this mechanism may be weaker in this case. As a result of these informational and organizational advantages, prisoners' relatives and friends became better able to participate in protest than they had previously been, increasing the likelihood that they would participate.

Integration into disciplinary institutions represents a difficult case for this book's theory. Whereas students are directly integrated into schools, prisoners' relatives and friends are only indirectly integrated into prisons and courts. As a form of state repression, integration into prisons and courts can also subject individuals to further control by the state and make them less likely to dissent. As a result, integration into these institutions could be expected to have only a weak effect on individuals' political behavior or to decrease the chance that they will participate in protest rather than increase it.

In contrast to these expectations, this chapter finds that the imprisonment of a family member or friend is associated with a significantly higher probability of participation in anti-regime resistance. Importantly, relatives and friends of prisoners were more likely to participate in resistance than other groups even after controlling for their general exposure to repression, family background, and other possible sources of politicization. Thus, the relationship between the imprisonment of a relative or friend and participation in protest does not appear to be due to higher pre-imprisonment levels of politicization among this group. Among previously politically inactive individuals, the imprisonment of a relative or friend also raised the probability that they would begin to participate in resistance for the first time. As a result, simple reverse causality also does not seem to account for this relationship.

In addition, this chapter also provides evidence that integration into disciplinary institutions provides prisoners' relatives and friends with informational and organizational advantages, which make them better able to participate in protest. This chapter argues that, like integration into schools, integration into prisons and courts joins individuals in wider, more information-rich social networks and promotes communication and coordination between them. Drawing on both qualitative sources and quantitative survey evidence, it shows that integration into these institutions linked prisoners' relatives and friends with others like themselves from all over the Palestinian Territories. With the rise of civil society in the early 1980s, the imprisonment of a loved one also brought individuals into contact with politicized civic networks. As a result, the survey evidence shows, the imprisonment of a relative or friend was associated with a large increase in the breadth of an individual's social networks and, in turn, their access to political information about protest.

One obvious alternative explanation for these findings is radicalization. Rather than improving individuals' capacity for protest, the imprisonment of a relative or friend could strengthen Palestinians' grievances against the Israeli military regime and make them more willing to protest against it. While not conclusive, this chapter's findings show more limited support for this mechanism than for the informational networks mechanism. Contrary to what this mechanism would imply, the imprisonment of a relative or friend is not consistently associated with reading a pro-PLO nationalist newspaper in our survey data. The available qualitative evidence also suggests that, while the imprisonment of a loved one may well intensify grievances against the state, these more intense grievances may not have been translated into action were it not for informational networks. Thus, while more research is needed to disentangle these two causal mechanisms, this chapter finds somewhat stronger support for a structural-institutional explanation than a grievance-based one.

These findings expand our understanding of the scope for protest in organizationally underdeveloped, authoritarian environments. In the absence of a strong, independent civil society, integration into those institutions most under the state's control – prisons, courts, and other disciplinary institutions – made individuals more likely to protest against the state. Integration into these institutions joined relatives and friends of prisoners in larger and more information-rich social networks and made them better able to participate in protest. As Palestinian civil society grew in strength, integration into these institutions also connected prisoners' relatives and friends to new, politicized civic networks, further increasing their capacity for protest. Importantly, however, these civic networks and structures did not precipitate unrest but, rather, emerged in response to protest. Thus, contrary to some influential perspectives, anti-regime resistance can occur even without the strong autonomous institutions and networks often regarded as necessary for protest.

These findings also have important implications for understanding how state repression and human rights abuses affect protest. Typically, scholars of human rights argue that government abuses tend to produce more conflict and violence by intensifying grievances, emboldening dissidents, or closing off other perceived outlets for achieving political change (White, 1989; Goodwin, 2001; Thoms and Ron, 2007). This perspective is also shared by other scholars of contentious politics, who similarly argue that state repression promotes protest by engendering or deepening grievances against the state (see e.g. Lichbach and Gurr, 1981; Longo, Canetti, and Hite-Rubin, 2014; Lawrence, 2017).[3] At the same time, this finding has also been widely disputed, with many scholars arguing that repression should and does deter open dissent (see e.g. McCarthy and Zald, 1977a; Lyall, 2009; Earl, 2011).

Consistent with the former perspective, this chapter suggests that, among a group with strong preexisting grievances, legal repression – via the imprisonment of a family member or friend – promotes individual participation in protest. However, this impact of repression is more likely due to the unintended informational and organizational benefits conveyed within repressive state institutions than to the intensification of group grievances. This suggests that mass imprisonment or other state policies that bring prospective dissidents together are likely to backfire, stimulating rather than suppressing protest. Yet it is possible that other forms of repression that do not confer such advantages for collective action may indeed deter protest, potentially explaining the divergent findings in the academic literature.[4]

4.2 INTEGRATION INTO DISCIPLINARY INSTITUTIONS, NETWORKS, AND PROTEST PARTICIPATION IN PALESTINE

As the Palestinian intifadah entered its second year in 1989, Israel's already high incarceration rate became the highest in the world (Hajjar, 2005, 3; Ron, 2000, 455). Due to the imprisonment of thousands of

---

[3] See also Jenkins and Schock (2003) for a similar argument based on Goodwin's logic (2001).

[4] See e.g. Earl (2003) and Oliver (2008) for other calls to disaggregate "repression" based on its perpetrators, their goals, or other factors.

Palestinians throughout the previous decade – many of them politically inexperienced youth – thousands of families with little prior history of political activism became indirectly integrated into the Israeli state's disciplinary structures for the first time. As this section will go on to show, this process of integration was a collective social experience that brought a diverse group of prisoners' relatives and friends into contact with one another and with more seasoned political activists. As a result of these new contacts and connections, in turn, prisoners' relatives and friends became better able and more likely to participate in mass resistance than before. In the next section, I trace this gradual process of mobilization using interviews, human rights reports, and other qualitative sources before, in the following sections, assessing the broader generalizability of these accounts using the survey data.

Since the beginning of the Israeli occupation in 1967, hundreds and thousands of Palestinians have been arrested by Israeli security forces (Hajjar, 2005).[5] In 1982, as the seeds of PLO institution-building began to bear fruit in a coordinated "mini-uprising," the number of Palestinians imprisoned in Israeli jails numbered at 500 per 100,000 residents – a rate higher than that of Northern Ireland and South Africa during the same period.[6] By 1989, as the first intifadah was entering its third year and unarmed protest gave way to armed resistance, that number had risen to over 13,000, rendering the Palestinian Territories one of the most heavily imprisoned societies in the world (Ron, 2000, 455).

As the Palestinian prisoner population grew, its composition also changed. The new prisoners were younger and less politicized than their predecessors, and their arrest brought families with little prior history of political activism into contact with the state's disciplinary structures for the first time. In the first decade of occupation, the prison population consisted primarily of members of PLO political-military factions who, in that period of time, were mainly militants. Political activists and those suspected of contact with political activists were also arrested and imprisoned, although the latter were typically detained for shorter periods of a year or less. The majority of those imprisoned were highly politicized

---

5 Between the beginning of the Israeli occupation in 1967 and the signing of the Oslo Accords between Israel and the PLO in 1993, approximately 813,000 Palestinians were arrested (Hajjar, 2005).

6 See "United Kingdom: Northern Ireland." World Prison Brief, Institute for Policy Research, www.prisonstudies.org/country/united-kingdom-northern-ireland (accessed May 20, 2017); "South Africa." World Prison Brief, Institute for Policy Research, www .prisonstudies.org/country/south-africa (accessed May 20, 2017).

before their imprisonment, and many came from families with a history of political involvement. In the colorful words of one Palestinian lawyer, they were "the lions and tigers of Palestinian society" (quoted in Hajjar, 2005, 11).

In contrast, as unarmed resistance to Israeli occupation began to stir in 1978, younger and more politically inexperienced Palestinians were increasingly arrested and imprisoned. Beginning in the early 1980s, intermittent arrests for periods of several weeks each became a common tactic used by Israeli authorities. According to Israeli sociologist Maya Rosenfeld, Israeli authorities used such arrests as a means of "punishment, intimidation, recruitment of informers, and the disruption of daily life" (Rosenfeld, 2004, 233). Their chief targets were preparatory and secondary school students – presumably because of this group's overall high rate of participation in protest. Many of these youths had never been arrested previously (Rosenfeld, 2004, 232–37), and their arrest exposed previously politically uninvolved families to Israeli prisons and courts for the first time.

Arrest and imprisonment widened still further during the first intifadah. With hundreds and thousands of Palestinians participating in the uprising, identifying and arresting those actually involved in protest activities came to prove increasingly challenging for the Israeli authorities. Faced with this difficult task, rank-and-file Israeli soldiers seemingly resorted to arresting young Palestinian men at random. According to James Ron, Israeli soldiers on routine street patrols responded to the swelling protests by grabbing young Palestinian men off the street, hauling them off to base, and charging them with fabricated offenses (Ron, 2000, 455). "You could arrest anyone you want, recalled a former IDF sergeant who served during this period. All you had to do was manufacture an excuse: 'Refused to obey an order' was something we used often" (quoted in Ron, 2000, 455). Those arrested in this manner were typically not highly politicized, nor did they come from politicized families. In many cases, their families were relatively disconnected from political networks and activities. However, with the imprisonment of their sons, this began to change.

Imprisonment was a collective social experience that affected not only the prisoner but also his wider circle of family and friends. With the imprisonment of a family member or friend, Palestinians were indirectly integrated into state disciplinary institutions. On regular, biweekly visiting days and court sessions, they passed long hours inside courtrooms and prison compounds waiting to see imprisoned relatives and friends.

Waits of eight to ten hours were not uncommon (B'Tselem, 1990; Rosenfeld, 2004). As a 1989 report published by the Israeli human rights organization B'Tselem documents, "Every day, dozens of relatives are to be found outside the fence, surrounding the court room, waiting for an opportunity to meet with defendants who are to stand trial... They wait there helplessly, not allowed to enter the court, and with no one to tell them when, or even if, they will be allowed to enter" (Golan, 1989, 24). A follow-up report published a year later stated, "Dozens of people still wait in the blazing sun with no shelter outside the court compound. There is no way of checking the order of hearings, of finding out which of their loved ones are present, or whose trial has been postponed. The suspense goes on for hours" (B'Tselem, 1990, 12).

Family members and friends of prisoners also spent long hours traveling to prisons and courts in the company of other prisoners' families. Palestinian prisoners were typically held far from their home communities, often in Israeli jails located outside the Palestinian Territories (i.e. within Israel's pre-1967 borders). As a result, relatives and friends were forced to travel long distances in order to visit their loved ones, attend court sessions, and meet with lawyers. The Palestinian Red Crescent, the Palestinian chapter of the International Red Cross and Red Crescent Movement, provided buses for this purpose. On visiting days, prisoners' family members and friends traveled to the nearest city or town, where they boarded Red Crescent buses that would take them the remaining distance to the military compound. On these buses, as well as at the compound, they interacted with other relatives and friends of prisoners from throughout the Palestinian Territories.

As a result of these experiences, prisoners' relatives and friends became joined in wider and more information-rich social networks, which increased their capacity for protest. In her book *Confronting the Occupation*, Israeli sociologist Maya Rosenfeld describes how incarceration linked prisoners' relatives and friends in new interfamilial networks of prisoners' families, which contributed to the politicization of the family and particularly its female members.[7] On visiting days, family members and friends of prisoners formed new bonds with like-minded people from

---

7 This chapter builds on Rosenfeld's argument yet departs from it in two key respects. First, the diverse mechanisms linking incarceration to politicization and political involvement in Rosenfeld's argument do not include informational or organizational factors that can overcome common barriers to collective action. Second, while Rosenfeld acknowledges that the imprisonment of a family member also likely affected political participation among his male relatives (Rosenfeld, 2004, 282), her analysis focuses on

all over the Palestinian Territories and, I argue, thereby gained access to new sources of information and opportunities for coordination. The story of Naʿim Abu-ʿAker, a prisoner's father interviewed by Rosenfeld, helps illustrate this process. Before the detention of his thirteen-year-old twin sons in 1983, Abu-ʿAker avoided any involvement in politics, going so far as to build a stone fence around his house to keep his children off the streets and out of trouble. Yet, after his sons were imprisoned, Abu-ʿAker joined a politicized network of prisoners' families: "On my first visits, I traveled by taxi. I wanted to get there before the others, to be the first visitor, to avoid standing in the long line. People didn't like this and said: 'What's the matter with you, Abu Nidal, don't go by taxi. Come with us in the Red Crescent bus.' And indeed I started taking the bus and *I linked up with the families of other prisoners in the camp. We would travel together to the prison and sit together in the afternoons and evenings*" (Rosenfeld, 2004, 275; my emphasis).

Similarly, in the book *The Lemon Tree* by Sandy Tolan, Khanom al-Khairi describes how the imprisonment of her brother, a suspected PFLP member, led to new social connections between her family and other prisoners' families. Al-Khairi recalled: "He forbade us from coming in a taxi. All other families came by public transport in buses, and we would refuse to take a bus. He refused to see us several times when we visited him because we had arrived in taxis – he was tough on us... So eventually we took the bus. He would always ask us to take something to other prisoners' families... He would ask for shoes for this family; clothes and medicine for that family. At the beginning of the school year, he would arrange for books for another family. Every time we visited, he asked us to do this" (Tolan, 2007, 183). Thus encouraged by their imprisoned son, the al-Khairi family eventually became part of a larger circle of prisoners' families.

These new relations between prisoners' families and friend groups widened their social networks beyond their immediate clan, village, or neighborhood. In contrast to many Palestinians' social networks, which were often based on more particularistic criteria, prisoners' networks were typically based on the prisoner's time of imprisonment or political affiliation. Family members and friends of prisoners came to associate with others whose sons were arrested around the same time or whose

women due (in large part) to methodological considerations. Using a different quantitative methodology, I am able to isolate the impact of the imprisonment of a loved one on men.

loved ones were affiliated with the same political faction (Rosenfeld, 2004, 294). The resulting social networks were geographically diverse. As Rosenfeld describes: "Visiting days in prison led to new social connections between families from the length and breadth of the West Bank" (2004, 293). Elsewhere Rosenfeld states: "There [on the grounds near the prison] they became friends with families from villages, towns and camps from all over the West Bank. Like the son who met fellow prisoners from Nablus, Jenin, Hebron and the Gaza Strip, the relatives, in the course of their visits, would get to know families from some locales they had barely known of previously" (Rosenfeld, 2004, 273). Indeed, despite this geographic distance, members of these new networks maintained regular, sometimes even daily, contact with one another (Rosenfeld, 2004, 293, 298). These contacts provided prisoners' relatives and friends with new sources of information about political events and activities far from their home, as well as facilitated communication, coordination, and a sense of "safety in numbers." In addition, because members of prisoners' networks often stayed in touch with one another even after the release of their sons (Rosenfeld, 2004, 293, 298), they became the basis for more lasting patterns of political participation.

Imprisonment also brought families and friends of prisoners into emergent civic networks. With the revival of Palestinian civic life in the early 1980s, a growing number of civic associations began engaging in outreach to families of prisoners and detainees. On Prisoners' Day and Prisoners' Week, civic associations distributed "material support" and gifts to families of detainees and organized ceremonies in their honor.[8] For example, in a typical report from 1982 to 1983, *al-Fajr* English reported that the Secondary School Students Committee in Tulkarm visited the families of prisoners being held in Qalqiliya jail and gave them gifts.[9] Women's associations were particularly active in such outreach activities. For example, a 1983 publication of the Union of Palestinian Women's Committees (UPWC) stated: "The UPWC is not isolated from the reality of life of our people in the Occupied Territories. Last year, after the Lebanon War, we conducted a campaign to collect donations in order to give gifts and aid to those of our people who were injured in

---

[8] See e.g. "Prisoners' Families Aided" 1982, April 29. *Jerusalem Dawn Palestinian Weekly* 3(103) 15; "Prisoners' Week" 1982, May 6. *Jerusalem Dawn Palestinian Weekly* 3(104), 2.

[9] "Students See Prisoners' Families" 1983, April 22. *Jerusalem Dawn Palestinian Weekly* 4(155), 15.

South Lebanon. *We also paid visits to families of Palestinian prisoners and gave them presents, expressing our solidarity with them on Prisoners' Day, 17 April.*" (quoted in Hiltermann, 1993, 169; my emphasis).[10] Similarly, Tahani Abu Daqa, a female DFLP activist, recalled: "When the intifadah broke out in December 1987, I started organizing women to support the wounded and assist them to get the medical treatment they deserved. *We also helped the families of Palestinians whom the Israeli military had imprisoned*" (quoted in Gordon, Gordon, and Shriteh 2003, 37; my emphasis).

As a result of such efforts, relatives and friends of prisoners became connected to politicized civic networks and gained access to reliable information about resistance. In some cases, political activists used civil society associations to mobilize prisoners' families and communicate and coordinate with them before protest events. Describing the process of preparing for demonstrations, former Shabiba and Fatah activist Adnan Milhelm noted the importance of visiting the families of prisoners and "martyrs" to gain their participation: "We used to prepare for certain national occasions for a while and not the night before; we had an agenda... Some of us will write a statement, or some of the statements come from other areas... Another section would buy paint cans and write graffiti ... *Another section was for visiting the prisoners' for example and martyrs' families* [my emphasis] and, on the day itself, there was a section responsible for the demonstrations... and another section for the schools, for recruiting the students" (Interview, A. Milhelm, Nablus, March 10, 2014).

Due to these new extra-local and civic networks, prisoners' relatives and friends became active participants in the burgeoning protests against the Israeli occupation. Relatives and friends of imprisoned Palestinians held frequent solidarity protests, strikes, and sit-ins in support of prisoners, often in parallel with prison strikes inside Israeli jails (Rosenfeld, 2004, 294). For example, in a typical report dated February 4, 1983, *al-Fajr* English reported that relatives of Palestinian prisoners in Israel's Nafha jail had been holding solidarity protests since January 22, when seventy-six Nafha prisoners began a hunger strike.[11] In general, prisoners' relatives formed the core of an active prisoners' movement that was integrated into the broader Palestinian national movement against

---

[10] The UPWC is the federation of women's working committees associated with the PFLP.
[11] "Nafha Prisoners Launch Hunger Strike" 1983, February 4. *Jerusalem Dawn Palestinian Weekly* 4(114), A.

Israeli occupation. According to Ibrahim Hamirshe, a former prisoner and director of the Palestinian Prisoner Club in Tulkarm, "The prison and prisoners have been and continue to have a large effect on motivating nationalist work outside the camps through the prisoners' movement and their integration into the greater nationalist movement. It still has a prominent role on the Palestinian street."[12]

For many Palestinian families, participation in solidarity protests like the Nafha protests was their first foray into political activism. As Maya Rosenfeld describes, "Men and women alike who had never in their lives joined protest activities over prisoners' issues, such as sit-down strikes, demonstrations and processions, told me how everything changed when their relatives were in prison" (Rosenfeld, 2004, 275). Importantly, however, political activism among prisoner's relatives and friends was not confined to prisoners' issues alone, nor did it typically end with the release of a prisoner. Family members and friends of prisoners also joined in nationalist demonstrations, processions, and other protest activities, further integrating them into the wider Palestinian national movement. After the release of their loved ones from prison, these families often remained in close contact with each other, as well as with nationalist activists they had come to know through their loved ones' incarceration and subsequent political activism (Rosenfeld, 2004, 280, 293–98). As a result of these ongoing contacts and their continued advantages for collective action, families and friends of former prisoners often remained politically active even after they were no longer integrated into disciplinary institutions.

These accounts suggest that integration into disciplinary institutions joined prisoners' relatives and friends in wider and more information-rich social networks and made them more likely to participate in anti-regime resistance. Integration into these institutions linked prisoners' relatives and friends in new, extra-local social networks and fostered communication and coordination between them, improving their capacity for protest. With the revival of Palestinian civil society in the early 1980s, integration into these institutions also brought these individuals into politicized civic networks rich in informational value. In the next section, I turn to the survey data to systematically test the relationship between integration into disciplinary institutions, social networks, and participation in resistance.

---

[12] "The Released Prisoner Ibrahim Hamarishe Discusses His Experiences of Struggle Inside and Outside Zionist Jails" (translated from Arabic). *Al-Quds Newspaper*, date unknown.

4.3 TESTING THE ARGUMENT

This section systematically examines the relationship between integration into disciplinary institutions and participation in anti-regime resistance using the survey data and measures described in the previous chapter. As in the previous chapter, the main dependent variable is a binary indicator of participation in anti-regime resistance.[13] The main independent variable is the imprisonment of a family member or close friend. To measure this variable, this chapter relies on respondents' self-reported answers to an open-ended survey question, which followed a series of questions about exposure to violence. Respondents were first asked if they had personally been the victims of violence perpetrated by Israeli soldiers or settlers, where violence was explicitly defined to include arrest. Respondents were next asked if they had a family member or close friend who had been a victim of violence perpetrated by Israeli soldiers or settlers. All respondents who answered "yes" were then asked to describe what happened, as in the following question. Respondents were coded as having a family member or close friend who had been imprisoned in a given year if they indicated that such a person was either imprisoned or arrested that year, as arrest typically involved detention of at least eighteen days and often longer (i.e. "administrative detention").

"If you said that any of your family members, friends, or associates were physically harmed by [Israeli] soldiers or settlers, would you mind telling us what happened?"

Drawing on this measure, Figure 4.1 shows the marginal effect of the imprisonment of a family member or friend on the likelihood that an individual will go on to participate in anti-regime resistance. As in the previous chapter, this effect is based on a multilevel logistic regression model with varying intercepts by locality (i.e. locality-level random effects). It controls for age, wealth, any secular trends in the prevalence of imprisonment and/or resistance, and duration dependence.[14] These results are robust to an alternative coding of the dependent variable

---

[13] As described below, the following results are also robust to an alternate coding of this variable, which excludes organized prison visits as a form of participation.

[14] The model controls for a secular trend through the inclusion of period dummy variables (i.e. period fixed effects) and duration dependence through the inclusion of cubic splines.

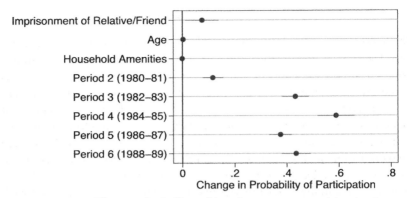

FIGURE 4.1 The marginal effect of imprisonment on participation in
anti-regime resistance
*Note: Marginal effects from multilevel logistic regression model with varying
intercepts by locality (i.e. locality-level random effects). Additional control
variables not shown include cubic splines to control for duration dependence.
N=2897 observations.*

excluding organized prison visits, as well as to two additional alternative
model specifications.[15]

Consistent with this chapter's argument, Figure 4.1 shows that the
imprisonment of a family member or friend is associated with a significantly higher likelihood of future participation in anti-regime resistance
($p < 0.05$). Specifically, having a family member or friend imprisoned
is associated with an 8 percentage point increase in an individual's
probability of participation. For a typical individual in the sample, the
imprisonment of a relative or friend raises the predicted probability of
participation from 37 percent to 45 percent.[16] At nearly 0.20 standard deviations, this effect is not only statistically significant but also
substantively important.

An immediate concern is that reverse causality could be driving the
relationship between imprisonment of a family member or friend and
participation in anti-regime resistance. For a number of reasons, participants in resistance are likely to have family members and friends who

[15] These alternative models include locality-level fixed effects instead of random
effects and individual-level robust clustered standard errors in place of cubic
splines. See Section A.2 in the online appendix for all robustness checks: www
.cambridge.org/TheRevolutionWithin

[16] Predicted probabilities were calculated by setting all continuous independent variables
at their means and all categorical variables at their modal value.

also become politically active and who, therefore, are also more likely to be arrested and imprisoned. As a result, participation in resistance could cause individuals to have a family member or close friend imprisoned and not the other way around. In the Palestinian context, participants in anti-regime resistance may also be more likely to have family members or friends imprisoned as a form of collective punishment. For example, anecdotal evidence exists that Israeli security forces sometimes detained activists' associates in the process of arresting activists. As described earlier, simply lagging the independent variable of imprisonment, as I have done so far, only partially addresses this problem.

Such issues of reverse causality affect nearly all existing research on the impact of repression on protest. Some innovative new research in political science has largely overcome these problems by making use of natural experiments that exploit random or quasi-random variation in specific instruments of repression such as indiscriminate shelling (Lyall, 2009) or military checkpoints (Longo, Canetti, and Hite-Rubin, 2014). However, given the nonrandom nature of imprisonment, it is difficult to conceive of a similar natural experiment that could be used to identify its causal impact.

In the absence of a plausible natural experiment, I take a statistical approach to correcting for possible reverse causality. Specifically, as in the previous chapter, I model the first onset of participation in anti-regime resistance among previously politically inactive individuals. In this model, I estimate the association between the imprisonment of a relative or friend in period t on the likelihood that a politically inactive individual first begins to participate in resistance in period $t+1$.[17] While this model does not rule out all forms of endogeneity, it eliminates the possibility of simple reverse causality – for example, due to the systematic arrest and imprisonment of political activists' friends and relatives.

Figure 4.2 shows the effect of the imprisonment of a family member or friend on the probability that a previously politically inactive individual first begins to participate in anti-regime resistance ("adjusted model"). For reference, it also displays the previously shown effect of the imprisonment of a family member or friend on the probability of future participation in resistance ("unadjusted model"). As Figure 4.2 shows, the effect of the imprisonment of a family member or friend is consistent across the two models. After correcting for reverse causality, the imprisonment of a family member or friend is associated with a 6 percentage

---

[17] Note that this is equivalent to a three-year lag in the independent variable.

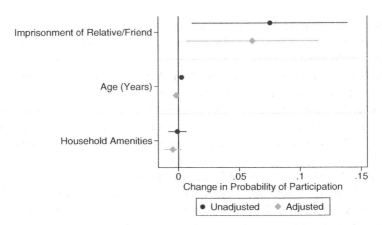

FIGURE 4.2 The marginal effect of imprisonment on participation in
anti-regime resistance (adjusted for reverse causality)
*Note: Marginal effects from multilevel logit model with varying intercepts by
locality (i.e. locality-level random effects). Additional control variables not
shown include period dummies and cubic splines. N=2897 observations
(unadjusted); N=1226 (adjusted).*

point increase in the probability of participation in resistance, and this
effect remains statistically significant at the 95 percent confidence level.

These results provide confidence that the observed association
between the imprisonment of a family member or friend and participation in anti-regime resistance is not due to simple reverse causality. However, it could still be due to selection bias stemming from a latent variable
that predicts both the imprisonment of a relative or friend and participation in protest. For example, if prisoners tend to come from more nationalist families, then this family background would predict both the imprisonment of a relative and participation in protest and, therefore, could
also potentially alter the relationship between them. The next section
thus evaluates the robustness of the results to controlling for a wide variety of such variables, including family background and political socialization within the family, general exposure to repression, and generational
effects.

4.3.1   Robustness Checks

This section tests the robustness of this chapter's main results to accounting for the political and social processes through which some individuals
come to have relatives and friends imprisoned while others do not.

Imprisonment in the Palestinian Territories was not a random occurrence. While indiscriminate arrests were not uncommon during the first intifadah (Ron, 2000, 455), many people – particularly those imprisoned in earlier periods – were arrested for their participation in, connection with, or proximity to some form of political activity. This fact suggests that there are common "risk factors" that predispose some individuals to both have a relative or friend imprisoned and participate in anti-regime resistance. As such, in order to prevent these factors from biasing the results, it is important to control for them in the statistical analysis.

The first such risk factor is political socialization within the family. Political socialization is the process by which individuals acquire their political beliefs, values, and behaviors. Families are powerful agents of political socialization. Individuals from nationalist families – that is, from families that have a history of support for or participation in nationalist resistance – are both more likely to have relatives and friends imprisoned for anti-regime activity and to participate in such activity themselves. As a result, when analyzing the relationship between the imprisonment of a relative or friend and an individual's participation in protest, it is important to control for his family's general political orientation.

To capture families' political orientations, I control for all relevant family-level characteristics on which survey data are available. Specifically, I control for refugee status stemming from the 1948 War, land alienation during the 1948 War, and fathers' level of education and profession. Refugees and individuals whose families lost land during the 1948 War should have more intense nationalist grievances, which they are likely to pass on to their children (see e.g. Khalidi, 2010). As a result, these children are both more likely to have a relative or friend imprisoned for nationalist political activity (e.g. a sibling or cousin) and to participate in such activity themselves. Moreover, in historically patriarchal societies such as Palestinian society, fathers' level of education and profession should also exert a strong influence on the political attitudes and behavior of other family members.[18]

A second possible risk factor is an individual's general vulnerability to state repression or violence. Individuals with relatives or friends who have been imprisoned may simply be more vulnerable or exposed to state repression in the first place. They may be more likely to have experienced,

---

[18] See the codebook for a description of these variables and how they are coded.

or to know others who have experienced, physical harm, land confiscation, or property damage. In this case, it is possible that these general
experiences of repression – rather than the specific experience of having a loved one imprisoned – may account for their greater propensity
to participate in protest. To some extent, the empirical analysis already
controls for this possibility by including locality-level fixed or random
effects that account for variation in exposure to repression across different localities (e.g. a refugee camp versus a remote village). However, it is
still possible that other group or individual-level differences in exposure
to repression could account for the observed relationship between the
imprisonment of a loved one and protest participation. To help rule out
this possibility, I thus include an index of exposure to repression in the
analysis.[19]

Finally, as described earlier, temporal dynamics could also account for
the patterns of participation in anti-regime resistance observed here. Due,
in part, to Israel's policy of using legal, if highly coercive, practices to put
down protest (Ron, 2000), incarceration rates grew in tandem with rates
of anti-regime resistance throughout the 1970s and 1980s. The empirical
analysis already presented controls for this secular trend in imprisonment
and resistance by including period fixed effects (i.e. dummy variables for
each period). However, the upward trend in imprisonment and resistance
presents an additional, inferential challenge: the relationship between the
two variables could be due to a "generational effect." To illustrate, members of what is known as "the intifadah generation" should be more
likely both to count prisoners among their relatives and friends and to
participate in anti-regime resistance themselves. Thus, in addition to controlling for an individual's age and for secular trends in the data, it is
also important to control for an individual's generation by including an
interaction term of age and time period.

Table 4.1 shows the relationship between the imprisonment of a relative or friend and future participation in anti-regime resistance after
controlling for all of the already-mentioned risk factors. To facilitate
comparison between statistical models and see how different control variables may influence the results, I present the results showing each group
of control variables separately, as well as all control variables together.
For reference, Column 1 shows the results from the baseline random

---

[19] This variable is measured as the average of respondents' answers to survey question 5.4
regarding indirect exposure to physical harm, land confiscation, or property damage.
See the survey questionnaire and codebook for additional details.

TABLE 4.1 *The effect of imprisonment on anti-regime resistance: robustness checks*

Participation	1	2	3	4	5
Imprisonment of Relative/Friend	0.07***	0.08***	0.05*	0.07***	0.08**
	(0.03)	(0.03)	(0.03)	(0.03)	(0.03)
Age (Years)	0.00***	0.00*	0.00***	0.01***	0.01***
	(0.00)	(0.00)	(0.00)	(0.00)	(0.00)
Wealth	−0.00	−0.00	−0.01**	−0.00	−0.00
	(0.00)	(0.00)	(0.00)	(0.00)	(0.00)
Socialization Controls					
Refugee Status		−0.05			−0.05
		(0.04)			(0.04)
Land Alienation		0.01			−0.02
		(0.05)			(0.05)
Father's Education		−0.01			−0.02
		(0.02)			(0.02)
Father's Profession		−0.05**			−0.05*
		(0.03)			(0.03)
Exposure to Repression					
Repression Index			0.08*		0.05
			(0.04)		(0.05)
Generational Effects					
Age × Period 2				−0.00	−0.00
				(0.00)	(0.00)
Age × Period 3				−0.01***	−0.01**
				(0.00)	(0.00)
Age × Period 4				−0.02***	−0.02***
				(0.00)	(0.00)
Age × Period 5				−0.02***	−0.01***
				(0.00)	(0.00)
Age × Period 6				−0.01***	−0.01***
				(0.00)	(0.00)
Constant	0.24***	0.28***	0.26***	0.05	0.13***
	(0.02)	(0.03)	(0.02)	(0.04)	(0.05)
Observations	2897	2363	2543	2897	2139

GLS regression coefficients with standard errors in parentheses.
All models include locality random effects, period fixed effects, and cubic splines.
*p<0.10 **p<0.05 ***p<0.01

effects model (i.e. Figure 4.1). Column 2 displays the results controlling for political socialization within the family. Column 3 displays the results controlling for general exposure to repression, and Column 4 shows the results controlling for generational effects. Column 5 shows the results when all control variables are included in the model together.[20]

As seen in the table, the relationship between the imprisonment of a relative or friend and participation in anti-regime resistance persists even after controlling for these possible risk factors, which could otherwise confound the analysis. In all of the models, the imprisonment of a loved one is associated with a 5 to 8 percentage point increase in the likelihood of participating in resistance in the future ($p<0.10$ or lower). The consistency of this association across diverse model specifications offers additional confidence that this statistical association is robust.

Overall, these results demonstrate that there is a strong and robust statistical association between the imprisonment of a relative or friend and future participation in anti-regime resistance. Because imprisonment does not occur completely at random, this analysis is unable to establish a causal effect of imprisonment on resistance. However, it does rule out the possibility that the relationship between the imprisonment of a loved one and protest participation is due to simple reverse causality or to the main "risk factors" for bias, including political socialization, general exposure to repression, and generational effects.

4.4 TESTING THE CAUSAL MECHANISMS

The preceding analysis demonstrates that integration into disciplinary institutions increases the probability of participation in anti-regime resistance. What accounts for this relationship? This chapter has argued that integration into state-controlled prisons and courts can paradoxically help individuals to overcome key informational and organizational barriers to collective action and, thus, renders them better able to participate in resistance. In particular, the imprisonment of a family member or friend joins individuals in wider, more information-rich social networks, which provide them with needed information about the occurrence, size, and scope of protests.

---

[20] Due to non-convergence of the maximum likelihood estimates in some specifications, multilevel generalized least squares (GLS) regression was used in place of multilevel logistic regression. GLS regression models produce consistent coefficient estimates for binary as well as continuous dependent variables.

In this section, I evaluate this causal mechanism by examining the relationship between the imprisonment of a relative or friend and the breadth of an individual's social networks. As in Chapter 3, I measure the breadth of an individual's social networks using two measures: the size of an individual's *extra-local networks*, or social ties outside his own family and community, and the size of an individual's *civic networks*. These measures capture the two key ways in which the imprisonment of a loved one is believed to broaden an individual's social networks. These ways are by creating extra-local networks of prisoners' families that cut across local and familial lines, as well as fostering contacts between prisoners' relatives and friends, on the one hand, and politicized members of civil society organizations on the other.

Figure 4.3 presents the marginal effect of the imprisonment of a relative or friend on the breadth of an individual's social networks.[21] The top panel of the figure shows the marginal effect of imprisonment on the size of an individual's extra-local networks, and the bottom panel shows the marginal effect of imprisonment on the size of his civic networks. As seen in the figure, the imprisonment of a relative or friend is associated with an increase in the size of both types of networks. Imprisonment is associated with a 0.25 increase in the size of an individual's extra-local networks and a 0.31 increase in the size of his civic networks. To help put these findings into perspective, these effects are equivalent to an approximately one-quarter standard deviation increase in the size of an individual's extra-local networks and an approximately one-third standard deviation in civic networks.[22] These results are robust to accounting for reverse causality using the same approach as in Section 4.3 and the previous chapter.[23]

In sum, the imprisonment of a relative or friend is associated with having wider social networks, which provide greater access to information and make individuals better able to participate in resistance. In addition to increasing individuals' capacity for protest, however, the

---

[21] Marginal effects from OLS regression model with locality and period fixed effects and robust clustered standard errors (i.e. clustered at the individual level).

[22] These figures are similar to the coefficients because the standard deviation of both variables is approximately equal to 1.

[23] The results of this analysis are generally consistent with my previous findings. After accounting for reverse causality, the effect of imprisonment on extra-local networks is consistent although it is slightly statistically weaker (p=0.13). The effect of imprisonment on civic networks is also similar as to before and remains statistically significant (p<0.10).

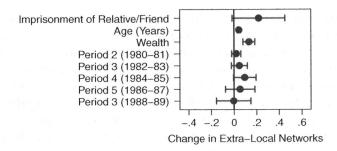

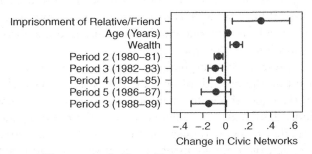

FIGURE 4.3 The marginal effect of imprisonment on social network size
Note: Marginal effects from OLS regression models with locality and period fixed effects and robust clustered standard errors (on individual). N=3054 (extra-local networks); N=2737 (civic networks).

imprisonment of a relative or friend could also radicalize individuals and make them more willing to resist state power. The next section examines this alternative causal mechanism.

4.4.1 Alternative Explanations: Radicalization

Radicalization is the most important alternative mechanism that could explain the relationship between integration into disciplinary institutions and participation in anti-regime resistance. As a form of state repression, integration into disciplinary institutions could politicize previously apathetic individuals or radicalize formerly more moderate ones, rendering them more willing to protest. A large and long-standing scholarly literature links state repression to higher levels of protest (see e.g. Lichbach and Gurr, 1981; Jenkins and Schock, 2003; Longo, Canetti, and Hite-Rubin, 2014; Lawrence, 2017). According to these works, repression makes individuals more willing to protest by undermining the legitimacy of the regime, strengthening anti-regime grievances, and radicalizing anti-regime opponents. The policy of repression may itself become a target of protest by anti-regime movements. As Lichbach and Gurr put it: "The apathetic become politicized, the reformers become radicalized and the revolutionaries double their efforts" (Lichbach and Gurr, 1981).

Testing the radicalization mechanism is challenging. An ideal test of this hypothesis would require collecting reliable data on individual political attitudes before and after the imprisonment of a family member or friend. Yet, due to the difficulties of conducting field research in conflict zones, most micro-level studies – including this one – are conducted only after conflict abates. While this makes collecting reliable data more difficult in general (see Chapter 3 for a discussion of this problem and this study's solution), it presents particular challenges for collecting attitudinal data, which are strongly shaped by present-day considerations. As a result, the survey questionnaire used in this study deliberately avoided including attitudinal questions in favor of asking more objective behavioral questions.

This section examines the impact of the imprisonment of a relative or friend on radicalization using such a behavioral measure. Specifically, it measures radicalization – the dependent variable or outcome of interest – using a binary indicator for reading a pro-PLO nationalist newspaper such as *al-Fajr*. As described previously, while Palestinian newspapers were censored during this time period and could not print any specific information about protest, they continued to print more general nationalist content. At the same time, consuming nationalist news media is an admittedly imperfect measure of radicalization, as grievances may not always influence media consumption habits. For example, it is conceivable that Palestinians could simultaneously harbor intense national grievances against Israeli occupation and pay little attention to the Palestinian nationalist media. However, to the extent that reading a nationalist newspaper is correlated with such strong grievances, it is a reasonable proxy variable for radicalization.

Figure 4.4 displays the association between the imprisonment of a relative or friend and radicalization, controlling for key confounding factors.[24] This figure shows mixed results for the proposition that the imprisonment of a relative or friend gives rise to more radical grievances

---

[24] As indicated in the figure, these factors include age, wealth, education, newspaper readership in general, locality, and time period (i.e. through the inclusion of locality and period fixed effects).

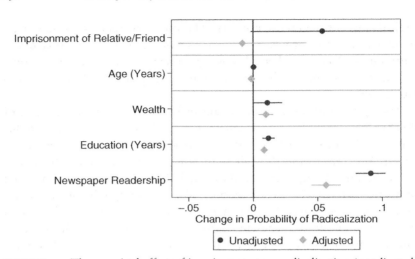

FIGURE 4.4 The marginal effect of imprisonment on radicalization (unadjusted and adjusted for reverse causality)
Note: Marginal effects from OLS regression models with locality and period fixed effects and robust clustered standard errors (on individual). N=3285 (unadjusted); N=1775 (adjusted).

or demands. The results of the baseline model indicate that imprisonment is associated with a large increase in the probability of reading a pro-PLO nationalist newspaper (i.e. the "unadjusted model"). However, after accounting for reverse causality using my previous approach, this finding disappears. The imprisonment variable switches signs from positive to negative, and it is no longer statistically significant. Importantly, accounting for reverse causality does not meaningfully alter the coefficients on the other variables in the model. For example, two main correlates of reading a nationalist newspaper – education and general newspaper readership – remain positive and statistically significant. These findings suggest that the adjusted model is statistically valid. Thus, while further research is needed, the results of the adjusted model cast some doubt on the radicalization hypothesis.

This, however, does not mean that the imprisonment of a relative or friend does not affect an individual's political interests in any way whatsoever. In particular, it seems very likely that the imprisonment of a loved one gives individuals a strong, direct stake in collective action, particularly solidarity actions undertaken in direct support of the prisoners' struggle. At the same time, it is unclear whether these "higher stakes" would have translated into participation in risky anti-regime resistance in the absence of informational networks. For example, Rosenfeld notes that, before the expansion of mass incarceration and the corresponding increase in prisoners' networks, many prisoners' families stayed away from any kind of collective activity (Rosenfeld, 2004, 294). Thus, while additional research is needed to assess the respective role of interests and networks, the available evidence suggests that interests alone may be insufficient to compel participation in high-risk protest.

4.5 CONCLUSIONS

Integration into disciplinary institutions made prisoners' family members and friends more likely to participate in anti-regime protests. Integration into these institutions joined prisoners' relatives and friends in new extra-local social networks and fostered communication and coordination across local lines, providing them with greater access to information about protest. As Palestinian civil society began to flourish again in the early 1980s, integration into these institutions also connected family members and friends of prisoners to emergent civic networks. As a result, they were more likely to participate in anti-regime resistance than before. Importantly, this newfound political activism did not end with a prisoner's release. Rather, qualitative evidence indicates that family members and friends of prisoners often continued to join in nationalist demonstrations and processions even after their loved ones were no longer incarcerated. Given the persistent impact of integration into educational institutions seen in the previous chapter, this suggests that integration into disciplinary institutions may also have a long-lasting effect.

One reason for this potentially long-standing impact of disciplinary institutions may be the civic networks to which they give rise. In the next chapter, I show that these new civic ties increased the probability that individuals would participate in anti-regime protest. Yet, contrary to studies that see such social structures and networks as necessary for protest to emerge, these civic networks did not precipitate resistance. Rather, as I describe in the following chapter, they evolved only after protest was well underway as, facing tightening repression, activists sought to build a communications network that could better sustain and spread resistance.

5

Beyond State Institutions: Civil Society
and the Coordination of Resistance

5.1 INTRODUCTION

Saturday, September 4, 1982: Over fifty youths belonging to the Youth Committees for Social Work spent the hottest part of the day moving stones, passing buckets, and providing water for workers in a clean-up and beautification campaign. The youths belonged to different neighborhood committees throughout the city of Jerusalem and its suburbs: Wadi Joz, Beit Hanina, Tur, Hizma, Qatanna, Silwan and Shuafat [refugee camp].[1]

Saturday, July 2, 1983: Over two hundred volunteers from the Tulkarm Union of Public Institutions and Construction Workers traveled to Barga, a village neighboring the city of Tulkarm, for a comprehensive clean-up campaign. According to Imad Labadi, the head of the Union's voluntary work committee, such work "reinforces relations between people and unites them against the occupation forces."[2]

Saturday, February 1984 (day unknown): A team of doctors, nurses, and staff belonging to the Makassed Hospital Medical Relief Committee traveled from Jerusalem to the Hebron area village of Idna to participate in a medical relief day. The visit took place in the headquarters of the local women's committee, and other local associations cooperated to spread the word. The team saw over two hundred patients and shared a

---

[1] Kuttab, Daoud. 1982, September 10–16. "Voluntary Work at al-Fajr." *Jerusalem Dawn Palestinian Weekly* 3(123), 7.

[2] Abdel Fattah, A. 1983, July 15. "Tulkarm Union of Public Institutions and Construction Workers: Serving the Community." *Jerusalem Dawn Palestinian Weekly* (4)167, 7.

meal with village residents, building "more casual relationships" between them.[3]

As the Israeli occupation entered its fifteenth year, Palestinian civil society was changing. After years of stagnation under authoritarian rule and occupation, independent civil society organizations began to flourish once more. As new organizations sprouted up and old ones gained new members, mass protests also became more coordinated and widespread. With new civic networks in place to join political activists to state institutions and local communities, as well as to connect these institutions and communities to one another, independent protests were fused into a nationwide protest campaign.

This book argues that, while state institutions facilitate mass protests among organizationally weak groups, civic organizations are needed to subsequently transform these protests into a nationwide uprising. As legal or quasi-legal structures, civic organizations serve as important conduits for political information in repressive regimes. By working within these organizations, political activists can reach into state institutions and local communities and openly forge ties with the individuals within them. Civic associations also serve as the connective tissue linking different state institutions, as well as the communities in which they are embedded, to one another. Without civic associations, in contrast, information about protest campaigns may not always enter institutional networks or travel between distant and unconnected state institutions. In this case, integration into state institutions should still promote participation in anti-regime protest, but these protests may remain relatively disconnected and uncoordinated.

This argument suggests two testable empirical implications that are situated at different levels of analysis. At the individual or "micro" level, individuals with wider civic networks – that is, with social ties connecting them to a larger number of civil society organizations – should be more likely to participate in protest than those with narrower ones. As a result of their informational advantages, these more networked individuals should be better able to protest and have a higher average probability of participation than those with fewer civic ties. Consistent with this hypothesis, this chapter finds that incorporation into civic networks significantly increases the probability of individual participation in protest. Importantly, it also shows that individuals within these networks were

---

[3] "West Bank Volunteers Offer Health Ed and Medical Relief." 1984, February 15. *Jerusalem Dawn Palestinian Weekly* 5(198), 7, 10.

more risk-averse than non-networked individuals and were also similar to them in many other respects. This suggests that these individuals' higher propensity for protest is due to their wider civic networks rather than to other preexisting characteristics or attributes.

Moving from the level of the individual to the "meso-level" of the political movement (Earl, 2011), the growth of civil society organizations and networks should also be associated with rising coordination among protestors. Consistent with this hypothesis, this chapter provides initial evidence that, as civil society associations grew and spread throughout the Palestinian Territories in the early 1980s, protests against the Israeli occupation also became more synchronized and widespread. While systematically testing the relationship between civil society strength and the degree of coordination within protest campaigns would require different data than my own, this chapter suggests that the two may well be linked.

Together with the previous chapters, this chapter's findings challenge our understanding of the relationship between a group's internal organizational strength and its propensity for unarmed protest. As described earlier, internal organizational strength, in the form of strong, independent civil society organizations, is often seen as a prerequisite for the emergence of unarmed protest (see e.g. McAdam, 2010; Tilly and Tarrow, 2007; Nepstad, 2011). Yet, as this chapter and volume demonstrate, a strong Palestinian civil society developed after, and in response to, an increase in protest activity rather than the other way around. While civil society associations were important players in the Palestinian national movement against Israeli occupation, they helped to spread and coordinate anti-occupation resistance rather than give rise to it. Thus, internal organizational strength may be more important for explaining the future growth and success of anti-regime movements than for predicting their initial emergence. As such, investigating the impact of civil society associations on the trajectory of unarmed resistance and how this impact varies over the life cycle of resistance movements represents a fruitful path for future study.

At a more "micro" level, this chapter's findings also improve our understanding of the mechanisms by which civil society organizations affect individual participation in anti-regime resistance. A large literature argues that membership in civil society organizations makes individuals more likely to participate in high-risk collective action by activating social norms and pressures (see e.g. Della Porta, 1988; Laitin, 1995; McAdam, 1986; Opp and Gern, 1993; Petersen, 2001; Scacco, n.d.). Strong ties between civil society members, this perspective holds, generate intense pressures for members to join the fray when their fellow members do. In contrast, this chapter shows that civic networks – relatively weaker social ties between civil society members and nonmembers – make nonmembers more likely to participate in protest. Whereas weak ties are not as powerful as strong ties for influencing behavior, they are arguably more important for disseminating information (Granovetter, 1973; Burt, 2009; McAdam, 1986). These findings provide more direct evidence for Beissinger's conclusions about the importance of weak ties in the Orange Revolution in Ukraine and the relative insignificance of stronger organizational affiliations (Beissinger, 2011; 2013). Taken together with prior work, they suggest that, while other mechanisms may be more important for motivating participation in violent resistance or different types of unarmed resistance,[4] civil society organizations play an important information and coordination role during mass protests. Therefore, theorizing about the interplay between a movement's tactics and organizations also offers a promising direction for future research.

5.2 THE RISE OF CIVIC NETWORKS AND A NATIONWIDE PROTEST MOVEMENT

As dissent began to swell in the late 1970s, Palestinian protests against the Israeli occupation tended to be localized and uncoordinated. School students, the prisoners' movement, and members of nascent civil society institutions all participated in protest in rising numbers, but these groups remained largely isolated and disconnected from one another as well as from the vast majority of Palestinians (see e.g. Taraki, 1984, 454). Yet, with the emergence of a new network of civil society associations over the following decade, these groups would join together in a coordinated national uprising against Israeli occupation.

This section traces the development of new civic networks over the decade leading up to the first intifadah and their role in fusing disparate groups together into a national protest movement. It shows that, in forming and working to grow civil society associations, Palestinian political activists aimed to build a new social and communications network that could better connect Palestinians across narrow and particularistic lines of social interaction. Using open and quasi-legal civic institutions, these activists worked to build top-down vertical ties to local communities

---

[4] For example, McAdam (1986) finds formal organizational affiliations were important for motivating participation in voter registration drives, educational activism, and other activities of the Freedom Summer Project.

and new horizontal relations between them through which information about protest could be disseminated and spread. By the mid-1980s, with this network in place, protests against Israeli occupation showed a new national scope and unity, which culminated with the outbreak of the first intifadah.

As Palestinian students, prisoners' families, and others began to protest against Israeli occupation in rising numbers, they initially lacked the means to coordinate their efforts. With Palestinian society divided along regional, local, and familial lines, no national communications network existed to bridge the different institutions and communities rising up in protest. In contrast to the case of the American civil rights movement, there were few strong autonomous institutions that could join Palestinians in a broad-based national movement. For example, as described in Chapter 2, civil society organizations were largely detached from other segments of Palestinian society as anti-occupation protest mounted. Confined to the main Palestinian cities and limited in size, they remained disconnected from the small villages and towns in which the vast majority of Palestinians still resided. As such, while their own members were politically active, they initially lacked the broader social constituency needed for mass mobilization.

Similarly, the National Guidance Committee also lacked widespread roots in Palestinian society at large. After its formation in 1978, the Committee briefly provided leadership to the nationalist opposition in the West Bank, unifying the mayors, emergent civic organizations, and other members of the new nationalist elite (Peretz, 1990, 389; Sahliyeh, 1988, 71–77). Yet, as a coalition of urban elites and professionals in large cities and towns, the NGC generally lacked ties to the vast majority of Palestinians living in more rural communities (Frisch, 1993, 260). Moreover, as a centralized, national political body, it was subject to increasingly heavy repression and harassment by the Israeli military authorities. By the summer of 1980, seven of the NGC's most active members were placed on town arrest, prohibited from attending political rallies and making political statements, and even barred from having a telephone (Sahliyeh, 1988, 83–84). With their telephone lines cut by military officials, they were literally cut off from communicating with the growing number of Palestinians willing to directly challenge Israeli authority.

In the absence of a preexisting communications network that could help coordinate the different groups now protesting against Israeli occupation, Palestinian nationalist factions sought to build a new network of civil society associations that could serve this purpose. Where they are allowed or tolerated, civil society associations provide opposition movements with unique advantages for communicating and coordinating under repression. As members of legal or quasi-legal civic associations, political activists can reach into state institutions and local communities and openly forge "vertical ties" with the individuals within them. Civic associations also provide activists with a diffuse and decentralized framework, which can better withstand state repression, for unifying and connecting different social groups and constituencies involved in protest. As a result, as unarmed protest gained ground in the Palestinian Territories, building civic associations became an important priority for local PLO activists, such as those that founded the Shabiba (youth) movement.

5.2.1 The Making of a Network: The Case of the Shabiba Youth Movement

The case of the Shabiba movement illustrates the connective function of civil society organizations and their role in unifying local and regional protests to form a nationwide movement. The Shabiba movement is a chapter-based youth movement associated with the Palestinian Fatah party, which first originated in 1980. With the resources and backing of Fatah, historically the largest and most politically powerful Palestinian faction, it became the largest of several such youth movements founded around this time. By 1983, it had more than one hundred local chapters in Palestinian cities, towns, and villages, which mobilized students in each community as well as worked in concert with one another.

The Shabiba movement began as a local initiative. In 1980, young Fatah activists from the northern West Bank village of Anabta founded the first local Shabiba committee in the Palestinian Territories. This founding group recruited over four hundred students and youth to join the committee and participate in its activities, which combined social welfare provision with political education and activism (Interview, A, Milhelm, Nablus, March 10, 2014).[5] Mimicking the strategy of the Communist Party before them, committee members – which included both young Fatah activists and non-affiliated youth – cleaned streets, restored graveyards, and assisted farmers with the olive harvest. These

---

[5] Shabiba membership was generally open to young men under thirty-five years old. Students were the main participants, although nonstudent youth also participated in smaller numbers.

formal members were often joined in their endeavors by a larger network of loose supporters or "friends," although the distinctions between
the two groups were somewhat blurry. Within a year of the founding
of the Anabta committee, Fatah supporters in the town of Beit Sahour
near Bethlehem and the Shuafat refugee camp in Jerusalem also formed
local committees in their communities (Jamal, 2005, 82; Interview 12,
Fatah/Shabiba activist, Shuafat Camp, March 7, 2014). By 1983, more
than one hundred local Shabiba committees had joined together to form
the General Federation for the Youth Committees of Social Work (Jamal,
2005, 81–82).

The Shabiba movement joined Palestinians in new vertical and horizontal relations, which transcended existing, more narrow and particularistic lines of interaction. Through their involvement in Shabiba,
seasoned Fatah activists formed new vertical ties to the politicized students and youth who joined the committees or participated in their
activities. This "middle layer" of civil society members and supporters, in turn, connected political activists to a broader spectrum of
Palestinian society. As I will describe, by working through Shabiba's
members and supporters, activists were able to reach within schools
and organize students to protest. Similarly, through the committees'
social welfare projects, activists also forged new vertical ties to prisoners' families and other social groups. As one former Fatah/Shabiba
member described: "We would organize projects for cleaning the streets,
for the olive harvest; we would provide support for the prisoners' families. This is what the Communists had been doing, so we tried to do
the same and do even more for the community than the Communists.
And people saw that now Fatah is doing this and this is something
new, and this is how we made the movement stronger" (Interview 17,
Tulkarm, October 29, 2014). Thus, as the Shabiba movement expanded
and matured, it came to serve as the connective tissue binding "the organization" – Fatah's formal political and military wings – to the wider
public.

In addition to these vertical ties, Shabiba also joined different state
institutions and local communities together in new horizontal webs of
relations. As the movement expanded, each local committee became part
of a regional committee or assembly that connected all local committees
within a given region. These regional bodies brought together students
and youth from different schools and communities. As a result, previously unconnected institutions and communities now became linked
to one another. According to Amal Jamal, this structure gave the local

committees a regional impact that extended beyond their local origins. As Jamal describes: "Although in the initial phase the committees were local initiatives at the village or neighborhood level, they quickly formed a very dynamic and interactive body on the regional level, which gave the local initiatives a comprehensive effect" (Jamal, 2005, 81).

This more comprehensive character of the committees was fostered by design. Consistent with this book's arguments about the connective function of civil society organizations, Shabiba leaders – like those of competing movements – deliberately set about to form a broad-based communications network that could cut across local lines and divisions. As outlined in the Shabiba Constitution and summarized by Amal Jamal:

> The fourth goal of the youth committees was to overcome the localist mentality that characterized the majority of Palestinians in rural society and to *create a regional social network, not only on the organizational-institutional level but also in terms of communication* [my emphasis]. The committees tried to break down the barriers between the village and the city as well as those that prevented contacts between the villages. For this purpose, they organized cultural, social, political and sporting events that brought people from the villages and cities together. Doctors and academics were invited to lecture in the villages, and sports clubs were organized in an attempt to extend the scope of contacts between villages and cities. These gatherings included cultural activities aimed at raising the sociopolitical awareness of the people in the villages and bringing them into a broader socionational web. (Jamal, 2005, 79)

As the youth movement affiliated with Fatah, the largest and most powerful political faction at that time, Shabiba was particularly successful in building this "broader socionational web." However, Fatah was neither the first nor only political faction to attempt to organize Palestinians across traditional, local and familial lines of interaction. According to a DFLP activist involved in the faction's civil society associations, forming wider social networks that cut across traditional cleavages was the first step toward mobilizing Palestinians to participate in protest: "When I was in charge of the student sector, I got people organized regardless of the specific demand being made – *anything to get them organized beyond their families and tribes* [my emphasis]. I would organize people according to their interests and then link their demands to the occupation. In this way, I would move them to participate in the movement against the occupation" (Interview 7, DFLP, Jerusalem, November 7, 2009).

As these remarks illustrate, building a communications network that could connect ordinary Palestinians across more narrow and particularistic lines of interaction was thus an important priority for Palestinian factions from across the political spectrum. The next section traces the formation of such a network, focusing on how political activists, working through the new civil society organizations, forged new relations between people that could be turned to political purposes.

5.2.2 The Expansion of Civic Networks

As the Israeli occupation of the Palestinian Territories continued into its fifteenth year, Palestinian civic organizations and networks underwent a dramatic expansion. By following *al-Fajr's* English-language coverage throughout the 1980s, we can see many examples of increasing linkages between politicized members of civil society associations, state institutions, and local communities, as well as across these groups. For example, a 1982 article on the Sa'ir Youth Committee for Social Work – the Shabiba committee in the Hebron area town of Sa'ir – reported that the committee offered lectures and free courses for high school students studying for their *tawjihi* (secondary school exit) exams and tried to organize local labor unions. These interactions allowed committee members to form new vertical ties to Sa'ir students and workers and forge stronger relationships with them. During this time, *al-Fajr* further reports, the committee also made contacts with nearby "national municipalities," scheduled soccer games with other West Bank clubs, and arranged for a medical relief committee from a Jerusalem hospital to visit Sa'ir.[6] These activities likewise connected Sa'ir and its residents to other communities throughout the West Bank, linking them in new, horizontal webs of relations.

The Makassed Hospital Relief Committee's visit to Sa'ir – one of hundreds such medical relief visits during this period – helps illustrate how civil society organizations and their members forged new bonds within and across local communities. In 1983, supporters of the Palestinian Communist Party founded the Union of Medical Relief Committees to provide medical care and health education in rural communities; over the next three years, other political factions also founded their own unions of health committees. Each health committee consisted of doctors, nurses, staff, and volunteers, who were typically sympathetic to the political faction with which the committee was affiliated. The committees generally

---

[6] "Sa'ir Voluntary Work." 1982, September 10–16. *Jerusalem Dawn Palestinian Weekly –* 3(123), 7.

worked with local civil society associations to organize medical relief visits such as the Sa'ir visit and educate the public about health issues. These interactions gave rise to new ties between political activists and local communities, cities and villages, and different social classes. According to an anonymous doctor interviewed by *al-Fajr*, "After a visit to the village, a new relationship develops between the doctors and the village people. When the villagers see the doctors at the hospital, they are usually afraid of them. But when they meet them at the village, this wall is removed and the relationship becomes more casual."[7]

These new, more casual relationships extended beyond the medical to the political sphere. As Glenn Robinson notes in his book *Building a Palestinian State*: "The relations forged between urban medical professionals and rural populations during the 1980s helped to overcome social fragmentation and intensify nationalist mobilization during this period. Throughout the 1980s, hundreds of health care professionals treated thousands of rural patients in the countryside and, in doing so, *created a network of contacts in hundreds of villages* [my emphasis]. The fact that women's committees often initiated and mediated this interaction helped to encourage more village women to associate with those professionals most active in the effort to recruit and mobilize Palestinians into the nationalist movement" (Robinson, 1997, 51).

Nearly all Palestinian civic associations conducted some kind of charitable or voluntary work both inside and outside their communities, fostering new vertical and horizontal networks. For example, a 1983 article on the Tulkarm Union of Public Institutions and Construction Workers noted that "its activities are not restricted to city workers but extend to most neighboring villages and the two refugee camps in the locale." In 1983, the article reported, the union's voluntary work committee recruited a labor force of 120 volunteers to build a road in the neighboring refugee camp of Nur al-Shams and helped farmers from various villages plant nine hundred olive trees. According to the head of the committee, Imad Labadi, such "voluntary work *reinforces relations between people* [my emphasis] and unites them against the occupation forces."[8]

[7] "West Bank Volunteers Offer Health Ed and Medical Relief." 1984, February 15. *Jerusalem Dawn Palestinian Weekly* 5(198), 7, 10.
[8] Abdel Fattah, A. 1983, July 15. "Tulkarm Union of Public Institutions and Construction Workers: Serving the Community." *Jerusalem Dawn Palestinian Weekly* 4(167), 7.

Similarly, Youth Activities Centres – youth centers located in Palestinian refugee camps – helped foster new relationships between their politicized members and other groups both inside and outside the camps. Although officially sponsored by UNRWA, such centers were often penetrated and coopted by political factions.[9] Thus, like other civic associations, these centers came to play an important connective role. For example, the Dheisheh Camp Center worked with the camp's education committee to recruit Bir Zeit University undergraduates to tutor students preparing for their *tawjihi* exams, linking politicized university students with younger high school students. The center also worked with "other camp communities" to provide aid for political prisoners and their families, hospital care for the ill, and other goods and services. Beyond the camp, the Dheisheh center maintained "strong links with nearby villages," and voluntary work groups from the Center assisted farmers from neighboring villages with clearing the land, planting, and harvesting.[10]

Through such activities, the Centres' members – and, through them, political factions – forged new ties with social groups both inside and outside the Palestinian Territories' refugee camps. As an *al-Fajr* article written about the Centres concluded: "The Youth Activities Centres, *the only organizations operating camp-wide in the West Bank*, are really just a bunch of kids that have organized themselves and others to create, develop, improve, and *protest*. With the barest of resources and the maximum of obstacles, *the camp youth have made their own infrastructure, not with buildings but by linking people* [my emphasis]."[11]

As the example of the Youth Activities Centres shows, by the mid-1980s, a communications network was in place linking political activists with school students, prisoners' families, and other groups, as well as connecting different local groups to each other. With its rise, the next section will also demonstrate, activists could spread information about protests more quickly and easily, and protests became more widespread and coordinated.

---

[9] For example, the youth center in Shuafat Camp was dominated by Fatah and Shabiba members. These groups' influence can be seen in the center's administrative committee: among its members were Talal Abu Afifeh, a Fatah supporter and the founder of the Shabiba committee in the camp (Interview 12, Fatah/Shabiba activist, Shuafat Camp, March 7, 2014; see also Interview, T. Abu Afifeh, Jerusalem, February 26, 2014).

[10] Yaffawi, A. E. 1984, February 29. "Camp Youth Activities Centers – Dealing With the Here and Now." *Jerusalem Dawn Palestinian Weekly* 5(200), 8–9.

[11] Yaffawi, A. E. 1984, February 29. "Camp Youth Activities Centers – Dealing With the Here and Now." *Jerusalem Dawn Palestinian Weekly* 5(200), 8–9.

5.2.3 Civic Networks as Information Conduits and Rising Protest Coordination

As civil society associations helped bridge traditional divisions within Palestinian society, civic networks became an important conduit for transmitting information about and coordinating protests. Information about protest was spread largely through word-of-mouth, and civic associations played a key role in passing this information onto their members, supporters, and the wider public. For example, when asked to describe the process of preparing for a demonstration from start to finish, a Fatah and Shabiba activist said: "We were five [in the leadership of the local Shabiba Committee], and each one of us had five people under him, for example. Meaning, in this way, we had twenty-five people [who were directly in contact with the main five]. Those twenty-five people, each one of them had under him five people. In this [way], we became 250! Each one of the 250 people had five persons with him. This is how it happened. Let's say there was an activity and we want one hundred people to participate [e.g. a confrontation]. It was easy for us to bring those one hundred people. And we said to each [Shabiba] member to bring with him not five but two people" (Interview 12, Shuafat Camp, March 11, 2014).

In this way, information about resistance traveled from outlawed nationalist factions to politicized civil society associations and, finally, to school students, prisoners' families, and other groups. Using civic networks, political activists were able to quickly reach different groups and inform them of impending demonstrations. A Fatah/Shabiba activist from a village near Tulkarm recalled: We would prepare for it [a mass demonstration] [with] flags and decorations, meaning we as the [Shabiba] committee prepare everything that relates to the start. We call our members and tell them to go hang flags and pictures so, when the event arrives, everything will be ready. If someone became a martyr, we call upon our members, telling them, 'Tomorrow, there is an event, and what you need to do is 1, 2, 3 [i.e. X, Y, Z]. *Each member would tell a certain group. For example, after someone was killed by the army, we used to tell the people [that] everyone has a responsibility to tell a group of people*" (Interview 23, Anabta, March 17, 2014; my emphasis).

This use of shared civic networks for mobilization brought added coherence and coordination to diffuse student protests. While students were leading participants in protests and demonstrations even before the development of these networks, "they had done so largely as an unorganized body lacking discipline and political direction" (Taraki, 1984, 454). With the formation of civic networks, previously unorganized student protests were joined into a coordinated and broad-based protest campaign. In the days leading up to a demonstration, civil society members contacted students who they knew from their associations' social welfare and other activities. These students would then circulate this information inside their schools and, in this manner, spread it to tens of thousands of other youth. As one Fatah/Shabiba activist described:

When demonstrations used to happen, all the schools participated in it. Shabiba would make the students exit the school and join the protest. We are part of the school students and they are part of us, *we communicate with them through voluntary work and the organizational work* [my emphasis], and even with some of the girls' schools at that time... *Within the schools, we have connections with older students who we trusted and could give to him [sic] the information so he [sic] can spread it inside the school.* We agreed among each other who is responsible for what so, for instance, I took responsibility for the girls' schools. I used to communicate with one girl from the school who spread the information about the next event. (Interview 11, Fatah/Shabiba activist Anabta, March 17, 2014; my emphasis)

As Shabiba and other civic organizations extended their reach into schools and communities in this manner, protests thus also became more synchronized and unified. In the spring of 1982, as PLO institution-building in the Occupied Territories intensified (see e.g. Taraki, 1984, 445–46), Palestinians came together in the most widespread, coordinated, and prolonged protests since the beginning of the Israeli occupation (Peretz, 1990, 389; Tessler, 1994, 562). In contrast to previous protests, which were more isolated and uncoordinated, simultaneous demonstrations took place in cities, villages, and refugee camps throughout the West Bank and Gaza Strip (Peretz, 1990, 389). For example, on April 25, 1982, *al-Fajr* English reported that "several people were shot and scores arrested, following demonstrations in the north, center, and south of the West Bank, as well as the Gaza Strip" (quoted in Tessler 1994, 563). For perhaps the first time, protests were reported not only in cities and refugee camps but also in some villages (Tessler, 1994, 562–63). Reflecting the strength of the new student and youth organizations, school students were among the main participants in such demonstrations. With rural youth now linked to urban activists via civic networks, student protests fanned out beyond the larger cities and towns to peripheral, and previously quiescent, villages.

When the first intifadah began in 1987, civic organizations played perhaps an even more important role in circulating information about the brewing uprising and organizing people to join it. In Yatta, a relatively large town of 30,000 people in the Hebron governorate, the local labor union organized the town's first meeting about the uprising and gave "accounts of what had been happening in Gaza and [elsewhere in] the West Bank." The labor union also formed a "Workers' Council" tasked with visiting members of the community and "discussing the current situation." According to the Yatta community diary published by the FACTS Information Committee: "Throughout the uprising, the community of Yatta has been informed and updated on the events taking place in other parts of the occupied territories. Accounts of what had been happening in Gaza and the West Bank were given during the first meeting held in Yatta and organized by the Labor Union of the town. This was followed by daily meetings for workers, students and others who were interested in discussing the direction of the uprising and its implications. A Workers' Council was formed whose task was to visit the houses of workers and their families as well as people from other sectors of the community. This council used to discuss the current situation, raise the political consciousness and press for the formation of popular committees" (FACTS Information Committee, 1990a, 30).

The events in Yatta illustrate a more general pattern whereby existing civil society associations gave rise to new local committees, which worked to inform residents about protest activities and mobilize them to participate. As Joost Hiltermann described: "Neighborhood committees sought to pinpoint problems in the community, *disseminate information on daily activities and to encourage the resident's participation in mass activities*" (Hiltermann, 1993, 194; my emphasis). For example, in Arroura, a village in the Ramallah governorate, labor union activists conducted an information campaign to educate village residents about Israeli policies and means of resisting them. A report from December 22, 1987, about two weeks after the start of the intifadah, states: "Union activists used to visit the houses to explain the political implications of current events, Israeli policies and means of counteracting them. Within time, the villagers became informed and ready to be mobilized" (FACTS Information Committee, 1990a, 79). This information campaign was part of a broader initiative to root out collaborators from the village and may have conveyed social pressure in addition to information. Regardless of the particular mix of information and coercion involved, however, this example illustrates the important informational function of civic networks and the informational advantages that those within them possess.

These accounts suggest that, as Palestinian civil society flourished and more Palestinians were incorporated into civic networks, resistance spread and became more coordinated. Vertical networks linking political activists to school students, prisoners' groups, and local communities allowed activists to spread information to these groups and unify them in protest. In addition, horizontal networks linking these groups to one another further diffused this information and spread it more widely across existing social and geographical boundaries. As a result, mass protests expanded and became more synchronized.

These arguments suggest two testable empirical implications that reside at different levels of analysis. First, at the individual or "micro" level, individuals in civic networks should be more likely to participate in protest than individuals outside these networks. As a result of their informational advantages, these individuals should be better able to participate in protest than less networked individuals and, in turn, have a higher average probability of participation. Second, at the level of the movement, or what Jennifer Earl calls the "meso-level" (Earl, 2011), the growth of civil society organizations and networks should also associated with rising coordination among the different groups or constituencies involved in protest. In the remaining sections, I use the survey data to systematically test the former, individual-level hypothesis. While these data are not suitable for testing the second, meso-level hypothesis in a more systematic fashion, I return to this hypothesis and discuss possible directions for future empirical research in the conclusion.

5.3 CIVIC NETWORKS AND PARTICIPATION IN RESISTANCE: AN EMPIRICAL ANALYSIS

This section systematically examines the relationship between incorporation into civic networks and participation in anti-regime resistance using my survey data. As in the previous chapters, participation in anti-regime resistance is measured as a binary variable indicating regular participation in risky unarmed collective action targeted against repressive regimes, such as demonstrations, sit-ins, and strikes. Incorporation into civic networks is also measured as in the previous chapters using a four-level categorical variable indicating the number of civic associations in which an individual personally knows a member.

5.3.1 Controlling for Selection into Civic Networks

Membership in civic organizations and networks is often treated as if it were exogenous or external to political conflict and violence. However, both previous research and contextual knowledge of the Palestinian case raise the possibility that individuals situated within these organizations and networks may have been more politicized than other individuals even before their incorporation into these structures; to the extent that this is true, their participation in protest may be due to the prior characteristics that brought them into these networks rather than the networks themselves. In other words, individuals may be systematically self-selecting or being selected into civic networks, which may result in selection bias. To prevent such bias, this section thus compares individuals who go on to join civic networks with those who never do and controls for *ex ante* differences between the two groups in the ensuing empirical analysis.

Civic organizations and networks can be both a cause and an outcome of conflict processes. In some cases such as the American civil rights movement, civil society organizations and networks predated the rise of social movement activism, arising earlier out of independent social processes and dynamics (McAdam, 2010). In other cases such as the Palestinian case, however, civic organizations and networks are themselves the outcome of conflict and contention. For example, in her influential study of El Salvador, Elisabeth Wood argues that, while social networks did facilitate insurgent collective action, "these networks were not based on strong antecedent communities but instead emerged in the mid-1970s as a result of the new pastoral practices by some Catholic priests and organizations, on the one hand, and initial organizing efforts by the then-tiny guerrilla organizations on the other" (Wood, 2003, 15). Similarly, in *Activists Beyond Borders*, Keck and Sikkink show that political entrepreneurship played a central role in the formation and spread of transnational human rights networks (Keck and Sikkink, 2014, 4, 12–14, 90). These perspectives suggest that, in many cases, civic networks have political origins. Empirical analyses of conflict that take such networks as their independent variable must thus take these political origins into account.

The previous chapters have shown how civic networks may be formed through integration into state institutions. These institutions offer important advantages for collective action that can be exploited by political activists, as well as by the ordinary people who are integrated into these institutions. As a result, political activists face strong incentives to foster relationships with individuals inside these institutions, and individuals integrated into these institutions will be more likely to become part of politicized civic networks.

One way that activists can forge ties with individuals inside state institutions, as well as with local communities, is through social welfare provision. As the previous accounts show, Palestinian civil society activists used social welfare provision to build relationships with individuals within state institutions and local communities, which they could subsequently deploy for political purposes. This implies that, at least in the Palestinian context, beneficiaries of social welfare services are more likely to be incorporated into civic networks than non-beneficiaries. As a result, I control for both integration into state institutions and the use of social welfare services in my analysis of the relationship between civic networks and protest participation.

In addition to their greater integration into state institutions and use of social welfare, individuals who join civic networks could also differ from those who do not in other important ways. In particular, individuals who come to join civic networks may already be more politicized than those who do not, rendering them more likely to participate in anti-regime resistance to begin with. As described earlier, many Palestinian civil society organizations were affiliated or associated with political factions in some way, and my survey data indicate that formal members of these organizations appear to have been highly politicized even before becoming members. Because people tend to associate with others like themselves, individuals in civic networks – that is, individuals who know members of politicized civil society organizations – may thus also have been more politicized to begin with. To the extent that linkages between civil society organizations and the PLO's political factions were known to the public (which appears to have varied widely across organizations and over time), it is also possible that more politicized individuals could have been self-selecting into these networks deliberately. As such, it is important to evaluate and control for such possible *ex ante* differences between individuals inside and outside civic networks.

Figure 5.1 compares individuals inside civic networks to those outside these networks on a number of observable indicators of politicization, in the period before the former group was incorporated into civic networks. That is, it compares individuals who would go on to join civic networks in the period before they did so with individuals who

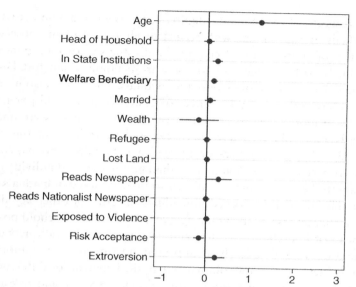

FIGURE 5.1 Are individuals in civic networks already more politicized?
Note: Results of difference in means tests comparing individuals in civic networks in the period before they joined with non-joiners on various observable indicators of politicization (i.e. in y-axis). 95% confidence intervals shown. 1201<N<1437 (varies by indicator).

never joined these networks.[12] Consistent with this book's arguments and my previous findings, the figure shows that networked individuals were more likely to have previously been integrated into state institutions, as well as to have benefited from social welfare services provided by civil society organizations. Two-thirds of networked individuals were previously integrated into state institutions, as compared with only 45 percent of non-networked individuals. Twenty-five percent had accessed social services provided by civil society organizations, compared with only 11 percent of those who were never incorporated into civic networks. These differences between networked and non-networked individuals are both statistically significant at the 95 percent confidence level.

Importantly, however, networked individuals do not appear to have been *ex ante* more politicized than non-networked individuals in most

[12] This comparison is based on the results of a difference in means test comparing these two groups.

other respects. As seen in the figure, networked and non-networked individuals appear similar with regard to almost all of my observable indicators of politicization. Networked individuals were not significantly more likely to be refugees or to come from families that lost land in the 1948 War than non-networked individuals. They were also no more likely to have other possible sources of grievance that could potentially make them more likely to protest: networked individuals were not significantly more likely to have been exposed to violence at the hands of Israeli soldiers or settlers or to read a nationalist newspaper, and they were actually *less* risk acceptant than non-networked individuals. In addition to these indicators of politicization, networked individuals were also similar to non-networked individuals in terms of other key demographic characteristics, including age, marital status, household position (i.e. head of household), wealth, and extroversion. Overall, networked and non-networked individuals appear quite similar to one another *a priori*. Nonetheless, in the following analysis, I control for differences in integration into state institutions, use of social services, and risk acceptance across these two groups. In addition, as in the previous chapters, I include controls for a secular time trend, generational effects, and duration dependence.

5.3.2   Civic Networks and Participation in Anti-regime Resistance

Having examined the origins of civic networks, I now turn to analyzing their impact on participation in anti-regime resistance. Figure 5.2 shows the association between incorporation into civic networks and participation in resistance, controlling for all statistically significant differences between networked and non-networked individuals. The figure shows that a one-unit increase in an individual's civic networks is associated with a 4 percentage point average gain in the likelihood that this individual participates in resistance (p<0.01).[13] That is, for each additional civic organization to which an individual is connected (i.e. by knowing a member), his probability of participation rises by an average of 4 percentage points. To help put the size of this effect into perspective, an increase from the minimum number of civic networks of zero to the maximum number of civic networks, equal to three or more, is associated with a 17 percentage point increase in the probability of participation. For

---

[13] This effect is equivalent to 0.10 standard deviations.

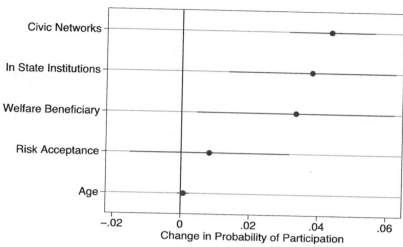

FIGURE 5.2 The marginal effect of civic networks on participation in
anti-regime resistance

*Note: Marginal effects from multilevel logistic regression model with varying intercepts by
locality. Additional control variables include secular trend variables (period dummies),
generational effects (age-period interaction terms), and cubic splines. N=2450
observations.*

the typical individual in the sample, the probability of participation in
protest is 35 percent if he is not networked and 52 percent if he is highly
networked.[14]

This association is also robust to controlling for two additional variables on which networked and non-networked individuals meaningfully
differ, but these differences fall short of conventional levels of statistical
significance: extroversion and newspaper readership. When controlling
for these additional variables, the association between incorporation into
civic networks and participation in anti-regime resistance remains the
same.[15] In addition, as shown in Figure 5.3, this association is also
robust to correcting for possible reverse causality between incorporation
into civic networks and participation in resistance using the approach
employed throughout this book. Applied to this chapter, this approach
models the relationship between incorporation into civic networks in a
given time period and the probability that a previously politically inactive
individual will begin to participate in resistance in the subsequent time

[14] Predicted probabilities calculated by setting all continuous variables at their means and
all other variables at their modal values.
[15] See Section A.3 in the online appendix: www.cambridge.org/TheRevolutionWithin

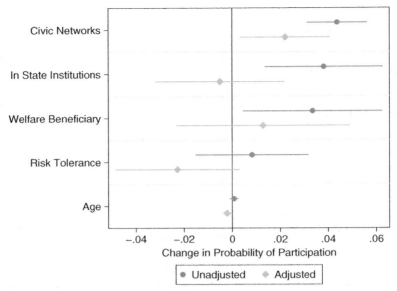

FIGURE 5.3 The marginal effect of civic networks on participation in
anti-regime resistance (adjusted for reverse causality)
*Note: Marginal effects from multilevel regression models with varying intercepts by
locality (i.e. locality-level random effects). Additional control variables not shown include
period dummies, generational effects, and cubic splines. N=2450 (unadjusted); N=1018
(adjusted).*

period (i.e. the initial onset of participation in resistance). After adjusting
for reverse causality in this manner, civic networks continue to have a
statistically significant effect on participation in resistance, although this
effect decreases slightly in size (see Figure 5.3).[16] Thus, while this analysis does not rule out all forms of endogeneity, the association between
civic networks and participation in resistance does not seem to be due to
simple reverse causality.

Overall, these results suggest that incorporation into civic networks
makes individuals more likely to participate in anti-regime resistance.
As shown earlier and in the previous chapters, Palestinians who were

---

[16] The coefficient on state institutions is expected to be smaller in this model, as integration
into these institutions increases participation in anti-regime resistance partly through the
mechanism of civic networks. Surprisingly, integration into state institutions does not
have a statistically significant effect in this model (i.e. a null finding). This may because,
since integration into state institutions is a control variable in the model, the model does
not further control for selection into these institutions: as shown in Chapters 3 and 4,
integration into these institutions does have a positive and statistically significant effect
in other models that account for reverse causality.

integrated into state institutions, such as school students and prisoners' family members and friends, were more likely to be incorporated into these networks and, therefore, to participate in resistance. However, civic networks were not made up of school students and prisoners' advocates alone. By using civic organizations to provide social services, political activists also forged new civic ties within local communities, which served as important conduits for political information and increased participation in protest. As these new civic networks grew in size and reach, the nationalist opposition thus also matured from a relatively fractured and disconnected set of groups into a broad-based and coordinated national protest movement.

5.4 CONCLUSIONS

As unarmed resistance to Israeli occupation intensified in 1978, Palestinians intitially lacked the organizational strength that is often believed to be necessary for protest. With civil society organizations limited in their size and influence, state institutions instead became the key nodes of protest. Without a broader communications network connecting these institutions to other groups, however, these protests remained relatively disconnected and uncoordinated.

This chapter shows that, with the revival of Palestinian civil society in the early 1980s, civil society organizations came to serve as the connective tissue in a broader communications network. Civil society organizations such as the Shabiba movement connected different schools to one another in new horizontal webs of relations, and they also joined local communities together in this fashion. Through these organizations, political factions also forged new vertical ties with school students, prisoners' groups, and local communities. As a result, civic networks connecting individuals to civil society members became important conduits for transmitting political information. Thus, despite their greater risk aversion, individuals who were connected to these networks were more likely to participate in protest than those who were not. These conclusions are supported by a combination of interviews, newspaper reports, survey evidence, and other sources.

This chapter also argues that, due to their connective function, civic networks increase coordination among different protest actors. It offers suggestive evidence that, as Palestinian civil society associations grew in number and size, resistance to Israeli occupation became more coordinated and widespread. Testing this argument systematically would require movement-level data rather than individual-level survey data and, as such, is beyond the scope of this book. Specifically, testing this argument would require temporal data on the degree of coordination within a protest movement, such as the number of simultaneous protests held in different locations or identifiable groups participating in the same protest campaign. It would also necessitate temporal data on the growth of civil society associations and, ideally, the spread of civic networks connecting these associations to other social groups. In recent years, scholars have begun to collect such data: for example, the updated NAVCO Dataset contains yearly information on the diversity of protest campaigns, which could potentially be used to gauge the level of coordination between different protest actors (Chenoweth and Lewis, 2013). However, to the best of my knowledge, there are currently no long-running time-series data on the growth of domestic civil society associations, either cross-nationally or in the Palestinian case. Developing such data would thus be an important first step toward more systematically testing the relationship between civic networks and protest coordination.

Beyond their importance for explaining the coordination of mass protests, the chapter's conclusions also have broader implications for understanding the trajectory of regime transitions. This chapter's arguments imply that, given the limitations of state institutions for supporting a nationwide uprising, anti-regime groups with low internal organizational strength will face strong incentives for institution-building. Lacking the strong independent organizations that are needed to coordinate and unify disparate groups into a more comprehensive protest campaign, they should seek to form new civil society associations that can fulfill this function. When anti-regime groups are able to do so, they will be more likely to succeed in achieving their political goals. At the same time, if such groups overthrow the ruling regime and assume power, the prospects for a full democratic transition may be imperiled. When anti-regime groups that have adopted an institution-building strategy come to power, civil society institutions will be particularly vulnerable to capture and cooptation by the state. Linked to regime officials through party ties and a shared history of struggle, they may fail to articulate the independent voice that they are intended to express. In this case, civil society may be more likely to sustain autocratic government than it is to promote democracy.

6

Conclusions

6.1 INTRODUCTION

State institutions in authoritarian regimes are typically regarded as sites of repression rather than sites of resistance. Through the strength or weakness of these institutions, states shape both the larger political opportunities available for resistance and the individual risks of participation in protest. State institutions also allow authoritarian regimes to better identify, register, and monitor the individuals situated inside them. Finally, integration into state institutions may also coopt and control citizens in other, more indirect, ways. For instance, state schools are often believed to transmit nationalist identities and official ideologies to their students, incorporating them into and binding them more fully to the nation-state.

In contrast to this perspective, this book argues that, under certain conditions, integration into state institutions can, paradoxically, make individuals more likely to resist state power. When groups have strong anti-regime grievances but low internal organizational strength, integration into these institutions provides individuals with informational and organizational advantages that make them better able to participate in anti-regime resistance. This, in turn, increases the likelihood that they will join in anti-regime protest. Using rare, original survey data on protest behavior, this book finds that individuals who were integrated into state institutions had a higher probability of participating in protest than otherwise similar individuals who were not exposed to this institutional context, and this greater propensity for protest tended to persist over time.

As this book describes, Palestinians had both strong anti-regime grievances and low internal organizational strength as new avenues for participation in unarmed resistance arose in Palestine in the late 1970s. By this time, public opinion data show, Palestinians expressed nearly unanimous support for the PLO and its goal of ending Israeli occupation and establishing an independent Palestinian state. Yet, after years of authoritarian rule and occupation, Palestinian civil society institutions remained weak and did not have the size or influence to promote mass participation. Under these conditions, schools, prisons, and courts became important if unlikely sites of protest. As a result, despite lacking the internal organizational strength that is often seen as necessary for protest, Palestinians were able to successfully mobilize against the much more powerful Israeli state.

This combination of strong anti-regime grievances and a weak civil society is not unique to Palestine. As this chapter will discuss, these conditions are also present in other repressive regimes, including the former apartheid regime in South Africa and the former Mubarak regime in Egypt. In the sections that follow, I show how, in these cases, state institutions also became important sites of mobilization and resistance against the ruling regime. Thus, while further research is needed to more fully situate these institutions in comparative perspective, they appear to have played a significant role in additional cases beyond Palestine as well.

6.2 ACADEMIC CONTRIBUTIONS AND IMPLICATIONS

This book contributes to our understanding of the conditions under which anti-regime resistance will occur. The question of when groups will rise up in protest against the prevailing political and social order has occupied successive generations of scholars. Since at least the 1960s, social movement theorists concerned with the origins of social movements have sought to understand when and why such movements arose in a wide variety of contexts (see e.g. McAdam, 2010; Tilly, Tilly, and Tilly, 1975; McCarthy and Zald, 1977a, 1977b). More recently, a growing literature in the social sciences has investigated the causes and consequences of nonviolent resistance (see e.g. Pearlman, 2011; Chenoweth and Stephan, 2011; Nepstad, 2011; Cunningham, 2013; Krause, 2017). Complementing the social movements literature, this literature also identifies a number of conditions under which opposition movements will use nonviolent tactics to achieve their goals and, in turn, unarmed resistance will occur (Pearlman, 2011; Cunningham, 2013; Asal et al., 2013; Dudouet, 2013; Krause, 2017).

Organizational strength has been central to the way scholars of social movement, revolution, and collective action conceive of the sources of anti-regime resistance. According to canonical social movement theories, social movements emerge among groups with internal organizational strength - strong autonomous institutions, organizations, and networks that provide groups with the capacity for protest (McAdam, 2010; Tilly, et al., 1975; Oberschall, 1973). For example, in the paradigmatic case of the American civil rights movement that helped shape this school of thought, scholars traced the movement's emergence to the growing strength of the southern black church and other "indigenous" institutions (McAdam, 2010; Morris, 1984). More recently, as Zhao has noted, a number of scholars have pointed to the rise of civil society to explain the Eastern European revolutions of 1989 (Di Palma, 1991; Ost, 1991), as well as the Chinese prodemocracy movement of the same year (Zhao, 1998, 1494). Subsequent revisions to social movement theory have taken a more dynamic approach, showing how, in the absence of strong preexisting organizations, such institutions can be appropriated or even created (McAdam, Tarrow, and Tilly, 2003). Yet, to a significant degree, the development of internal organizational strength is still seen by many social movement scholars as a prerequisite for protest (see e.g. Tilly and Tarrow, 2007, Nepstad, 2011, 6).[1]

Political scientists studying the sources of nonviolent resistance have also pointed to the importance of group organization. A group's internal structure, these studies argue, powerfully shapes its capacity to use and sustain nonviolent tactics. For example, in an in-depth longitudinal analysis of the Palestinian national movement, Wendy Pearlman persuasively argues that strong autonomous institutions help foster the internal cohesion that is necessary for opposition movements to engage in nonviolent resistance (Pearlman, 2011). Likewise, in a comprehensive cross-national analysis, Kathleen Cunningham finds that internally fragmented movements are more likely to use armed violence relative to other political strategies (Cunningham, 2013). To the extent that strong institutions indeed underpin group cohesion or fragmentation, this also implies that organizational strength is critical for unarmed protest. Along

---

[1] See also Diani and McAdam's review of this literature (2003).

with the social movements literature, these newer works thus also suggest that unarmed resistance is unlikely to occur among organizationally weak groups without strong autonomous institutions and organizations of their own.

Yet, in contrast to the case of the American civil rights movement, organizational strength is often lacking in the authoritarian environments in which anti-regime resistance tends to take place. In these more typical environments for anti-regime protest, any kind of independent organization is often banned or strongly discouraged. As a result, independent political parties, civil society associations, and other organizations tend to have low membership and only limited penetration into society. In many cases, they are simply too weak to promote wide participation in unarmed resistance. What explains participation in resistance under such difficult conditions? How do groups mobilize in the absence of internal organizational strength?

This book provides a new answer to these questions that centers on the critical role that state institutions can play in facilitating collective action. To date, little research has examined how integration into state institutions may affect participation in collective protest. State strength is widely argued to shape the larger political opportunities that groups face for protest and rebellion (see e.g. Kitschelt, 1986; Fearon and Laitin, 2003). State repression also shapes the incentives (or disincentives) that individuals have to participate in high-risk collective action. In contrast, the role of state institutions as possible "mobilizing structures" has received relatively little attention. Some newer social movement theories have adopted a more expansive definition of the institutional underpinnings of protest that includes "elements of the state structure" (McCarthy, 1996). Yet, while this definition acknowledges that state institutions may also play a role in mobilization, little work has explored the dynamics of mobilization and participation within such institutions. For example, in McCarthy's extensive review of the different mobilizing structures identified in the literature, state or state-controlled institutions are not mentioned once (McCarthy, 1996).

State institutions figure more prominently in Adrienne LeBas' recent book *From Protest to Parties* (2013). In *From Protest to Parties*, LeBas shows how state-controlled trade unions gradually evolved into platforms for oppositional politics during political openings in sub-Saharan Africa. Although these unions were subject to corporatist controls, they provided incipient opposition parties with organizational resources and pan-ethnic constituencies that, ultimately, allowed them to emerge as strong and effective parties. In contrast to Israeli-dominated institutions in the Palestinian Territories, however, African trade union structures were generally less subject to coercion by ruling regimes and enjoyed more independence from them. In both Zambia and Zimbabwe, for example, trade unions retained control over their internal governance, which they used to elect more confrontational leadership and, gradually, challenge state control. In contrast, as described in Chapter 3, Palestinian schools lacked such organizational autonomy. By showing how state institutions can emerge as hubs for mobilization and resistance even under these arguably more difficult conditions, this book thus further expands our understanding of the conditions that support anti-regime protest.

This book's conclusions are also consistent with those of some other empirical studies of anti-regime movements, which suggest that even tightly controlled state institutions could play an important role in mass mobilization. For example, in his study of the 1989 Chinese prodemocracy movement, Zhao describes how Chinese universities under the state's control served as the initial locus for mobilization (1998). More recently, Joel Beinin has traced the roots of the Egyptian revolution of 2011 to workers' protests that originated in state-owned factories and industries in the 2000s (Beinin, 2015). Consistent with Beinin's analysis, Beissinger, Jamal, and Mazur find that, during the Egyptian revolution, government employees were more likely to participate than the general population (Beissinger, Jamal, and Mazur, 2015). Although these studies do not focus on state institutions as an analytical category, they nonetheless imply that these institutions could play an important and underappreciated role in facilitating anti-regime resistance.

Building on these insights, this book develops and tests a general theory of how and why integration into state institutions promotes individual participation in protest. It argues that integration into state institutions helps individuals to overcome informational and organizational obstacles to collective action, making them better able and therefore more likely to participate in anti-regime protest. This argument suggests that anti-regime resistance can occur even when groups lack the internal organizational strength that some scholars regard as necessary for protest (McAdam, 2010; Tilly and Tarrow, 2007; Nepstad, 2011).[2] In the absence of strong autonomous institutions and organizations, state institutions may instead function as sites of mobilization and

---

[2] See also Diani and McAdam's review of this literature (2003).

resistance. As a result of their informational and organizational advantages, these institutions provide aggrieved but organizationally weak groups with the capacity to protest against the state. Thus, in contrast to some existing perspectives, anti-regime protest can occur even when groups lack strong independent civil society organizations of their own.

This perspective helps to explain the occurrence of protest in at least two important cases beyond Palestine, which are under-predicted by the existing literature: the 1976 Soweto Uprising against South Africa's apartheid regime and the Egyptian labor movement of the 2000s. In the absence of internal organizational strength, existing theories would largely predict little or no anti-regime mobilization in both of these cases. Yet, in both South Africa and Egypt, schoolchildren and government workers situated inside the state apparatus staged the largest mass demonstrations against their ruling regimes to take place in decades. In the following sections, I discuss how this book's theory helps us to understand mobilization in these unlikely cases, as well as its ongoing relevance for understanding individual participation in the present day and beyond.

6.3 BEYOND PALESTINE: STATE INSTITUTIONS AND RESISTANCE IN COMPARATIVE PERSPECTIVE

This book's arguments were honed through close engagement with the Palestinian case. By focusing on a single geographic and temporal setting – the Palestinian Territories between 1978 and 1989 – I was able to compare Palestinians who were similar to each other in many ways other than their political participation and, thus, to better determine the individual-level factors that shaped their participation decisions. In other words, by narrowing in on a single case, I was able to achieve greater *internal validity* or confidence in the validity of my argument for understanding the dynamics of the particular setting under study.

At the same time, like other recent scholars of Palestine (Ron, 2003; Jamal, 2007; Pearlman, 2011; Krause, 2017; Manekin, in press), I do not see the Palestinian case as exceptional or so fundamentally different from other organizationally weak authoritarian settings in ways that would limit its *external validity* or broader generalizability. While a full test of the generalizability of this book's arguments would require collecting additional fine-grained survey data from multiple countries – and thus lies significantly beyond the scope of this project – the following sections thus probe the plausibility of these arguments in two other important cases: South Africa and Egypt. I conclude by considering the ongoing relevance of the book's arguments for understanding participation in anti-regime protest in the future, as new technologies both provide opposition movements with newfound opportunities for protest and present them with novel challenges.

6.3.1 State Schools in South Africa's Struggle against Apartheid

State schools were key sites of resistance during the resurgence of the anti-apartheid movement in South Africa (1976–1994). In the Soweto Uprising of 1976, schoolchildren launched a series of protests against South Africa's apartheid regime and its policies, igniting a months-long national uprising with students at its head. The roots of the uprising can be traced to a wave of student strikes in June 2016. In response to the apartheid regime's plan to introduce compulsory instruction in Afrikaans in black South African schools, seven higher primary and junior secondary schools went on strike (Ndlovu, 2006, 335).[3] Three days later, on June 16, fifteen thousand school children marched in Soweto in the largest anti-regime demonstration in the last sixteen years (Glaser, 1998, 15).[4] After the Soweto march, waves of student-led protests engulfed the rest of the country (Ndlovu, 2006, 350).

Schoolchildren in Soweto benefited from the same informational and organizational advantages for collective action that aided Palestinian students. As in Palestine, integration into educational institutions joined South African students in wide, information-rich social networks that provided information about dissent under conditions of state repression and censorship. Under South Africa's apartheid regime, individuals were legally and spatially segregated by both "race" and "ethnicity"; for example, the "black" township of Soweto was further divided along into separate Zulu, Sotho, and other "ethnic" areas.[5] In an exception to this

---

[3] Consistent with the level of schooling among Palestinian participants, higher primary school included the fifth to seventh grades and junior secondary school the eighth to eleventh grades (Ndlovu, 2006, 323).

[4] For a comparison of the Soweto Uprising with previous protests, see also Brewer (1986, 1–3) and Hirson (1979).

[5] See "Never Forget Those Who Were Killed in the 1976 Soweto Uprising." 2017. Daily Vox. www.thedailyvox.co.za/never-forget-killed-1976-soweto-uprising/ (accessed June 2018).

general "divide and conquer" strategy, however, post-primary schools drew students from diverse ethnic backgrounds and wide geographic areas (Glaser, 1998, 309, 322; Glaser, 2015, 167). For example, secondary school students from Alexandra – a black township 16 kilometers north of Johannesburg and 30 to 40 kilometers from Soweto – commuted to schools in Soweto and other nearby townships, bringing them into contact with a wide network of youth (Ndlovu, 2006). Extracurricular activities and inter-school competitions further broadened students' circle of acquaintances and allowed them to exchange information and ideas (Glaser, 1998, 303, 307; Glaser, 2015, 166–67). Thus, as some Soweto students began to protest against the apartheid regime's educational policies, news of the strike traveled rapidly to other students in the township, as well as to neighboring townships.

In contrast to students, youth outside schools had more narrow and parochial social networks and, therefore, were worse able to participate in anti-apartheid protests. Whereas students spent much of their lives in the school space (Glaser, 2015, 167), nonstudents spent most of their time at home caring for their siblings while their parents were working long days (Ndlovu, 2006, 319). Outside of the home, they were involved in narrow, neighborhood-based networks that, as they grew older, blurred into local street gangs (Glaser, 1998; Ndlovu, 2006). In contrast to schools, which knit together large numbers of students from diverse backgrounds, these gangs were small, neighborhood-based, homogenous, and cohesive. Absorbed in localized territorial competition, their members had little contact with school-going students or with political activists and organizations (Glaser, 1998). Indeed, gang members even spoke a different dialect – *tsotsitaal* or gangster argot – that school students did not (Glaser, 1998, 313). As a result of the separation and sometimes even outright hostility between the two groups, nonstudents joined the Soweto protests later than students did, and their subsequent participation was "spontaneous and sporadic" (Glaser, 1998, 320).

In addition to their wider social networks, South African school students could also communicate and coordinate with one another more easily than nonstudents could and enjoyed greater safety in numbers. Like Palestinian schools, the schools attended by South Africa's black majority were large and overcrowded. As a result of apartheid-era policies that limited school construction and funds for the education of black students, by 1970 classroom sizes reached as high as seventy or eighty students per classroom (Glaser, 2015, 162). By 1976, the year of the uprising, secondary school enrollment outpaced the number of available seats by a factor of over six to one, and overcrowding reached new heights (see e.g. Ndlovu, 2006, 321–23). These crowded conditions hampered formal learning but facilitated the sharing of sensitive, political information. As a result, in the early days of the uprising, its leadership "explicitly called for a return to schools because it felt unable to regroup and organize outside of school networks" (Glaser, 1998, 318). With few channels with which to reach constituencies other than students, it remained "largely dependent on the school institution to mobilize students and disseminate information" (Glaser, 1998, 318). Consequently, while some non-students did join the growing protests against the apartheid regime, the Soweto Uprising "was an uprising of school students rather than 'the youth'" (Glaser, 1998, 301).

The theory advanced in this book predicts that schools and other state institutions should become key sites for protest under two conditions: when anti-regime sentiment is pervasive among members of a group; and when the group has low organizational strength. These conditions were both satisfied in the years leading up to the Soweto Uprising in South Africa. By the mid-1970s, the ideas of the black consciousness movement and its anti-apartheid message had become popular among black South African students. Influenced by black theology and the black power movement in the United States, the black consciousness movement preached a message of black pride, self-awareness and -reliance, and resistance to racial oppression (Marx, 1992, 47–59).[6] While the movement was primarily influential among urban, middle-class intellectuals and professionals, its basic themes filtered down to a much broader and more diverse group (Hirschmann, 1990, 8). By 1975, these ideas, had also permeated to black South African students. As black consciousness leader Ben Khopa wrote of this period, "The youngsters were then [by 1975] very angry and began to formulate their own description of what black consciousness was" (quoted in Marx, 1992, 65). In the 1976 Soweto Uprising, these black consciousness-inspired ideas were manifest in the rhetoric used by student protestors (Marx, 1992, 65).

Thus, in the years leading up to the Soweto Uprising, anti-apartheid sentiment was high. However, in contrast to school students, most black South Africans lacked the organizational capacity for protest. This

---

[6] See also "Defining Black Consciousness." 2011. South African History Online. www.sahistory.org.za/topic/defining-black-consciousness (accessed March 15, 2017).

organizational weakness is evident in the lack of trade union activity, which offers a good barometer of the overall degree of organizational strength within a society. At the time of the Soweto Uprising, African trade unions were illegal and could not register or collectively bargain, limiting their size and influence (Gould, 1981, 124; Macun, 2000, 59). Despite these restrictions, black unions initially grew in the 1930s and 1940s in tandem with the rapidly growing South African manufacturing industry (Macun, 2000, 59; Fine and Davis, 1991). However, after a miners' strike in 1946 and a change in the overall political climate, the South African government cracked down on black unions, and their membership sharply declined (Lichtenstein, 2005, 298). Following the banning of the African National Congress (ANC) and other political organizations in 1960, what little labor mobilization there was all but disappeared (Baskin, 1991; Friedman, 1987). As a result, although some individual factories did unionize and became the basis for strikes, total union membership and density remained low (Macun, 2000, 60). In 1981, two years after the legalization of black unions, black union membership was estimated at only 1 percent of the population – a rate even lower than that of the Palestinian Territories (Gould, 1981, 135).

Churches and student groups were somewhat stronger than trade unions and played a leading role in spreading black consciousness ideas in the late 1960s and early 1970s. In 1969, the South African Students' Organization (SASO) was formed (Marx, 1992, 52). The SASO was an organization of university students and the main formal organization of the black consciousness movement. By 1973, it had a membership of six thousand university students, which, although not large in absolute terms, encompassed about 50 percent of all black college students.[7] However, beginning in 1973, SASO was subjected to increasing state repression. By 1975, twenty-nine previous leaders of the organization had been "banned", and from 1973 to 1977 many of the organization's members were forced into exile (Badat, 2016, 133). As SASO members came under increasing repression, participation in the organization inevitably declined. While SASO chapters continued to exist on university campuses, SASO leaders reported considerable "difficulty in harnessing the students' cooperation" (1974 SASO president, quoted in Badat, 2016, 135). As a result, while some individual SASO members

---

[7] In 1977, the closest year for which I could find data, the total number of black university students was 11,516 and the total number of nonwhite students was 25,104 (Badat, 2016, 198).

were involved in the 1976 protests in Soweto, the organization did not play a large part in the uprising (Badat, 2016, 138).

As a result, until the uprising in Soweto, the period from 1960 to 1976 saw only muted resistance against the apartheid regime. After the banning of the ANC in 1960, ANC leaders formed a separate armed wing – uMkhonto we Sizwe (MK) – that engaged in acts of sabotage against the South African government throughout the decade. Some unarmed resistance also continued to occur, namely strikes at factories with unionized work forces (Macun, 2000, 60). However, until South African schoolchildren initiated their protest in Soweto, there had been no single mass demonstration against apartheid rule since the Sharpeville anti-pass protests over fifteen years earlier.

The case of South Africa thus illustrates the broader applicability of the book's theory to cases in which groups have high anti-regime sentiment and low organizational strength. As already described, by the mid-1970s, black consciousness ideas had filtered down to wide segments of black South African society. Yet, from 1960 onward, and particularly after the repression of SASO in 1973, South Africans generally lacked the organizational capacity for protest. In this context of strong anti-regime sentiment and weak internal organization, black South African schoolchildren initiated one of the largest mass demonstrations against the apartheid regime to date. Aided by information-rich school networks, institutional channels for communication and coordination, and safety in numbers, they boldly challenged the apartheid regime and reinvigorated the anti-apartheid movement. Thus, as in Palestine, regime-controlled schools were, paradoxically, at the forefront of anti-regime protest.

6.3.2 State Institutions and Protest against Egypt's Mubarak Regime

State institutions were also at the vanguard of protest during the last decade of the Mubarak regime in Egypt. State workers and civil servants staged both the largest industrial strike and the "largest collective actions" directed against the Mubarak regime until the Egyptian revolution of 2011 that toppled it from power (Beinin and Duboc, 2013, 222). As in Palestine, participants in these illegal strikes and demonstrations lacked the strong autonomous institutions that are often regarded as necessary for protest. Yet, as this case study will show, Egyptian state workers and employees did benefit from informational and organizational advantages for collective action that were not available to all Egyptians. In the section that follows, I discuss how these advantages enhanced workers' capacity for protest and, therefore, increased the odds that they would participate.

In January 2011, millions of Egyptians took to the streets to demand the ouster of then Egyptian President Hosni Mubarak. While unprecedented in its size and scope, the roots of this revolution can be traced back to an earlier wave of mobilization that began within state institutions. From 1998 to 2010, Egyptian workers participated in over three thousand strikes, demonstrations, and other forms of collective action (Beinin and Duboc, 2013, 205). The majority of strikes, including the largest and most impactful actions, were conducted by public sector workers employed by state firms and factories (Beinin, 2015, 68). These actions inspired a small group of Egyptian youth activists calling themselves the April 6 Youth Movement to launch their own revolt, which would eventually help bring down the Mubarak government. When the Egyptian revolution began in January 2011, state workers were quick to join the uprising. As the protests in Tahrir Square intensified, workers at Egypt's national telecommunications company and other state-owned industries went on strike (Beinin and Duboc, 2013, 223–24). Throughout the uprising, Egyptian government employees participated at significantly higher rates than the general Egyptian population (Beissinger, Jamal, and Mazur, 2015, 15).

The largest industrial strike in Egypt during the 2000s erupted at the Misr (Egypt) Spinning and Weaving Company, also known as Ghazl al-Mahalla. Ghazl al-Mahalla is a state-owned textile factory with a work force of over twenty thousand employees – nearly a quarter of all public-sector textile and clothing workers in Egypt. Ghazl al-Mahalla has a storied history: established in 1927 by Tal'at Harb, a hero of Egyptian economic nationalism, it was one of the first factories to be nationalized by the Nasser regime in the 1960s. As Beinin and Duboc note, as a political symbol, it is a potent one (2013, 218).

The first strike at Ghazl al-Mahalla erupted on December 7, 2006, when workers at the company discovered they had been underpaid. On that day, thousands of workers began assembling opposite the entrance to the factory's mill in [the city of] Mahalla's Tal'at Harb Square. As production at the faculty slowly ground to a halt, three thousand female garment workers left their stations and marched to the spinning and weaving sections, where their male colleagues were still at work. Chanting "Where are the men? Here are the women!," they incited the men to join in the strike. Around ten thousand male and female workers then gathered in the central square of the factory complex, shouting "Two months [bonus pay]! Two months!"(Beinin, 2015, 76). Black-clad riot police were quickly deployed to quell the growing demonstration, but they did not act. According to strike leader Muhammad 'Attar, "They were shocked by our numbers" (Beinin and El-Hamalawy, 2007).

After night fell and most of the demonstrators had dispersed, riot police rushed the mill compound, where seventy workers and strike leaders 'Attar and Sayyid Habib had barricaded themselves inside. "They told us we were few and better get out," recalled 'Attar. "But they did not know how many of us were inside. We lied and told them we were thousands" (Beinin and El-Hamalawy, 2007). To foster the illusion of large numbers and bring other workers to their aid, the strikers also began banging loudly on iron barrels. "We woke up everyone in the company and the town," 'Attar said (Beinin and El-Hamalawy, 2007).

Meanwhile, the strikers started calling every worker they knew to hurry to the factory and join the strike. By the end of the day, twenty-two thousand workers had joined in the demonstration, and elementary school pupils and students from the nearby high schools had also taken to the street in support of the strikers. With so much power in numbers, 'Attar stated, "Security did not dare to step in," (Beinin and El-Hamalawy, 2007). Inspired by the success of the Ghazl al-Mahalla workers, who went on to win significant concessions, as many as thirty thousand Egyptian textile workers would participate in strikes, work slowdowns, and other forms of collective action over the following three months (Beinin, 2015, 76–77).

While the unrest at Ghazl al-Mahalla erupted over localized economic issues, the specific grievances that fueled the strike would subsequently evolve into more general anti-regime sentiment. In fall of 2007, workers at Ghazl al-Mahalla went on strike again to pressure the government to honor its promises during the 2006 labor action. This time, their demands were more explicitly political. As Joel Beinin describes, the striking workers raised chants and banners opposing the regime and its economic policies. In a video uploaded by one worker, workers could be seen chanting "We will not be ruled by the World Bank! We will not be ruled by colonialism!" (quoted in Beinin, 2015, 78). Strike leaders also stated their demands in national political terms, framing their grievances in terms of corruption and urging action not only from the factory management but also their allies within the government and security forces and even Egyptian president Hosni Mubarak himself (Stack and Mazen,

2007). As strike leader Sayyid Habib told Voice of America directly, "We are challenging the regime" (Sayyid Habib, quoted in Beinin, 2015, 78). Similarly, speaking to a packed crowd in Mahalla's Tal'at Harb Square, al-'Attar told the assembled workers, "I want the whole government to resign... I want the Mubarak regime to come to an end. Politics and workers' rights are inseparable. Work is politics by itself" (Muhammad al-'Attar, quoted in Beinin, 2015, 78–79).

As Ghazl al-Mahalla's workers began to challenge the regime more overtly, other state employees also began to mobilize against it. In September 2007, real estate tax collectors in Egypt's Giza province staged a one-day strike and demonstration for greater wage parity. Relying primarily on face-to-face contacts, they organized Giza's tax collectors to march from the central administration building and into the streets to demand a raise and other reforms. Although riot police locked the building's doors to prevent other employees from joining in the protest, five thousand government employees participated in the march. Inspired by this action, tax collectors from other provincial offices contacted the Giza strike leaders. Together, they began organizing local demonstrations in different provinces with the goal of amassing large enough numbers to stage a national strike in Cairo (Lachapelle, 2012). By the end of the campaign, over fifty thousand tax collectors would participate in what became the largest collective action against the Mubarak regime until the Egyptian revolution of 2011 (Beinin and Duboc, 2013, 222).

Buoyed by their large numbers and organizational capacity, Egypt's tax collectors moved their campaign from the provinces into the capital. On December 3, 2007, five thousand tax collectors from as many as fourteen provinces converged on Husyan Higazi Street in downtown Cairo. Although protestors initially planned to demonstrate on Husayn Higazi for only a few hours before decamping to the relative safety of a sit-in at the Egyptian Trade Union Federation (ETUF) office in Cairo, they were emboldened by their large numbers. When strike leader Kamal Abu Eita asked each provincial delegation if they wanted to move to ETUF headquarters, they unanimously voted to stay (Lachapelle, 2012).

Meanwhile, strike leaders sought to display their power in numbers and, thereby, convince their more reticent colleagues to join the fray. With this goal in mind, they asked arriving protestors to lock their doors behind them and bring their keys to the sit-in. As each new group added their keys, Abu Eita triumphantly displayed the growing set. By December 9, the crowd's size had swelled to eight thousand (Lachapelle, 2012). The tax collectors then asked their families to participate in the sit-in with them, bringing their numbers to over ten thousand (Beinin and Duboc, 2013, 222). Fearing an even more massive demonstration, the regime gave in and acceded to most of the strikers' demands. Following the strike, organizers successfully transformed the strike committee into an independent union, ending the Egyptian regime's monopoly on organizing labor and establishing Egypt's first independent union in over half a century (Beinin, 2015, 82).

Why did Egyptian tax collectors – "civil servants strategically located in the state's apparatus" – rise up in protest against it (Beinin and Duboc, 2013, 222)? Scholars of the Egyptian revolution and the labor movement that preceded it often attribute protests among Egyptian government employees to the Mubarak regime's neoliberal economic policies and their adverse impacts on state workers (Beinin and Duboc, 2013, 216; Beissinger, Jamal, and Mazur, 2015, 15). And, indeed, such protests were often a response to the regime's economic policies, which resulted in privatizations and layoffs at state firms, low wages, and fewer of the allowances and benefits needed to raise incomes to a living wage (Beinin and Duboc, 2013; Beinin, 2015). Yet, state workers were not uniquely affected by these policies. Between 2005 and 2008, inflation and food prices skyrocketed, real wages stagnated, and economic inequality widened, impacting the vast majority of Egyptians (Beinin and Duboc, 2013, 211–12). As the gap between Egypt's haves and have-nots grew larger, many Egyptians thus came to harbor strong economic grievances against the regime. To explain why state workers took to the streets when most Egyptians did not, we thus need to look not only to workers' grievances against the regime but also to their capacity to mobilize against it.

At first glance, Egyptian workers would also seem to lack this capacity. Contrary to what existing theories would suggest, they did not have strong autonomous institutions that could channel their dissatisfaction into an organized campaign of protest. While both the Ghazl al-Mahalla workers and municipal tax collectors were organized into trade unions, the ETUF served as an official arm of the Egyptian regime rather than an independent interest group. And, unlike the trade union structures that LeBas (2013) studied in sub-Saharan Africa, it had little real autonomy or independence from the regime. In contrast to their counterparts in Zimbabwe and Zambia, Egypt's local union committees worked to prevent rather than promote strikes (Beinin and Duboc, 2013, 208). For example, the official local union committee representing Ghazl al-Mahalla workers failed to support their demands during their 2006 strike, leading workers to call for the committee's impeachment and, eventually, to resign from its rolls (Beinin and Duboc, 2013, 219).

Workers were also not organized into other civil society organizations that could support protest. Responding to domestic and international pressures, the Mubarak regime had began allowing Egyptian civil society associations more freedom to operate in the 2000s, including labor-oriented associations such as the Center for Trade Union and Worker Services and the Coordinating Committee for Trade Union and Workers Rights and Liberties. Some of these organizations provided legal advice and other forms of technical support to workers, aiding them in their mobilization against the regime (Beinin, 2015, 70). However, these organizations employed only a handful of people between them. They had few organizational resources to speak of to lend the labor movement. While they supported striking workers, they did not initiate or organize collective action, and participants in protest were not drawn from their ranks (Beinin and Duboc, 2013, 208–9).

As such, as Egyptian workers began to mobilize against the regime and its economic policies, they lacked the strong autonomous institutions traditionally thought to be necessary for protest. As Joel Beinin writes, "The upsurge in workers' protest did not rely on 'movement entrepreneurs' or 'professional movement organizations' or previously existing 'bases', which some social movement theorists have regarded as necessary to form a movement... The movement had meager financial resources, no national organizational infrastructure, and no national-level leadership or coordination. E-mail and Internet contacts were uncommon, though a few workers blog in Arabic. Irregular face-to-face meetings and mobile telephones were the main means of communication" (Beinin and Duboc, 2013, 208–9). How, then, did thousands of ordinary Egyptian workers come to protest against the Mubarak regime and its policies?

While they lacked strong independent institutions of their own, state workers did have substantial informational and organizational advantages for collective action. With thousands and sometimes even tens of thousands of workers concentrated in a single factory or office, workers could communicate and coordinate with one another easily even without the access to the internet or social media that most workers lacked. For example, strike leaders in Ghazl al-Mahalla relied on leaflets and word-of-mouth to reach the more than twenty thousand workers employed at the faculty, not online networks (Beinin and El-Hamalawy,

2007). Similarly, the organizers of the first tax collectors' strike at Giza also relied primarily on face-to-face communications. Indeed, their initial choice of tactics – a one-day strike in Giza – was based on the fact that the organizing could be done face-to-face and did not require coordination with other provinces (Lachapelle, 2012).

Perhaps more importantly, the "ecological concentration" of many workers in a single factory or firm provided state workers with a relative degree of safety in numbers. Ghazl al-Mahalla is one of the largest factories in Egypt, employing nearly a quarter of all public-sector textile and clothing workers in Egypt – over twenty thousand people in all. The Giza tax authority office also employed thousands of civil servants. As a result of these large numbers, employees at Ghazl al-Mahalla and Giza were able to mobilize against the regime at relatively low risk to themselves. As described earlier, the riot police dispatched to stop the initial demonstration at Ghazl al-Mahalla "were shocked by our [the workers'] numbers" (Beinin and El-Hamalawy, 2007). Faced with a crowd of around ten thousand employees, they did not move against them. This inaction by the police was not an isolated occurrence. In general, whether due to their large numbers, economic importance, or both, the regime rarely used violence against large numbers of striking workers (Beinin and Duboc, 2013, 212).

In addition, labor movement organizers were keenly aware of the power of numbers, displaying and publicizing their large numbers (e.g. displaying keys at the tax collectors' sit-in) and also manipulating them (e.g. banging on iron barrels during the first Ghazl al-Mahalla strike). While such manipulation was carried out by a relatively small number of workers, it would not have been credible without the threatened participation of thousands. The large numbers of workers in state-owned factories and firms thus helped them to mobilize against the regime even in the absence of autonomous trade union structures or strong independent civil society organizations.

In contrast, social networks may have played a less important role in facilitating protest among Egyptian state workers. Like state institutions in Palestine, state-owned factories and firms in Egypt did join individuals from diverse backgrounds in wider and more information-rich social networks than their peers. For example, from its foundation in 1927, Ghazl al-Mahalla has recruited rural peasants from the villages surrounding the factory to work alongside urban workers from the city itself (Beinin and El-Hamalawy, 2007). Similarly, as employees situated within large provincial offices, Egypt's tax collectors would also likely have had a broad range of acquaintances and contacts. As the initial strikes at Ghazl al-Mahalla and Giza were local labor actions staged over local demands, however, these networks may not have been as important for facilitating participation in these actions as they were in the Palestinian case. Without more in-depth research, which is beyond the scope of this book, it is difficult to establish the precise impact of wide social networks on participation in the Egyptian labor movement. Nonetheless, Egyptian state workers were situated within such networks, and these networks may have aided in the movement's broader diffusion.

In sum, as economic grievances intensified among Egyptian government workers and other Egyptians, workers generally lacked the strong autonomous institutions that are often regarded as necessary for protest. Yet, in comparison to other aggrieved groups, Egyptian state workers did possess important informational and organizational advantages for collective action. As workers at public factories and firms employing thousands of people, they could easily communicate and coordinate with one another even without access to information technology, and they benefited from safety in numbers that deterred harsh police action and encouraged wide participation in their campaign. Workers were also joined in large and diverse social networks, which may have helped their movement to spread. As a result, Egyptian state workers were better able to protest and, consequently, may also have been more likely to participate than many other economically aggrieved Egyptians.

Why, then, did protest emerge in state-owned factories and firms in Egypt but not in the Occupied Palestinian Territories? As described earlier in the book, in the 1970s and 1980s, the Palestinian Territories was still a predominantly rural society with low levels of industrialization. With few workplaces employing more than twenty workers (Hiltermann, 1993, 19), there were simply no factories or firms large enough to support mass mobilization. If Israeli authorities had developed an industrial sector in the Palestinian Territories, the theory advanced in this book predicts that Israeli state-owned industries would also have become sites of resistance to Israeli rule. While it is impossible to assess this counterfactual, the Egyptian case suggests that the particular configuration of state institutions involved in protest may be context-specific. Regardless of the particular institutions at work, however, comparative analysis indicates that state institutions are also likely to play an important mobilizing role in other cases where groups possess strong anti-regime grievances but lack internal organizational strength.

6.3.3 State Institutions and Technological Change

Consistent with this book's findings in the Palestinian case, state institutions were also key sites of protest in the 1976 Soweto Uprising and the Egyptian workers' movement of the 2000s. Yet, to what extent do these findings help explain participation in mass protest in the present day? Have new forms of information technology rendered state institutions obsolete as sites of mobilization and resistance? Or will such institutions continue to play an important role even as new information technologies become more prevalent? Inspired by these questions, this section explores the utility of the book's arguments for understanding individual participation in protest not only across space but also moving forward across time.

Academic and media accounts of recent uprisings and upheavals around the world often give pride of place to the mobilizing power of social media and other information technologies. For example, writing in the *Atlantic* about the 2009 protests in Iran, Andrew Sullivan called Twitter "the critical tool for organizing resistance in Iran" (quoted in Morozov, 2009, 10). Likewise, two years after the proclamation of this first "Twitter Revolution," commentators widely hailed the Arab uprisings as, alternately, some combination of "The Twitter/Facebook Uprisings/Protests/Revolutions" (Little, 2016).

Information technology did play an unprecedented role in the Arab uprisings, helping to transform what began as local demonstrations in Tunisia into a regional wave of protest (Lynch, 2013, 76, 81–82). At the same time, the rise of new information technologies is unlikely to render state institutions irrelevant as sites of mobilization and resistance. This is the case for at least three reasons. First, across much of the developing world, internet penetration is still far from complete. For example, in the Egyptian labor movement of the 2000s, email and internet contacts were uncommon: face-to-face meetings and mobile phone calls were the dominant modes of communication (Beinin and Duboc, 2013, 209). When the Egyptian revolution erupted several years later in 2011, Facebook penetration remained at merely 5.5 percent of the population (Mourtada and Salem, 2011). Most Egyptians continued to get their news from traditional television and radio outlets, many of them under the regime's control (Arab Barometer, 2011).

Similarly, Evgeny Morozov notes that, despite the heady media coverage of Iran's "Twitter Revolution" in 2009, very few Iranians were actually on Twitter. In a country of more than seventy million people, less than twenty thousand were Twitter users before the protests began (Morozov, 2009, 12). Likewise, even in Tunisia, where the internet is demonstrated to have played an important coordinating role, Marc Lynch writes that "there were simply not enough Arab users of social media for that alone to have made a difference" (Lynch, 2013, 82). While social media did allow images of Tunisian protestors to spread despite regime repression, it was neither necessary nor sufficient for organizing protests (Lynch, 2013, 81).

Second, just as activists can, authoritarian regimes and their supporters can also exploit new information technologies to pursue their own strategic ends. Whereas state intelligence services may once have been relatively ignorant of these technologies, they now routinely use them to monitor activists and prospective dissidents. Indeed, social media platforms like Facebook and Twitter may allow intelligence services to gather open-source intelligence about future revolutionaries and their networks more easily than before. Once obtainable only by torture, this information is now available at the click of a button (Morozov, 2009, 12). As a result, Morozov argues, political activists are unlikely to use the internet to coordinate with one another. Writing about the role of the internet in the 2009 protests in Iran – often labeled "the Twitter Revolution" – he states: "That the Iranian opposition would venture into Twitter territory to deliberate about the best venue for its next march is ridiculous, not only because it seems pointless... but because the Iranian secret services would probably read these deliberations before anyone else did – and then take preemptive action" (Morozov, 2009, 12).

Government authorities can preempt protests by spreading false information about them online or, as with more traditional media sources, limiting access to this information altogether. For example, writing about Iran, Morozov reports that online "citizen vigilantes" – presumably regime supporters – spread misinformation about the times and venues of protests, as well as about the reaction of state authorities (Morozov, 2009, 13).[8] State authorities can also censor the internet or shut it off entirely. On January 26, 2011, the second day of the Egyptian revolution, the Egyptian government closed off access to the internet nationwide. Vodafone, the largest Egyptian cell phone carrier and a company with

---

[8] Similarly, activists can also deliberately spread false information about protests online. For instance, Lynch reports that Egyptian revolutionaries posted fake venues and locations of protests online and then circulated the real information via text message shortly before the events (Lynch, 2013, 88).

close ties to the regime, also shut down its networks (Lynch, 2013, 89). As Marc Lynch points out, these actions did not succeed in crippling the protest movement: due to heavy coverage of the protests on Al Jazeera, many Egyptians could simply turn on their televisions to find out when and where demonstrations were happening (Lynch, 2013, 90). However, the Egyptian case is somewhat unusual due to Egypt's size and historical importance and the unique timing of the protests, which immediately followed Tunisia's successful revolution. In cases where there is no alternative media outlet like Al Jazeera or media coverage is less extensive, these measures would likely have been more debilitating. Where these conditions are coupled with a weak civil society, state institutions are therefore likely to remain at the locus of resistance.

Consequently, even as information technology continues to gain in reach and sophistication, state institutions should continue to serve as important sites for mobilization and resistance. Like social media usage, integration into these institutions gives rise to new social networks and facilitates rapid communication and coordination. However, unlike online networks that can be easily monitored and surveilled by the state at the click of a button, these face-to-face networks may, paradoxically, be more difficult for the state to penetrate. In addition, real-world networks may also be less susceptible to manipulation and the spreading of misinformation, rendering the information they provide more credible. Finally, to the extent that the internet fragments users into small, homogenous online communities (see e.g. Ginsburg, Abu-Lughod, and Larkin, 2002), online networks may potentially be smaller, less diverse, and lower in information value than the wide social networks formed through integration into state institutions.

For these reasons, perhaps, face-to-face networks have remained important channels of protest mobilization in a number of more recent cases. For example, in the Egyptian revolution of 2011, political activists spread information about protests by text message, not online, and most participants were mobilized through more traditional offline networks (Lynch, 2013, 88; Berman and Nugent, 2018). In an age of state surveillance and censorship and tightening restrictions on global civil society, state institutions that connect people in new and wider social networks should thus continue to be at the forefront of resistance.

7

Methodological Appendix

7.1 SURVEY DESIGN

This book draws on an original large-scale survey of former participants and nonparticipants in unarmed resistance in the Palestinian Territories. The survey was conducted in sixty-eight localities across the West Bank, including Palestinian cities, towns, villages, and refugee camps. Figure 7.1 displays the localities included in the survey, which are marked with triangles. As seen in the figure, these localities are representative of the West Bank's three regions: north, center, and south.

Although the survey was conducted in the West Bank alone, omitting the Gaza Strip and parts of East Jerusalem, its conclusions are expected to generalize to the Palestinian Territories as a whole. Due to access restrictions, the survey did not include localities in the Gaza Strip. East Jerusalem neighborhoods on the Israeli side of the separation barrier were also excluded due to the well-known problem of high survey refusal rates in these neighborhoods. However, because East Jerusalem and the Gaza Strip were only sharply differentiated from the West Bank *after* the time period covered by the survey, their exclusion should not affect its findings. Specifically, because East Jerusalem neighborhoods were only recently cut off from similar neighborhoods sampled on the other side of the barrier (which, in some cases, divided existing neighborhoods in two), omitting them should not affect conclusions about participation in resistance long before the barrier was built. Similarly, because the West Bank and Gaza Strip were under the same administration during the time period studied and movement was not restricted between them, the determinants of participation in resistance in the Gaza Strip should

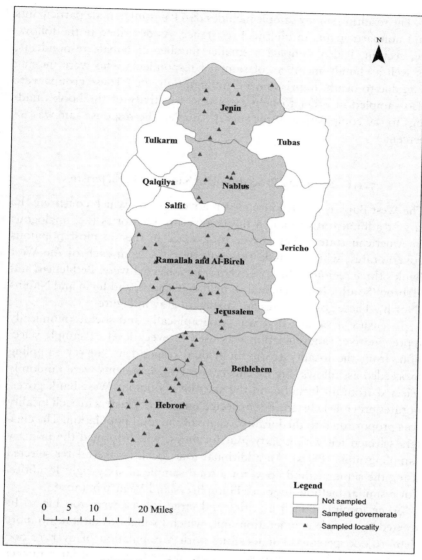

FIGURE 7.1 Localities sampled for survey

be generally similar to those identified in the West Bank. Indeed, as I show using administrative data, the survey sample closely resembles the population of the entire Palestinian Territories on available demographic and socioeconomic indicators.

The resulting survey sample includes 646 Palestinian male participants and nonparticipants in unarmed resistance. As described in the following section, I also sampled a smaller number of female respondents, as well as family members of sampled respondents who were missing (e.g. due to death, imprisonment, immigration, etc.) These groups were also sampled in order to help assess the sensitivity of the book's findings to the composition of the survey sample. The response rate was 68 percent.[1]

7.1.1 Sampling Procedure and Sample Characteristics

The West Bank is divided into eleven governorates, which constitute the largest administrative unit in the Palestinian Territories (i.e. analogous to American states). The survey took place in the six most populous governorates, which include two governorates from each of the West Bank's three regions. The six governorates selected were: Bethlehem and Hebron (South), Jerusalem and Ramallah (Center), and Jenin and Nablus (North). These governorates are shaded in gray in Figure 7.1.

To ensure a sample that was geographically and socioeconomically representative, randomization was used at every level of sample selection, from the locality to the individual respondent. Survey sampling proceeded as follows. Eighty clusters of ten respondents were randomly selected from all localities in the six most populous West Bank governorates previously listed. The expected number of clusters in each locality was proportional to the locality's share of the total population. The clusters selected fell within sixty-four localities, which formed the primary sampling units (PSUs). An additional four localities were later selected using the same methodology, for a total sample of sixty-eight localities. For a similar methodology, see Humphreys and Weinstein (2008).

Some localities, such as cities and large towns, were too big to be treated as a single enumeration unit, which I sought to limit at no more than 10,000 persons. For localities with a population of over 10,000 persons, the following procedure was adopted. As I will later further describe, localities with a population of over 20,000 persons were divided into smaller enumeration units, and cluster(s) were then randomly sampled from within these units. Localities with populations between ten

---

[1] AAPOR response rate category 2. Since this response rate includes all households of unknown eligibility in the denominator, the true response rate may be higher. The response rate was estimated based on a subsample of all household contact attempts.

and twenty thousand persons were also divided into smaller enumeration units if the population of each of the resulting units would be closer to 10,000 persons than if the locality were left undivided.

In localities that were too large to be treated as a single enumeration unit, an additional stage of sample selection was undertaken. All such localities were first divided into smaller enumeration units, which were no bigger than 0.75 kilometers across their furthest points – the largest geographical area that could reasonably be covered by each team of interviewers (i.e. "enumeration team"). To divide localities into enumeration units, I used a scale ruler to divide census maps of each locality purchased from the Palestinian Central Bureau of Statistics (PCBS). Importantly, while these maps were useful for defining and selecting enumeration units, they were not sufficiently up-to-date to permit sampling of households. Thus, as I will describe, a separate procedure was used to sample households from within each enumeration area.

After dividing each large locality into smaller enumeration units, enumeration units were sampled as follows. In those localities that were assigned one cluster, one enumeration unit was randomly selected from the set of all 0.75 kilometer enumeration units. In localities assigned multiple clusters, the locality was first divided into the assigned number of clusters. If the resulting clusters were still too large, an enumeration unit was then randomly selected from each cluster.

Within each enumeration area, households were sampled from a map sampling frame created by the enumeration team. Enumerators drew a map of all residential buildings lying on a randomly chosen axis located between the geographical center of the enumeration area and its borders. This was achieved as follows. Enumerators began at the geographical center of the locality. For larger localities, this was identified by the PI on maps handed to the enumeration team. For smaller localities (i.e. smaller than 10,000 persons), the enumeration team identified the geographical center by asking local residents. After identifying the geographical center of the locality, enumerators used a random number table to randomly select one of eight compass directions: north, south, east, west, northeast, northwest, southeast, southwest. After randomly selecting a compass direction, enumerators used a wristband compass provided by the PI to locate this compass direction. Finally, respondents walked along this compass direction and marked each residential building lying on the compass direction as they went. A random number table was then used to select which households to visit based on the number of households included in the sampling frame. This procedure was designed to result in a more representative sample of households than would typically result from a simple random walk procedure.

The final stage of sample selection involved randomly selecting an individual respondent from each randomly selected household. After verifying that the household was present in the Palestinian Territories during the period covered by the study (1978–89) and that at least one member of the household satisfied the eligibility requirements for the survey, enumerators worked with the head of the household to construct an anonymous household roster. The head of the household was asked to think of all members of the household who satisfied the residency and age requirements for participation in the survey. A respondent was then selected from this list using a random number table. If the selected respondent had passed away, was no longer living in the household, or would be away from the household beyond the duration of the fieldwork, the head of household was asked to complete an absentee questionnaire. As in Blattman (2009) and Scacco (n.d.), this latter step was intended to assess any potential selection bias stemming from the absence of individuals more active in anti-regime resistance due to death, imprisonment, or deportation.

As participation in anti-regime resistance was relatively rare, particularly before the first intifadah, a simple random sample of households and individuals may not have produced a sufficient number of participants to allow for meaningful causal inference. To ensure that a sufficient number of participants would be included in the sample, eligibility for participation in the survey was restricted to males between the ages of six and thirty-five years old in 1978 (i.e. the first year of the study period).[2] Despite the unprecedented nature of women's participation in demonstrations within conservative Palestinian society and the considerable attention given to women's participation, female participation rates remained quite low – 10 percent compared to the overall participation rate of 35 percent by my estimates. Participation in protests and demonstrations also declined with age, becoming much less common after middle age. For these reasons, the survey sample was limited to younger males. In order to assess the sensitivity of the findings to these characteristics of the survey sample, a small sample of women was also surveyed using the same general procedures as the main sample already described.

---

[2] This resulted in a survey sample that was between the ages of six and forty-six years old during the study period (1978–89).

TABLE 7.1 *Descriptive statistics*

Variable	Mean	Standard Deviation	Median	Min.	Max.	N
Main Outcome of Interest						
Participation in Anti-Regime Resistance	0.36	0.48	0	0	1	3074
Main Independent Variables						
Educational Institutions						
Preparatory	0.57	0.50	1	0	1	3857
Secondary	0.37	0.48	0	0	1	3857
University	0.13	0.33	0	0	1	3857
Schooling (in Years)	9.12	4.38	9	0	23	3751
Disciplinary Institutions						
Imprisonment of Relative/ Friend	0.05	0.21	0	0	1	3495
Non-state Structures						
Civic Networks	0.73	1.00	0	0	3	2914
Key Demographic/Control Variables						
Age	26.31	7.94	26	6	45	3857
Wealth/Household Amenities	3.32	2.19	3	0	9	3839
Family Status/Father's Education	0.24	0.43	0	0	1	3587

Table 7.1 presents key descriptive statistics on the main survey sample of male respondents. As described in Section 7.2, the survey collected data on individuals over the period between 1978 and 1989, resulting in multiple observations for each respondent. The statistics below are thus for respondent-years. As seen in the table, the mean age of respondents during the period from 1978 to 1989 was 26.31 years old. The mean number of years of schooling was 9.12 years, which is almost exactly equal to preparatory school completion (nine years). 57 percent of respondents, or slightly over half of the sample, completed preparatory school, 37 percent completed secondary school, and 13 percent completed university.

Respondents experienced the imprisonment of a family member or close friend in approximately 5 percent of all respondent-years. That is, respondents had a family member or friend enter or be placed in prison in 5 percent of all respondent-years, with the proportion of respondents with a family member or close friend imprisoned at any time between 1978 and 1989 consequently higher. On average, respondents knew a

TABLE 7.2 *Survey and CBS population proportions*

	Survey Sample	West Bank	Palestinian Territories
Household Size			
Household Size: 1	0.01	0.05	0.04
Household Size: 2	0.05	0.08	0.08
Household Size: 3	0.05	0.07	0.07
Household Size: 4	0.09	0.08	0.09
Household Size: 5	0.14	0.10	0.10
Household Size: 6	0.16	0.10	0.10
Household Size: 7+	0.49	0.51	0.51
Profession[1]			
Employer or Manager	0.02	0.01	0.01
Professional	0.13	0.08	0.08
Office Worker	0.02	0.03	0.03
Skilled Worker	0.24 – 0.35[1]	0.26	0.27
Farmer or Agricultural Worker	0.20	0.28	0.25
Other Statistics			
Unemployed[2]	0.03	0.01	0.01
Monthly Income[3] (NIS)	900+	2100	2084
Refugee	0.16	0.42	0.56

Notes: Population proportions calculated using the Statistical Abstracts of Israel prepared by the Israeli Central Bureau of Statistics (CBS). CBS figures for the Palestinian Territories exclude East Jerusalem. All survey and population proportions are reported for 1978.
[1] Profession data drawn from CBS data on employed persons by occupation. The percentage of skilled workers in our survey data ranges from 0.24 to 0.35 depending on whether or not semiskilled workers are also included; CBS did not include a semiskilled category.
[2] CBS unemployment rate calculated by dividing the total number of unemployed persons by the total number of persons in the labor force.
[3] Population monthly income calculated by taking CBS average daily wage in Israeli pounds, converting to new Israeli shekels (NIS) and multiplying by 20 (days). Sample income is the modal income bracket; 900+ was the highest income bracket included in the survey.

member of 0.73 civil society organizations – fewer than one organization. Finally, respondents reported participating in anti-regime resistance, the main dependent variable of the study, in 36 percent of all respondent years. In 1988–89, the peak year of participation in the sample, 43 percent of respondents reported participating in anti-regime resistance.

Table 7.2 further compares the survey sample to the Palestinian population of the Occupied Territories in 1978. Historical data on the Palestinian population were obtained from the Israeli Central Bureau of Statistics, which is the only available data source of which I am aware. Table 7.2 compares the survey sample to the population on all indicators for which comparable data were available.[3] As seen in the table, the survey sample closely resembles the population as a whole in terms of its demographic and socioeconomic characteristics. However, the survey sample includes a significantly lower proportion of refugees than the population as a whole. While I expected to find that refugees participated in anti-regime resistance at higher rates than non-refugees, this did not turn out to be the case: refugee status was not significantly associated with participation in anti-regime resistance in any of the analyses I conducted. Thus, the lower proportion of refugees in the survey sample seems unlikely to bias the conclusions of the study regarding the determinants of participation in anti-regime resistance.

7.2 SURVEY ADMINISTRATION, QUESTIONNAIRE DESIGN, AND DATA STRUCTURE

The survey consisted of a closed-ended questionnaire that was administered to respondents in person by a Palestinian enumerator from their home region. As previously described in this volume, survey responses to questions about participation in anti-regime resistance may be biased due to social desirability concerns, leading respondents to overreport and/or potentially underreport their participation. To mitigate such social desirability bias as well as limit any possible risks to respondents, all questions regarding participation were self-administered by the respondent. Self-administration is the gold standard for collecting sensitive individual-level data that cannot be collected using group-level methods like list experiments (Corstange, 2009; Groves et al., 2011). Using techniques adapted from Scacco's innovative study of riot participation (n.d.), all sensitive questions were contained in a separate questionnaire, which included no other personal information and was linked to the main questionnaire by a random number known to the principal investigator alone. The respondent completed this separate questionnaire by himself while the survey enumerator waited, usually in a separate room, and then placed it into a separate envelope from the main questionnaire that also contained other respondents' questionnaires. If the respondent was illiterate, the survey enumerator read the survey questions, answer choices,

---

[3] The population data are for males as well as females. However, since most Palestinian women did not work outside the home (i.e. were not in the labor force), data on individuals' professions (i.e. employed persons by profession/occupation), unemployment, and monthly income should be similar for men and women.

and instructions aloud while sitting sufficiently far away to allow the respondent privacy. All answer choices were numbered in such a way as to allow illiterate respondents to complete the survey independently in response to the enumerator's verbal instructions. Thus, for all respondents, the enumerator did not view the respondent's answers to sensitive questions and could not link these answers to other characteristics of the respondent recorded in the main survey questionnaire. These steps were carefully explained to all respondents during the informed consent process.

The survey collected data on individual participation in anti-regime resistance during the period from 1978 to 1989, over twenty years before the survey was conducted in 2011. Retrospective surveys such as this one may be subject to recall bias, even when they are conducted closer in time to the events they study: prior research shows that recall substantially deteriorates as little as one year after a given event and subsequently stabilizes (Groves et al., 2011, 213–18). To mitigate these problems of accurate recall and collect reliable, time-sensitive information about individual behavior during conflict, the survey used an event history calendar or life history calendar ("LHC") questionnaire design. Life history calendars have been widely used in sociology, public health, and other fields, and, in a direct experimental comparison, they have been shown to yield more complete and accurate reports of retrospective behavior than standard question list surveys (Belli, Shay, and Stafford, 2001). Yet, to my knowledge, this is the first political science study to use a life history calendar to study past political behavior.

In contrast to a traditional survey questionnaire, an event history calendar takes the form of a two-dimensional grid. The vertical dimension is divided by the variables of interest, for example marital status or income. The horizontal dimension is divided into the time units used in the study. These serve as timing cues that respondents can use to help them recall the timing of life events (Belli, 1998).[4] The introduction to the survey also included a variety of "cognitive landmarks" – national and regional events, as well as local and personal events filled in before the survey interview – as additional timing cues (Belli, 1998; Axinn, Pearce, and Ghimire, 1999). Figures 7.2 and 7.3 depict a sample question from the survey questionnaire in event history format, as well as the introduction to the survey with cognitive landmarks.

---

[4] For more information on why LHCs help improve recall in retrospective surveys, see Chapters 1 and 3.

1.1	In year [1978...], were you single, married, widowed, divorced or separated?											
Marital Status	1978	1979	1980	1981	1982	1983	1984	1985	1986	1987	1988	
Single	O		O		O		O		O		O	
Married	O		O		O		O		O		O	
Widowed	O		O		O		O		O		O	
Divorced	O		O		O		O		O		O	O DK
Separated	O		O		O		O		O		O	O RF

FIGURE 7.2 Survey question in event history calendar layout

Gregorian Year	1978	1979	1980	1981	1982	1983	1984	1985	1986	1987	1988
Islamic Year	1398	1399	1400	1401	1402	1403	1404	1405	1406	1407	1408
Respondent Age											
Regional Events	Camp David Accords signed			Sadat assass- inated	Second Israeli invasion of Lebanon	U.S. Marine barracks in Lebanon bombed		Achille Lauro incident			PNC meets in Algiers
National Events										First intifada begins	
Locality Events											
Personal Events											

FIGURE 7.3 Landmarks domain of survey

In this study, the LHC collected data on respondents over six two-year periods between 1978 and 1989. Data on participation was collected on the six two-year periods from 1979 to 1989, and data on the independent variables was collected on the six two-year periods from 1978 to 1988. This approach allows for lagging the independent variables in the analysis without having to truncate the time period covered by the survey. As previously mentioned in this volume and reported in the online appendix, my main results are also robust to grouping the data into wider four-year periods, which allow respondents more room for error in recalling the timing of their participation.

The unit of analysis in the resulting dataset is thus the individual-period. For each individual respondent, there are six observations corresponding to six periods: 1978–79, 1980–81, 1982–83, 1984–85, 1986–87, and 1988–89. As already described, data on the independent variables was collected on the first (even) year of each period, and data on the dependent variables was collected on the second (odd) year of each period. The resulting dataset thus includes six observations on 646 respondents for a total of 3876 complete observations.

Bibliography

Abu-Amr, Ziad. 1994. *Islamic Fundamentalism in the West Bank and Gaza: Muslim Brotherhood and Islamic Jihad.* Indiana University Press.

Al-Sha'bani, B., and S. Khadr. 1982. "Al-Khadamat al-'ama fi qura al-Difa al-Gharbiyya wa Qita' Ghaza [Public services in the villages of the West Bank and the Gaza Strip]." Technical report, Office of Literacy and Adult Education, Birzeit University. Birzeit, Palestine.

Alimi, Eitan. 2007. "Discursive Contention: Palestinian Media Discourse and the Inception of the 'First' Intifada." *Harvard International Journal of Press/Politics* 12(4):71–91.

Alwin, Duane F., and Jon A. Krosnick. 1991. "Aging, Cohorts, and the Stability Of Sociopolitical Orientations over the Life Span." *American Journal of Sociology* 97(1):169–95.

Alzaroo, Salah, and Gillian Lewando Hunt. 2003. "Education in the Context of Conflict and Instability: The Palestinian Case." *Social Policy & Administration* 37(2):165–80.

Andersen, Benedict. 1983. *Imagined Communities.* Verso.

Asal, Victor, Richard Legault, Ora Szekely, and Jonathan Wilkenfeld. 2013. "Gender Ideologies and Forms of Contentious Mobilization in the Middle East." *Journal of Peace Research* 50(3):305–18.

Axinn, William G., Lisa D. Pearce, and Dirgha Ghimire. 1999. "Innovations in Life History Calendar Applications." *Social Science Research* 28(3): 243–64.

Badat, Saleem. 2016. *Black Student Politics: Higher Education and Apartheid from SASO to SANSCO, 1968–1990.* Routledge.

Baskin, Jeremy. 1991. *Striking Back: A History of Cosatu.* Raven Press.

Beck, Nathaniel, Jonathan N. Katz, and Richard Tucker. 1998. "Taking Time Seriously: Time-Series-Cross-Section Analysis with a Binary Dependent Variable." *American Journal of Political Science* 42(4):1260–88.

Beinin, Joel. 2015. *Workers and Thieves: Labor Movements and Popular Uprisings in Tunisia and Egypt.* Stanford University Press.

Beinin, Joel, and Hossam El-Hamalawy. 2007. "Egyptian Textile Workers Confront the New Economic Order." *Middle East Report Online* 25.

Beinin, Joel, and Marie Duboc. 2013. "A Workers' Social Movement on the Margin of the Global Neoliberal Order, Egypt 2004–2012." In *Social Movements, Mobilization, and Contestation in the Middle East and North Africa*, ed. Joel Beinin and Frédéric Vairel. Stanford University Press, pp. 205–27.

Beissinger, Mark R. 2011. "Mechanisms of Maidan: The Structure of Contingency in the Making of the Orange Revolution." *Mobilization: An International Quarterly* 16(1):25–43.

Beissinger, Mark R. 2013. "The Semblance of Democratic Revolution: Coalitions in Ukraine's Orange Revolution." *American Political Science Review* 107(3):574–92.

Beissinger, Mark R., Amaney A. Jamal, and Kevin Mazur. 2015. "Explaining Divergent Revolutionary Coalitions: Regime Strategies and the Structuring of Participation in the Tunisian and Egyptian Revolutions." *Comparative Politics* 48(1):1–24.

Belli, Robert F. 1998. "The Structure of Autobiographical Memory and the Event History Calendar: Potential Improvements in the Quality of Retrospective Reports in Surveys." *Memory* 6(4):383–406.

Belli, Robert F., William L. Shay, and Frank P. Stafford. 2001. "Event History Calendars and Question List Surveys: A Direct Comparison of Interviewing Methods." *Public Opinion Quarterly* 65(1):45–74.

Benvenisti, Meron, and Shlomo Khayat. 1988. *The West Bank and Gaza Atlas*. West Bank Data Base Project.

Berman, Chantal, and Elizabeth Nugent. 2018. "Ctrl-Alt-Revolt? Online and Offline Networks during the 2011 Egyptian Uprising." Middle East Law and Governance 10(1):59–90.

Berman, Eli, Michael Callen, Joseph H. Felter, and Jacob N. Shapiro. 2011. "Do Working Men Rebel? Insurgency and Unemployment in Afghanistan, Iraq, and the Philippines." *Journal of Conflict Resolution* 55(4):496–528.

Blair, Graeme, C. Christine Fair, Neil Malhotra, and Jacob N. Shapiro. 2013. "Poverty and Support for Militant Politics: Evidence from Pakistan." *American Journal of Political Science* 57(1):30–48.

Blattman, Christopher. 2009. "From Violence to Voting: War and Political Participation in Uganda." *American Political Science Review* 103(2):231–47.

Brady, Henry E., Sidney Verba, and Kay Lehman Schlozman. 1995. "Beyond SES: A Resource Model of Political Participation." *American Political Science Review* 89(2):271–94.

Brancati, Dawn. 2016. *Democracy Protests*. Cambridge University Press.

Brand, Laurie A. 1991. *Palestinians in the Arab World: Institution Building and the Search for State*. Columbia University Press.

Brand, Laurie A. 2014. *Official Stories: Politics and National Narratives in Egypt and Algeria*. Stanford University Press.

Brewer, John D. 1986. *After Soweto: An Unfinished Journey*. Oxford University Press, USA.

Brown, Nathan J. 2003. *Palestinian Politics after the Oslo Accords: Resuming Arab Palestine*. University of California Press.

B'Tselem. 1990. "The Military Judicial System in the West Bank: Followup Report", ed. Daphna Golan. Technical report, B'Tselem - The Israeli

Information Center for Human Rights in the Occupied Territories. Technical report.

Burt, Ronald S. 2009. *Structural Holes: The Social Structure of Competition.* Harvard University Press.

Campante, Filipe R., and Davin Chor. 2012. "Why Was the Arab World Poised for Revolution? Schooling, Economic Opportunities, and the Arab Spring." *The Journal of Economic Perspectives* 26(2):167–87.

Campbell, Angus. 1980. *The American Voter.* University of Chicago Press.

Cederman, L. E., N. B. W. Weidmann, and K. S. Gleditsch. 2011. "Horizontal Inequalities and Ethno-nationalist Civil War: A Global Comparison." *American Political Science Review* 105(3):478–95.

Chenoweth, Erica, and Maria J. Stephan. 2011. *Why Civil Resistance Works: The Strategic Logic of Nonviolent Conflict.* Columbia University Press.

Chenoweth, Erica, and Orion A. Lewis. 2013. "Unpacking Nonviolent Campaigns: Introducing the NAVCO 2.0 Dataset." *Journal of Peace Research* 50(3):415–23.

Collier, Paul, and Anke Hoeffler. 2004. "Greed and Grievance in Civil War." *Oxford Economic Papers* 56(4):563–95.

Collins, John. 2004. *Occupied by Memory: The Intifada Generation and the Palestinian State of Emergency.* New York University Press.

Corstange, Daniel. 2009. "Sensitive Questions, Truthful Answers? Modeling the List Experiment with LISTIT." *Political Analysis* 17(1):45–63.

Cunningham, Kathleen Gallagher. 2013. "Understanding Strategic Choice: The Determinants of Civil War and Nonviolent Campaign in Self-determination Disputes." *Journal of Peace Research* 50(3):291–304.

Darden, Keith. 2013. "Resisting Occupation: Mass Schooling and the Creation of Durable National Loyalties." Book manuscript.

Davenport, Christian, and Priyamvada Trivedi. 2013. "Activism and Awareness: Resistance, Cognitive Activation, and 'Seeing' Untouchability among 98,316 Dalits." *Journal of Peace Research* 50(3):369–83.

Della Porta, Donatella. 1988. "Recruitment Processes in Clandestine Political Organizations: Italian Left-wing Terrorism." *International Social Movement Research* 1:155–69.

Di Palma, Giuseppe. 1991. "Legitimation from the Top to Civil Society: Politico-cultural Change in Eastern Europe." *World Politics: A Quarterly Journal of International Relations* 44(1):49–80.

Dudouet, Véronique. 2013. "Dynamics and Factors of Transition from Armed Struggle to Nonviolent Resistance." *Journal of Peace Research* 50(3):401–13.

Earl, Jennifer. 2003. "Tanks, Tear Gas, and Taxes: Toward a Theory of Movement Repression." *Sociological Theory* 21(1):44–68.

Earl, Jennifer. 2011. "Political Repression: Iron Fists, Velvet Gloves, and Diffuse Control." *Annual Review of Sociology* 37:261–84.

FACTS Information Committee. 1988. "Towards a State of Independence – The Palestinian Uprising: December 1987–August 1988." *Jerusalem: Facts Information Committee.*

FACTS Information Committee. 1990a. "Diaries." In *The Palestinian Uprising,* eds. Samir Abed-Rabbo and Doris Safie. Belmont, MA: The Association of Arab-American University Graduates, pp. 55–130.

FACTS Information Committee. 1990*b*. "Fear of Education." In *The Palestinian Uprising*, eds. Samir Abed-Rabbo and Doris Safie. Belmont, MA: The Association of Arab-American University Graduates, pp. 307–48.

FACTS Information Committee. 1990*c*. "Physical Measures." In *The Palestinian Uprising*, eds. Samir Abed-Rabbo and Doris Safie. Belmont, MA: The Association of Arab-American University Graduates, pp. 175–248.

Falloon, Virgil. 1986. *Excessive Secrecy, Lack of Guidelines: A Report on Military Censorship in the West Bank*. AL-HAQ Law in the Service of Man (West Bank affiliate of the International Commission of Jurists).

Fearon, James D., and David D. Laitin. 2003. "Ethnicity, Insurgency, and Civil War." *The American Political Science Review* 97(1):75–90.

Fine, Robert, and Dennis Davis. 1991. *Beyond Apartheid: Labour and Liberation in South Africa*. Ravan Press.

Freeman, Jo. 2015. "The Women's Movement." In *The Social Movements Reader*, eds. Jeff Goodwin and James M. Jasper. John Wiley & Sons, pp. 13–23.

Friedman, Robert I. 1983. "Israeli Censorship of the Palestinian Press." *Journal of Palestine Studies* 13(1):93–101.

Friedman, Steven. 1987. *Building Tomorrow Today: African Workers in Trade Unions, 1970–1984*. Ravan Press of South Africa.

Frisch, Hillel. 1993. "The Palestinian Movement in the Territories: The Middle Command." *Middle Eastern Studies* 29(2):254–74.

Frisch, Hillel. 1996. "From Repression to Facilitation: The Effects of Israeli Policies on Palestinian Mobilization in the West Bank, 1967–1987." *Terrorism and Political Violence* 8(1):1–21.

Frisch, Hillel. 2012. *Countdown to Statehood: Palestinian State Formation in the West Bank and Gaza*. SUNY Press.

Gazit, Shlomo. 2003. *Trapped Fools: Thirty Years of Israeli Policy in the Territories*. Vol. 38 Psychology Press.

Gellner, Ernest and John Breuilly. 2008. *Nations and Nationalism*. Cornell University Press.

Gelman, Andrew. 2007. *Data Analysis Using Regression and Multilevel/Hierarchical Models*. Cambridge University Press.

Gelvin, James L. 2012. *The Arab Uprisings: What Everyone Needs to Know*. Oxford University Press.

Gerber, Alan S., Donald P. Green, and Ron Shachar. 2003. "Voting May Be Habit-forming: Evidence from a Randomized Field Experiment." *American Journal of Political Science* 47(3):540–50.

Ginsburg, Faye D., Lila Abu-Lughod, and Brian Larkin. 2002. *Media Worlds: Anthropology on New Terrain*. University of California Press.

Glaser, Clive. 1998. " 'We Must Infiltrate the Tsotsis': School Politics and Youth Gangs in Soweto, 1968–1976." *Journal of Southern African Studies* 24(2):301–23.

Glaser, Clive. 2015. "Soweto's Islands of Learning: Morris Isaacson and Orlando High Schools under Bantu Education, 1958–1975." *Journal of Southern African Studies* 41(1):159–71.

Golan, Daphna. 1989. "The Military Judicial System in the West Bank." Technical report, B'Tselem – The Israeli Information Center for Human Rights in the Occupied Territories Jerusalem.

Goldstone, Jack A. 1994. "Is Revolution Individually Rational? Groups and Individuals in Revolutionary Collective Action." *Rationality and Society* 6(1):139–66.

Goodwin, Jeff. 2001. *No Other Way Out: States and Revolutionary Movements, 1945–1991.* Cambridge University Press.

Gordon, Haim, Rivca Gordon, and Taher Shriteh. 2003. *Beyond Intifada: Narratives of Freedom Fighters in the Gaza Strip.* Greenwood Publishing Group.

Gordon, Neve. 2008. *Israel's Occupation.* University of California Press.

Gould, William B. 1981. "Black Unions in South Africa: Labor Law Reform and Apartheid." *Stanford Journal of International Law.* 17:99.

Graham-Brown, Sarah. 1984. *Education, Repression & Liberation, Palestinians.* World University Service (UK).

Granovetter, Mark. 1978. "Threshold Models of Collective Behavior." *American Journal of Sociology* 1420–43.

Granovetter, M.S. 1973. "The Strength of Weak Ties." *American Journal of Sociology* 78(6):1360–80.

Groves, Robert M., Floyd J. Fowler Jr, Mick P. Couper, James M. Lepkowski, Eleanor Singer, and Roger Tourangeau. 2011. *Survey Methodology.* Vol. 561 John Wiley & Sons.

Gurr, T.R. 1970. *Why Men Rebel.* Princeton University Press.

Hajjar, Lisa. 2005. *Courting Conflict: The Israeli Military Court System in the West Bank and Gaza.* University of California Press.

Halabi, Rafik. 1985. *The West Bank Story.* Houghton Mifflin Harcourt Press.

Hasso, Frances S. 1998. "THE 'WOMEN'S FRONT': Nationalism, Feminism, and Modernity in Palestine." *Gender & Society* 12(4):441–465.

Hasso, Frances Susan. 2005. *Resistance, Repression, and Gender Politics in Occupied Palestine and Jordan.* Syracuse University Press.

Hiltermann, Joost R. 1993. *Behind the Intifada: Labor and Women's Movements in the Occupied Territories.* Princeton University Press.

Hirschmann, David. 1990. "The Black Consciousness Movement in South Africa." *The Journal of Modern African Studies* 28(01):1–22.

Hirson, Baruch. 1979. *Year of Fire, Year of Ash: The Soweto Revolt, Roots of a Revolution?* Vol. 3, Zed Press.

Hodgson, Geoffrey M. 1988. "Economics and Institutions." *Journal of Economic Issues.* Citeseer.

Hoffman, Michael, and Amaney Jamal. 2014. "Religion in the Arab Spring: Between Two Competing Narratives." *Journal of Politics* 76(3): 593–606.

Hoffman, Michael T., and Elizabeth R. Nugent. 2017. "Communal Religious Practice and Support for Armed Parties: Evidence from Lebanon." *Journal of Conflict Resolution* 61(4):869–902.

Horowitz, D. L. 1985. *Ethnic Groups in Conflict.* Vol. 387. University of California Press.

Humphreys, Macartan, and Jeremy M. Weinstein. 2008. "Who Fights? The Determinants of Participation in Civil War." *American Journal of Political Science* 52(2):436–55.

Jackson, Philip Wesley. 1990. *Life in Classrooms*. Teachers College Press.

Jaeger, David A., Esteban F. Klor, Sami H. Miaari, and M. Daniele Paserman. 2012. "The Struggle for Palestinian Hearts and Minds: Violence and Public Opinion in the Second Intifada." *Journal of Public Economics* 96(3–4):354–368.

Jamal, Amal. 2005. *The Palestinian National Movement: Politics of Contention, 1967–2005*. Indiana University Press.

Jamal, Amaney A. 2007. Barriers to Democracy: The Other Side of Social Capital in Palestine and the Arab World. Princeton University Press.

Jencks, Christopher, et al. 1972. "Inequality: A Reassessment of the Effect of Family and Schooling in America."

Jenkins, J. Craig, and Kurt Schock. 2003. "Political Process, International Dependence, and Mass Political Conflict: A Global Analysis of Protest and Rebellion, 1973–1978." *International Journal of Sociology* 33(4):41–63.

Kalyvas, Stathis N. 2006. *The Logic of Violence in Civil War*. Cambridge University Press.

Kam, Cindy D., and Carl L. Palmer. 2008. "Reconsidering the Effects of Education on Political Participation." *The Journal of Politics* 70(3):612–31.

Kapiszewski, Diana, Lauren M. MacLean, and Benjamin L. Read. 2015. *Field Research in Political Science: Practices and Principles*. Cambridge University Press.

Keck, Margaret E. and Kathryn Sikkink. 2014. *Activists beyond Borders: Advocacy Networks in International Politics*. Cornell University Press.

Kepel, Gilles. 1985. *Muslim Extremism in Egypt: The Prophet and Pharaoh*. University of California Press.

Khalidi, Rashid. 2010. *Palestinian Identity: The Construction of Modern National Consciousness*. Columbia University Press.

Khawaja, Marwan. 1995. "The Dynamics of Local Collective Action in the West Bank: A Test of Rival Explanations." *Economic Development and Cultural Change* 44(1):147–79.

King, Gary, Robert O. Keohane, and Sidney Verba. 1994. *Designing Social Inquiry: Scientific Inference in Qualitative Research*. Princeton University Press.

Kitschelt, Herbert P. 1986. "Political Opportunity Structures and Political Protest: Anti-nuclear Movements in Four Democracies." *British Journal of Political Science* 16(1):57–85.

Knight, Jack. 1992. *Institutions and Social Conflict*. Cambridge University Press.

Krause, Peter. 2017. *Rebel Power: Why National Movements Compete, Fight, and Win*. Cornell University Press.

Krosnick, Jon A., and Duane F. Alwin. 1989. "Aging and Susceptibility to Attitude Change." *Journal of Personality and Social Psychology* 57(3):416.

Kuran, T. 1989. "Sparks and Prairie Fires: A Theory of Unanticipated Political Revolution." *Public Choice* 61(1):41–74.

Kuran, Timur. 1991. "Now out of Never: The Element of Surprise in the East European Revolution of 1989." *World Politics* 44(01):7–48.

Kurzman, Charles. 1994. "A Dynamic View of Resources: Evidence from the Iranian Revolution." *Research in Social Movements, Conflicts and Change* 17:53–84.

Kuttab, Daoud. 1988. "A Profile of the Stonethrowers." *Journal of Palestine Studies* 17(3):14–23.

Kuttab, Daoud. 1998. "The Palestinian Media and the Peace Process." *Palestine-Israel Journal* 5(3–4).

Lachapelle, Jean. 2012. "Lessons from Egypt's Tax Collectors." *Middle East Report* 42(264):38–41.

Laitin, David D. 1995. "National Revivals and Violence." *European Journal of Sociology* 36(1):3–43.

Lavine, A. n.d. Social Services in the Administered Territories.

Lawrence, Adria. 2013. *Imperial Rule and the Politics of Nationalism: Anti-Colonial Protest in the French Empire.* Cambridge University Press.

Lawrence, Adria K. 2017. "Repression and Activism among the Arab Spring's First Movers: Evidence from Morocco's February 20th Movement." *British Journal of Political Science* 47(3):699–718.

LeBas, Adrienne. 2013. *From Protest to Parties: Party-building and Democratization in Africa.* Oxford University Press.

Lee, Alexander. 2011. "Who Becomes a Terrorist? Poverty, Education, and the Origins of Political Violence." *World Politics* 63(2):203–45.

Levi, Sasson. 1982. "Local Government in the Administered Territories." in *Judea, Samaria and Gaza: Views on the Present and Future,* pp. 103–123.

Lichbach, Mark I. 1998a. "Contending Theories of Contentious Politics and the Structure-Action Problem of Social Order." *Annual Review of Political Science* 1(1):401–24.

Lichbach, Mark Irving. 1998b. *The Rebel's Dilemma.* University of Michigan Press.

Lichbach, Mark Irving, and Ted Robert Gurr. 1981. "The Conflict Process: A Formal Model." *Journal of Conflict Resolution* 25(1):3–29.

Lichtenstein, Alex. 2005. "Making Apartheid Work: African Trade Unions and the 1953 Native Labour (Settlement of Disputes) Act in South Africa." *The Journal of African History* 46(2):293–314.

Lipset, Seymour Martin. 1964. "University Students and Politics in Underdeveloped Countries." *Minerva* 3(1):15–56.

Lipset, Seymour Martin. 1971. *Rebellion in the University.* Transaction Publishers.

Little, Andrew T. 2016. "Communication Technology and Protest." *The Journal of Politics* 78(1):152–66.

Lockman, Zachary, and Joel Beinin. 1989. *Intifada: The Palestinian Uprising against Israeli Occupation.* South End Press.

Lohmann, Susanne. 1994. "The Dynamics of Informational Cascades: The Monday Demonstrations in Leipzig, East Germany, 1989–91." *World Politics* 47(1):42–101.

Longo, Matthew, Daphna Canetti, and Nancy Hite-Rubin. 2014. "A Checkpoint Effect? Evidence from a Natural Experiment on Travel Restrictions in the West Bank." *American Journal of Political Science* 58(4): 1006–23.

Lyall, Jason. 2009. "Does Indiscriminate Violence Incite Insurgent Attacks? Evidence from Chechnya." *Journal of Conflict Resolution* 53(3):331–62.

Lynch, Marc. 2013. *The Arab Uprising: The Unfinished Revolutions of the New Middle East.* PublicAffairs.

Macun, I. 2000. "Growth, Structure and Power in the South African Union Movement." In *Trade Unions and Democratization in South Africa, 1985–97,* ed. Glenn Adler and Eddie Webster. St. Martin's Press, pp. 57–74.

Manekin, Devorah. In press. Regular Soldiers, Irregular War: Violence and Restraint in the Second Intifada. Cornell University Press.

Manski, Charles F. 1995. *Identification Problems in the Social Sciences.* Harvard University Press.

Marx, Anthony W. 1992. *Lessons of Struggle: South African Internal Opposition, 1960–1990.* Oxford University Press on Demand.

McAdam, Doug. 1986. "Recruitment to High-risk Activism: The Case of Freedom Summer." *American Journal of Sociology* 92(1):64–90.

McAdam, Doug. 2003. "Beyond Structural Analysis: Toward a More Dynamic Understanding of Social Movements." In *Social Movements and Networks: Relational Approaches to Collective Action,* ed. Mario Diani and Doug McAdam. Oxford University Press, pp. 281–98.

McAdam, Doug. 2010. *Political Process and the Development of Black Insurgency, 1930–1970.* University of Chicago Press.

McAdam, Doug, and Ronnelle Paulsen. 1993. "Specifying the Relationship between Social Ties and Activism." *American Journal of Sociology* 99(3): 640–67.

McAdam, Doug, Sidney Tarrow, and Charles Tilly. 2003. "Dynamics of Contention." *Social Movement Studies* 2(1):99–102.

McCarthy, John D. 1996. "Constraints and Opportunities in Adopting, Adapting, and Inventing." *Comparative Perspectives on Social movements: Political Opportunities, Mobilizing Structures, and Cultural Framings.* Cambridge University Press, pp. 141–51.

McCarthy, John D., and Mayer N. Zald. 1977a. "Resource Mobilization and Social Movements: A Partial Theory." *American Journal of Sociology* 82(6):1212–41.

McCarthy, John D., and Mayer N. Zald. 1977b. "The Trend of Social Movements in America: Professionalization and Resource Mobilization."

Migdal, Joel S. 2014. *Palestinian Society and Politics.* Princeton University Press.

Mishal, Shaul, and Avraham Sela. 2006. *The Palestinian Hamas: Vision, Violence, and Coexistence.* Columbia University Press.

Mishal, Shaul, and Re'uven Aharoni. 1994. *Speaking Stones: Communiqués from the Intifada Underground.* Syracuse University Press.

Morozov, Evgeny. 2009. "Iran: Downside to the 'Twitter Revolution.'" *Dissent* 56(4):10–14.

Morris, Aldon. 1984. "The Origin of the Civil Rights Movement." The Free Press.

Mourtada, Racha, and Fadi Salem. 2011. "Civil Movements: The Impact of Facebook and Twitter." *Arab Social Media Report* 1(2):1–30.

Mueller, Lisa. 2013. "Democratic Revolutionaries or Pocketbook Protesters? The Roots of the 2009–2010 Uprisings in Niger." *African Affairs* 112(448):398–420.

Muslih, Muhammad. 1993. "Palestinian Civil Society." *Middle East Journal* 47(2):258–74.

Nachtwey, Jodi, and Mark Tessler. 2002. "The Political Economy of Attitudes toward Peace among Palestinians and Israelis." *Journal of Conflict Resolution* 46(2):260–85.

Najjar, Orayb Aref. 2015. "Israel and the Occupied Territories: The Palestinian Press." In *Censorship: A World Encyclopedia*, ed. Derek Jones. Routledge, 1236–38.

Nashif, Esmail. 2008. *Palestinian Political Prisoners: Identity and Community*. Routledge.

Ndlovu, Sifiso Mxolisi. 2006. "The Soweto Uprising." *The Road to Democracy in South Africa* 2:1970–1980.

Nepstad, Sharon Erickson. 2011. *Nonviolent Revolutions: Civil Resistance in the Late 20th Century*. Oxford University Press.

Niemi, Richard G., and Mary A. Hepburn. 1995. "The Rebirth of Political Socialization." *Perspectives on Political Science* 24(1):7–16.

North, Douglass C. 1994. "Economic Performance through Time." *American Economic Review* 84(3):359–68.

Oberschall, Anthony. 1973. *Social Conflict and Social Movements*. Prentice-Hall.

Oliver, Pamela. 2008. "Repression and Crime Control: Why Social Movement Scholars Should Pay Attention to Mass Incarceration as a Form of Repression." *Mobilization: An International Quarterly* 13(1):1–24.

Olson, Mancur. 1965. *The Logic of Collective Action: Public Goods and the Theory of Groups*. Vol. 124. Harvard University Press.

Opp, Karl-Dieter, and Christiane Gern. 1993. "Dissident Groups, Personal Networks, and Spontaneous Cooperation: The East German Revolution of 1989." *American Sociological Review* 58(5):659–680.

Ost, David. 1991. *Solidarity and the Politics of Anti-politics: Opposition and Reform in Poland since 1968*. Temple University Press.

Paige, J. M. 1978. *Agrarian Revolution: Social Movements and Export Agriculture in the Underdeveloped World*. Free Press.

Pearlman, Wendy. 2011. *Violence, Nonviolence, and the Palestinian National Movement*. Cambridge University Press.

Pearlman, Wendy. 2013. "Emotions and the Microfoundations of the Arab Uprisings." *Perspectives on Politics* 11(2):387–409.

Peretz, Don. 1990. "The Intifada and Middle East Peace." *Survival* 32(5):387–401.

Peteet, Julie. 1994. "Male Gender and Rituals of Resistance in the Palestinian Intifada: A Cultural Politics of Violence." *American Ethnologist* 21(1):31–49.

Peteet, Julie Marie. 2005. *Landscape of Hope and Despair: Palestinian Refugee Camps*. University of Pennsylvania Press.

Petersen, Roger D. 2001. *Resistance and Rebellion: Lessons from Eastern Europe*. Cambridge University Press.

Petersen, Roger D. 2002. *Understanding Ethnic Violence: Fear, Hatred, and Resentment in Twentieth-Century Eastern Europe*. Cambridge University Press.

Pilger, John. 2007. *Freedom Next Time: Resisting the Empire*. Nation Books.

Popkin, Samuel L. 1979. *The Rational Peasant: The Political Economy of Rural Society in Vietnam*. University of California Press.

Poropat, Arthur E. 2009. "A Meta-analysis of the Five-Factor Model of Personality and Academic Performance." *Psychological Bulletin* 135(2):322.

Pressman, Jeremy. 2017. "Throwing Stones in Social Science: Non-violence, Unarmed Violence, and the First Intifada." *Cooperation and Conflict* 52(4):519–36.

Rabah, J., and N. Fairweather. 1993. *Israeli Military Orders in the Occupied Palestinian West Bank, 1967–1992*. Jerusalem Media & Communication Centre.

Rekhess, Elie. 1975. "The Employment in Israel of Arab Labourers from the Administered Areas." *Israel Yearbook on Human Rights* 5:389–412.

Robinson, Glenn E. 1997. *Building a Palestinian State: The Incomplete Revolution*. Indiana University Press.

Ron, James. 2000. "Savage Restraint: Israel, Palestine and the Dialectics of Legal Repression." *Social Problems* 47(4):445–72.

Ron, James. 2003. *Frontiers and Ghettos: State Violence in Serbia and Israel*. University of California Press.

Rosenfeld, Maya. 2004. *Confronting the Occupation: Work, Education, and Political Activism of Palestinian Families in a Refugee Camp*. Stanford University Press.

Roy, Sara M. 1995. *The Gaza Strip: The Political Economy of De-development*. Institute for Palestine Studies.

Sahliyeh, Emile F. 1988. *In Search of Leadership: West Bank Politics since 1967*. Brookings Institution Press.

Salem, Walid. 2012. "Civil Society in Palestine: Approaches, Historical Context and the Role of the NGOs." *Palestine-Israel Journal of Politics, Economics, and Culture* 18(2/3):17.

Sapiro, Virginia. 2004. "Not Your Parents' Political Socialization: Introduction for a New Generation." *Annual Review of Political Science* 7:1–23.

Sayigh, Yazid. 1997. *Armed Struggle and the Search for State: The Palestinian National Movement, 1949–1993*. Oxford University Press.

Scacco, Alexandra. n.d. Anatomy of a Riot: Participation in Ethnic Violence in Nigeria. Manuscript.

Schiff, Zeev, and Ehud Yaari. 1991. *Intifada: The Palestinian Uprising – Israel's Third Front*. Touchstone Books.

Scott, J. C. 1976. *The Moral Economy of the Peasant: Rebellion and Subsistence in Southeast Asia*. Yale University Press.

Sears, David O., and Carolyn L. Funk. 1999. "Evidence of the Long-Term Persistence of Adults' Political Predispositions." *Journal of Politics* 61(1): 1–28.

Seawright, Jason. 2016. *Multi-method Social Science: Combining Qualitative and Quantitative Tools*. Cambridge University Press.

Seawright, Jason, and John Gerring. 2008. "Case Selection Techniques in Case Study Research: A Menu of Qualitative and Quantitative Options." *Political Research Quarterly* 61(2):294–308.

Shamir, Jacob, and Khalil Shikaki. 2002. "Determinants of Reconciliation and Compromise among Israelis and Palestinians." *Journal of Peace Research* 39(2):185–202.

Shapiro, Jacob N., and C. Christine Fair. 2010. "Understanding Support for Islamist Militancy in Pakistan." *International Security* 34(3):79–118.

Sharp, Gene. 1973. *The Politics of Nonviolent Action*. 3 vols. Porter Sargent.

Shehadeh, Raja, and Jūnāthān Kuttāb. 1980. *The West Bank and the Rule of Law: A Study*. Vol. 88. International Commission of Jurists.

Shelef, Nadav G., and Yael Zeira. n.d. "International Recognition and Support for Violence among Nonpartisans."

Small, Mario Luis. 2011. "How to Conduct a Mixed Methods Study: Recent Trends in a Rapidly Growing Literature." *Annual Review of Sociology* 37:57–86.

Stack, Liam, and Maram Mazen. 2007. "Striking Mahalla Workers Demand Govt. Fulfill Broken Promises." *Daily Star Egypt*.

Staniland, Paul. 2014. *Networks of Rebellion: Explaining Insurgent Cohesion and Collapse*. Cornell University Press.

Stewart, Frances. 2008. *Horizontal Inequalities and Conflict*. Palgrave Macmillan.

Tamari, Salim. 1981. "Building Other People's Homes: The Palestinian Peasant's Household and Work in Israel." *Journal of Palestine Studies* 11(1): 31–66.

Taraki, Lisa. 1984. "Mass Organizations in the West Bank." In *Occupation: Israel over Palestine*, ed. Naseer Hasan Aruri. Zed Books, pp. 431–63.

Telhami, Shibley. 2010. "2010 Israeli Arab/Palestinian Public Opinion Survey." Brookings Institution, http://www.brookings.edu/~/media/research/files/reports/2010/12/09-israel-public-opinion-telhami/israeli_arab_powerpoint.pdf

Tessler, Mark A. 1994. *A History of the Israeli–Palestinian Conflict*. Indiana University Press.

Tessler, Mark, and Michael D. H. Robbins. 2007. "What Leads Some Ordinary Arab Men and Women to Approve of Terrorist Acts against the United States?" *Journal of Conflict Resolution* 51(2):305–28.

Thoms, Oskar N. T., and James Ron. 2007. "Do Human Rights Violations Cause Internal Conflict?" *Human Rights Quarterly* 29(3):674–705.

Tilly, Charles, Louise Tilly, and Richard Tilly. 1975. *The Rebellious Century, 1830–1930*. Vol. 1 Harvard University Press.

Tilly, Charles, and Sidney Tarrow. 2007. *Contentious Politics*. Vol. 1. Paradigm.

Tolan, Sandy. 2007. *The Lemon Tree: An Arab, a Jew, and the Heart of the Middle East*. Bloomsbury Publishing.

Tucker, Joshua A. 2007. "Enough! Electoral Fraud, Collective Action Problems, and Post-communist Colored Revolutions." *Perspectives on Politics* 5(3):535–51.

White, Robert W. 1989. "From Peaceful Protest to Guerrilla War: Micromobilization of the Provisional Irish Republican Army." *American Journal of Sociology* 94(6):1277–1302.

Wickham-Crowley, Timothy P. 1992. *Guerrillas and Revolution in Latin America: A Comparative Study of Insurgents and Regimes since 1956*. Princeton University Press.

Wiktorowicz, Quintan. 2004. *Islamic Activism: A Social Movement Theory Approach*. Indiana University Press.

Wolfinger, Raymond E. 1980. *Who Votes?* Vol. 22. Yale University Press.

Wood, Elisabeth Jean. 2003. *Insurgent Collective Action and Civil War in El Salvador*. Cambridge University Press.

Yom, Sean. 2015. "From Methodology to Practice: Inductive Iteration in Comparative Research." *Comparative Political Studies* 48(5):616–44.

Zald, Mayer N., and John David McCarthy. 1987. *Social Movements in an Organizational Society: Collected Essays*. Transaction Publishers.

Zeira, Yael. 2018. "From the Schools to the Streets: Education and Anti-regime Resistance in the West Bank." *Comparative Political Studies* 52(8):1131–1168.

Zhao, Dingxin. 1998. "Ecologies of Social Movements: Student Mobilization during the 1989 Prodemocracy Movement in Beijing 1." *American Journal of Sociology* 103(6):1493–1529.

Index